MARIE HENRY BEYLE—STENDHAL

Nach dem Relief von David d'Angers, gestochen von Collas (1829)

BY GILBERT D. CHAITIN

The Unhappy Few

A PSYCHOLOGICAL STUDY OF THE NOVELS OF STENDHAL

INDIANA UNIVERSITY PRESS
BLOOMINGTON AND LONDON

Indiana University Humanities Series Number 69
Indiana University, Bloomington, Indiana

PUBLICATION COMMITTEE
David H. Dickason, Norbert Fuerst,
Rudolf B. Gottfried

The Indiana University Humanities Series was
founded in 1939 for the publication of occasional papers
and monographs by members of the faculty.

*The pictures of Stendhal on the half title and page
xii of this monograph were reproduced with the permission of the Bettman Archive and Culver Pictures,
respectively.*

TO

My Parents

Contents

Introduction

At Destutt de Tracy's house one day, a stranger approached Stendhal and asked him, "What is your profession?" Stendhal replied, "I am simply an observer of the human heart." At this remark, so the story goes, the stranger took fright and fled to the farthest corner of the drawing room.[1] The poor fellow's behavior reminds me of the reaction of many of Stendhal's critics who, while paying lip service to his psychological genius, turn tail and run each time he disturbs their dogmatic slumbers by probing the darker, more hidden recesses of the mind.

Student of the human heart? It would be more accurate to say, "student of his own heart," for Stendhal was above all a master of introspection, as the 1,500 pages of diaries and autobiographical essays collected in the Pléiade edition of his *Oeuvres Intimes* testify. Not even his greatest predecessors in the French literary tradition, Montaigne and Rousseau, display the depth of self-perception and often brutal honesty that make *Souvenirs d'Egotisme* and *La Vie de Henry Brulard* such fascinating and valuable human documents. Henri Martineau, the dean of Stendhal studies, gives a just evaluation of the extent of Stendhal's self-revelation in the Foreword of the *Oeuvres Intimes:*

Stendhal s'est beaucoup raconté. Un lecteur averti est certain de le retrouver en personne à chaque page pour ainsi dire de ses écrits. A toutes les étapes de ses déplacements, dans les protagonistes de ses romans, en marge des livres de sa bibliothèque qu'il couvrait de notes, jusque dans les remarques les plus objectives en apparence de ses ouvrages de critique.[2]

If even Stendhal's most objective remarks are revelations of self, it is still more likely that not only the protagonists of his novels but the total content and deepest meaning of his fiction are reflections of the author's personality. Nowhere more than in Stendhal are life and work so inextricably entwined. This is such an obvious fact that it has become a platitude of Stendhal criticism. In the introductory chapter of one of the most recent books on the subject, Wallace Fowlie has described the relationship with admirable precision:

The fundamental life of Beyle, the biography of his feelings and thoughts and fantasies, is in each of his novels he signed Stendhal. These novels narrate the same story of the same young man. They are compositions about Henri Beyle's fantasies, richly documented, placed in a variety of settings, each evocative of a different world, but each the same story of a young man who is unable or who refuses to grow into adulthood.[3]

So much for the lip service. When it comes to actual analysis of the novels, Mr. Fowlie, like the vast majority of his predecessors, takes only a passing glance at plot sources, models of characters and biographical similarities between author and character. The nature and meaning of Beyle's innermost phantasies is not even touched upon. Why Stendhal should rewrite the same story of the same young man still remains a mystery. After closing Mr. Fowlie's book, the reader has no greater understanding of the "fundamental life" of Beyle than he had before opening it.

In Freud's words, there is a big difference between flirting with an idea and marrying it. In this book I propose to do the latter, to explore the subterranean connections between Beyle's life and Stendhal's novels. Through the findings and methods of psychoanalysis, I hope to arrive at an understanding of some of the problems that have perplexed the critics. What is the cause of Octave de Malivert's impotence in *Armance*? Why did the stories of Berthet and Laffargue stimulate Stendhal's imagination to create *Le Rouge et le Noir?* Why does the denouement of that novel defy credibility? Why is the beginning of *La Chartreuse de Parme* esthetically defective? What are the source and meaning of Stendhal's fascination with prisons? Why is the protagonist of his last novel a female version of the earlier heroes? Why do all his novels tell the same story?

It is my contention that the psychic content of the novels—the deepest, often unconscious desires and fears, phantasies and conflicts represented by the characters in their various relationships, thoughts, feelings and actions toward one another—arises from and accurately depicts the rich emotional life of Henri Beyle. In the present study the heaviest emphasis lies on the fiction and artistic career of Stendhal. Therefore, I consistently use the facts and phantasies of Beyle's life to illuminate the meaning of his novels. In particular, I try to show that the psychic content of these novels remains substantially the same, but that the extent and manner of its expression vary in a fairly regular and identifiable way.

Along with Stendhal's own autobiographical works, the most valuable sources for this book have been the biographical studies by Henri Martineau, especially *Le Coeur de Stendhal,*[4] and Edmund Bergler's psychograph of the author.[5]

I would like to thank the Woodrow Wilson Fellowship Foundation whose generous Dissertation Fellowship made this book possible; Professor Albert Sonnenfeld for his helpful suggestions and moral support in difficult times; and most of all my wife Joy for her long hours of proofreading, editing, and typing, and for her love.

On the 8th of October, 1841, Stendhal wrote to his cousin Romain Colomb: "Did I tell you that my portrait, painted by Mr. Södermark, a Swedish colonel and painter, is a masterpiece. It was a big attraction [Il était roi] at the Roman exhibition, at the Porta del Popolo."

I

The Secret Sin

In discussing *Armance*, critics generally concentrate their attention on two aspects of the novel: the psychological study of an unusual character (or of two unusual characters), and the social criticism.[1] When interested primarily in Octave's character, they inquire into the causes of his impotence or the development of his love for Armance. Several important critics, such as Turnell, Martineau, and Prévost,[2] have expressed doubts as to the value of a novel whose major preoccupation is the analysis of a pathological character.[3] They seem to feel that a literary work should have a wider appeal to the public than a case history would ordinarily command. Before dismissing *Armance* as a mere study in pathology, therefore, they attempt to relate the psychological problem of the novel to Stendhal's description of contemporary society.

Jean Prévost sees the uniqueness of Octave's view of society as the crucial connection between the two aspects of *Armance*:

Il ne s'agit pas d'exposer aux yeux des curieux un cas de physiologie et de médecine mentale. Il s'agit de juger la société, le monde et le bonheur par les yeux d'un être qui se croit séparé sans retour du monde et du bonheur, d'un moine malgré lui, cloîtré au milieu des hommes par son corps imparfait. C'est une nouvelle vue sur l'ensemble des choses, et non pas seulement un détail curieux, que ce roman prétend nous offrir.[4]

There are several objections to this interpretation. In the first place, is Octave's impotence due to physical rather than psychological causes? There is no indication within the novel that this is so, whereas there are good reasons, which I will go into later, for accepting the second view. Let it be said parenthetically that one of the critics who have devoted the most detailed studies to this question, Martineau, has opted for the second alternative. And if Octave's impotence is the result of psychological factors, the novel loses much of its aura of strangeness. Certainly the field of abnormal psychology has often been a source for novelists—Proust and Joyce, for example.

Secondly, although almost everyone has a great deal of interest in and sympathy for "strangers" these days (for all of us feel alienated from society in one way or another), why should anyone be interested in judgments made by a character such as Octave on society, the world, and happiness? The implication seems to be that, because he is cut off from these things, his ideas about them are somehow truer. Prévost apparently has in mind the objective scientist who does not let himself become emotionally involved in a situation, in order to judge it the better. Yet Octave's case is quite different. His emotional disturbance, whether caused by, or the cause of, his impotence, makes him the worst possible judge of other people and happiness. He is precisely the sort of person whose intellectual attitudes are mere manifestations of his own personality. They are not objective evaluations of a situation. Their only claim to other people's interest is their peculiar nature.

Finally, Prévost's account neglects a crucial point: why, if his purpose was to give an outsider's point of view on life and society, did Stendhal choose precisely this type of outsider rather than any other, especially since he was well aware that the nature of Octave's malady would arouse only repugnance and distaste in most readers? Certainly he must have realized that Octave's reason for remaining outside the pale of ordinary life would influence his views in a particular direction, differentiating him from other outsiders. Since the greater part of the novel describes Octave's personal life, his thoughts and feelings about himself, and his love for Armance, it seems evident that character study was at least as important to the author as social criticism.

In contrast to Prévost's interpretation, Martineau feels that each of the themes in *Armance* is independent of the others:

Une des principales difficultés d'*Armance* consiste en réalité dans la multiplicité de ses thèmes. Il apparaît verrouillé sous une triple serrure . . . le point de départ demeuré trop obscur sous la plume du romancier, devait être la peinture d'un malheureux à qui la nature refuse de prouver l'amour qu'il peut encore néanmoins ressentir. Sur ce premier motif . . . l'auteur avait greffé un second . . . l'affrontement de deux âmes mues par une passion réciproque, mais d'une essence si rare que leur malheur constant ne provient que de leurs scrupules poussés à l'extrême . . . De plus il a entendu représenter du même coup les moeurs de son époque.[5]

If this view is correct, it brings to light something more than one of the novel's "principal difficulties"; it reveals a basic flaw, the complete lack of integration of the three supposed themes. In fact, two of these themes are not independent. The distinction between the subject of Octave's impotence and that of his love for Armance is spurious. For how could an author hope to portray the hero's impotence without putting him in the one situation where the full significance of his illness could manifest itself? It would seem to require a special effort to avoid seeing the connection between Octave's trouble and the "rare essence" and "exaggerated scruples" of his love. Surely the way a man is in love is not unrelated to his emotional makeup.

The question of the relation between Octave's impotence and the representation of contemporary manners is not so easily answered, even in a general way. It is quite possible that Stendhal had no clear idea of this relation, or that he failed to give adequate expression to his idea, but this can be determined only after defining the manner in which society is portrayed in the novel. Merely praising or criticizing the acuity of Stendhal's description on the basis of its correspondence with what is known of that society from other sources does not help us at all to understand the novel. If these are the two subjects of the novel, then the following questions arise: Are they of equal importance or is one subordinated to the other? If they are equal, do they exist separately, side by side? If one is subordinated to the other, which one, how, and why? Making lists and distinctions, if they are correct, is a fine beginning for an analysis, but it is just a beginning.

Atherton's approach attempts to unite the subjects of Octave's impotence and the description of manners in a symbolic frame of reference. Octave's impotence becomes a symbol of the sterility of his social class, while at the same time his social position becomes symbolic of, and the cause for, his detachment from life:

One of the strong points of *Armance* is precisely the attempt to join a psychological study of character to a historical analysis of class structure. It is this double view of the hero that provides the opportunity for irony. Octave's elaborate theories are of central importance to any understanding of his character, yet at the same time the lack of connection between his subtle thinking and the prosaic problems of society explains the failure of his class to engage in any meaningful form of political activity.[6]

Atherton thus implies that the disparity between Octave's way of thinking and the real problems that face him is symbolic of the outmoded attitudes of the Restoration nobility in dealing with the political realities of a postrevolutionary society. There is certainly an analogy here, but I cannot agree that it is strong, enough for the one fact to "explain" the other. Stendhal repeatedly insists that Octave is an outsider to his society, that is, to Restoration society. However much the nobility desired to restore the past, they did not simply construct complicated theories about it; they actually succeeded, for a time, in changing the political structure of France. Atherton himself sums up the most decisive argument against his own interpretation:

Stendhal had tried to portray his hero as both a representative of his society and as a rebel against it, and the two themes were not well joined. In reading the novel as social criticism one is perplexed by the abnormality of the hero; in reading it as a psychological study one is inclined to resent the foppishness of the world in which it occurs.[7]

At this point I might be content to end my inquiry, satisfied that I have determined what *Armance* is about. In reviewing the steps in this line of reasoning, however, I find one very vulnerable point. The entire argument rests on the assumption that Stendhal started out with two more or less independent themes which he felt would reinforce each other when united symbolically. But perhaps the relationship of these two subjects is of a different sort, one that would not require us to suppose that Stendhal was unaware of the contradiction inherent in portraying an outsider as a representative of the society from which he feels alienated. If I assume that the theme of social criticism is not an independent element but serves some unconscious purpose related to the psychological theme, then the pieces of the puzzle begin to fall into place. The social criticism, which amounts to nothing more than generalizing individual guilt, would then be a defensive measure against an internal emotional conflict. Stendhal overlooked the contradiction for the same reason that everyone "overlooks" similar contradictory aspects of his behavior and opinions—because of the unconscious needs of his personality.

One might contend that Stendhal really held these opinions concerning the young nobles of his time; they were not merely a promising topic for a novel. In fact, he even published an article on the subject, based on his observations of French society—"D'un nouveau complot contre les industriels." Quite so. But here I must ask whether his observations were just, or were the result of a similar defense mechanism he actually employed in his own life. At least one of his friends was convinced of the latter hypothesis:

Dès 1817, peu après la publication de *Rome, Naples et Florence,* Adolphe de Mareste se moquait de son "ami Henri Beyle qui, s'asseyant aux Tuileries après son déjeuner à la fourchette et dans les horreurs d'une digestion laborieuse, se persuadait sérieusement que les jeunes gens qui se promenaient devant lui étaient *tous mortellement ennuyés.*"[8]

Far from being an "historical analysis of class structure," Stendhal's ideas on the young nobility resemble much more a projection, according to the formula: it is they, not I, who are bored, unable to act, who often think of suicide, etc. Since Stendhal identified closely with his hero, as is evident from the fact that he attributed so many of his own character traits and opinions to Octave, it becomes easily understandable that the latter should share this defense mechanism.

In terms of the previous discussion, I am suggesting that the idea that Octave is symbolic of his class be regarded as subordinate to the primary theme of his story. The various opinions he emits concerning contemporary society will then be considered as indicators of his character. In this way I may hope to penetrate the smoke screen set up by Stendhal's conscious intention to represent him both as representative of and rebel against his class. In keeping with this suggestion, I will now direct my attention to the psychological theme of *Armance*.

To begin with, why did Stendhal choose to call his novel "Armance" rather than "Octave?" Surprisingly enough, no critic, to my knowledge, has even raised this question in other than a cursory manner. Yet it can hardly be without significance that a novel whose central preoccupation is the life of one character should be named after a second character of lesser importance.[9]

In Stendhal's own notes on the so-called Bucci edition, there are only two references to the title: "*Olivier*—such was the name of the novel till the parere of Clara Gaz."[10] *Parere* is, of course, the Italian word for "opinion," and Clara Gaz is an abbreviation of *Clara Gazul*, which Stendhal used to designate the author of that work, his friend Mérimée. From this cryptic remark it appears that it was on Mérimée's advice that Stendhal changed the title of the novel, presumably in order to avoid any reference to the novels of the Duchess of Duras and Hyacinthe Thabaud de La Touche on the subject of an impotent in love. However, there is no indication of his reason for choosing *Armance* rather than *Octave* as title. Nor is the second reference of much use in this respect: "Le titre était *Armance, anecdote du XIXe siècle*. Le second titre a été inventé par le libraire; sans emphase, sans charlatanisme, rien ne se vend, disait M. Canel."[11] The second title referred to is the one actually employed in the first and all subsequent editions: *Armance, ou quelques scènes d'un salon de Paris en 1827.* The point at issue here is the trivial question of selecting a subtitle that would help the novel to sell better.

In his Introduction to the Garnier edition of *Armance*, Martineau points out: "[Mérimée] obtint seulement que le héros fut débaptisé: *Olivier* lui semblait avec raison un peu suranné. *Ce nom fut donc changé contre celui d'Octave et l'ouvrage s'appela désormais Armance.*"[12] The little word "and" that connects the two clauses in the italicized sentence seems to imply that rechristening the hero entailed, as a natural consequence, changing the title to *Armance*. But this is obviously not the case. Yet the fact that Martineau, along with the other critics, takes this title for granted, must mean that for some reason he feels it to be appropriate, or at least not inappropriate.

Since I have received no help in clearing up this enigma from Stendhal or the critics, I will examine the circumstances under which the book was written, in the hopes of finding a clue to the solution of the problem. Here, at least, there is no room for doubt.

Stendhal . . . songea à écrire *Armance* en janvier 1826, après avoir lu le roman de la Touche: *Olivier*. Il en commença la rédaction le 30 ou le 31, et il la poussa fort activement jusqu'au 8 février. A ce jour, le premier jet en étant à peu près terminé, il s'arrêta brusquement sans que nous sachions au juste pour quelle cause, et si son incapacité lui vint des difficultés de son sujet ou de ses chagrins intimes.

Car cette même année voyait la fin de ses amours avec la comtesse Curial qu'il appelle d'ordinaire Menti. Il était en froid avec elle depuis octobre 1825 déjà. Le désaccord ne fit ensuite que s'accentuer. . . . Le 15 septembre marque le point culminant de la crise sentimentale de Beyle. Alors, complètement désespéré, il songea au pistolet. Il lui fallait un dérivatif, une puissante distraction; dès le 19 septembre, il reprit *Armance* et se sauva à force de travail. Le 10 octobre il avait terminé son livre; il n'eut plus ensuite qu'à le polir.[13]

According to this account, which there is every reason to believe, Stendhal's decision to write *Armance* had two principal causes: his reading of La Touche's novel, *Olivier,* and his feelings about the loss of the Countess Curial's affections. It is clear that reading La Touche's book would not have spurred Stendhal's imagination if its subject had not had some special appeal for him. This subject can be divided into two distinct, but related parts: the problem of impotence, and the more general problem of lack of success in love. It is well known that Stendhal was more than once preoccupied with what he called the "fiasco," and that he had suffered from this unpleasant experience several times. It is not at all unlikely that he had a few fiascos with Countess Curial, or at least worried about this possibility, although the assertion cannot be proved. In any case, this fear must have been intensified when he realized that Menti was about to break off with him. The second element has an even more obvious relationship to Stendhal's emotional state at that time. He knew that his current love affair was coming to a disastrous end, and he was consequently in a state of depression which became one of almost total despair when the inevitable finally took place. This new defeat reopened his past wounds suffered on the battlefield of love. As he puts it, in a marginal comment to *Armance:*

> Three great despairs
> abandon of Gina 1817
> impossible of Métilde 1820
> abandon of Menti 1826
> *all by love.*[14]

The effect of La Touche's novel on Stendhal can be summarized by saying that in it he saw an image of his own fears about his potency and of his lack of success in love.

It is doubtful, although not impossible, that the effect of La Touche's book alone would have been enough to move Stendhal to write a novel. However, this can never be known, since he was concurrently under the influence of a much stronger emotional impetus. As noted above, at that time he was in the process of losing Countess Curial's love. Significantly, although he started to write while there was still a faint hope for a reconciliation, he did not finish the novel until the break was final. Martineau surmises that Beyle completed *Armance* in order to save himself from committing suicide. This hypothesis can be accepted only if writing the novel served, in the following manner, as a psychological substitute for taking his own life. Beyle contemplated suicide because things were not going well for him; that is, he saw no possibility for satisfying his strongest desires. If these desires could be satisfied at least in phantasy, in his fiction, then life would become more bearable. Comparing the story related in *Armance* with the real course of events, I find two striking discrepancies between them. In real life Countess Curial ceased loving Stendhal and rejected him; in the novel, Armance continues to love Octave, and it is he who withdraws from her, even though it costs him his life. In the novel Octave commits suicide, whereas in reality Stendhal merely wrote a novel.

It might seem farfetched to interpret Octave's suicide as a means of rejecting Armance, since he professes to love her still on his death bed and he certainly had other, less drastic means at his disposal for rejecting her love if he had so desired. After all, by killing himself, he could not even savor his supposed revenge as he could have done if, for instance, he had merely jilted her. Nevertheless, I feel that this is a valid interpretation of his suicide. It is true that Octave does not live to observe the results of his action, but care must be exercised not to confuse Octave with Stendhal. For Stendhal does "live to see the results," and, what is more, he carries out the revenge by despatching Armance and Mme de Malivert off to a convent in the very last line of the novel. Here the revenge motif becomes clear. In life Countess Curial went off with another lover, while Stendhal was left in despair. In the novel, Octave dies, to be sure, but Stendhal is left as a spectator and Armance is locked up in a nunnery. By thus considering the actual results of Octave's death, without bothering about the alleged reasons, one can easily ascertain the presence of the revenge idea behind it. However, this still does not explain why he chose suicide rather than some other means to this end. Indeed this choice must have been motivated by other factors as well. What these other factors are will become clear subsequently. At this point it is better not to enter into a lengthy discussion of them so as not to interrupt the present line of argument. But one of the statements above can at least give a clue as to the direction in which to look for them. Stendhal remained as a spectator after his fictional death by proxy in the form of Octave. Psychoanalysis has shown that this corresponds to man's deepest convictions about his own death:

Our own death is indeed unimaginable, and whenever we make the attempt to imagine it we can perceive that we really survive as spectators. Hence the psychoanalytic school could venture on the assertion that at bottom no one believes in his own death, or to put the same thing in another way, in the unconscious every one of us is convinced of his own immortality.[15]

But in granting that in the unconscious one's own death is inconceivable, one is forced to the conclusion that imagining one's own death must have a very different meaning to the unconscious from the idea of annihilation it carries for the conscious ego. It is in this meaning that the supplementary motivations for Octave's suicide are found.

Returning to the original contention, that Octave's suicide is a type of revenge, I find that there is one more objection left unanswered. Is it not being unjust to Octave to impute evil motives to him just at the time when his love for Armance seems purest? Indeed, Stendhal relates, as Octave is writing his farewell confession to Armance: "Jamais Octave n'avait été sous le charme de l'amour le plus tendre comme dans ce moment suprême" (p. 245). But this does not contradict the hypothesis. The fact that Octave's love for Armance is strongest precisely at the moment when he is hurting her the most merely confirms the highly ambivalent nature of his feelings toward her. The phenomenon of ambivalence, the existence of contradictory feelings toward the same person, is an indisputable fact in man's emotional life. That it plays an inordinately large role in Octave's relationship with Armance can be seen most clearly perhaps in their meeting shortly before Octave's duel with the Marquis de Crêveroche. Octave has decided that he must never see Armance again, but instead of explaining his reasons to her, he tries to convince her that he does not love her.

The scene reaches its climax when Octave makes the following speech:

"Je vais partir, je dois partir pour un long voyage en Amérique. . . . Quant à vous, mademoiselle, on a prétendu que j'avais de l'amour pour vous; je suis bien éloigné d'avoir une telle prétention. D'ailleurs, l'ancienne amitié qui nous unit devait suffire, ce me semble, pour s'opposer à la naissance de l'amour." [p. 139]

The effect on Armance of this bit of planned cruelty is devastating:

En ce moment Armance se trouva hors d'état de marcher; elle releva ses yeux baissés et regarda Octave; ses lèvres tremblantes et pâles semblaient vouloir prononcer quelques mots. Elle voulut s'appuyer sur la caisse d'un oranger, mais elle n'eut pas la force de se retenir; elle glissa et tomba près de cet oranger, privée de tout sentiment. [p. 139]

As Martineau succinctly puts it: ". . . Octave piétine à plaisir l'amour sincère d'Armance."[16] Yet this scene comes immediately after Octave's touching burial of Armance's purse: "Adieu, adieu pour la vie, chère Armance! Dieu sait si je t'ai aimée" (p. 136). These phrases show how strong his love was at that time. Indeed, on closer examination, the scenes evoked turn out to parallel the final sequence of events in the most striking fashion. In both cases Octave has decided to *leave* Armance; in both his love for her reaches its highest intensity; and in both he acts toward her in the cruelest way. And if there could be any doubts remaining about the similarity of the two situations, they are completely dispelled by Octave's thoughts just after he has buried Armance's purse, before he tells her of his plan to travel:

Si quelque enfant maladroit, en tirant un oiseau derrière une haie, pouvait me tuer, je n'aurais aucun reproche à me faire. Dieu! quelles délices de recevoir un coup de fusil dans cette tête brûlante! Comme je le remercierais avant que de mourir si j'en avais le temps! [p. 137]

In other words, he wishes to kill himself at this point also, but cannot bear the burden of guilt involved. Given that Octave can experience these emotions, have these ideas, and then hurt Armance so deeply (pp. 136–39), there is no reason why he should not do so again at the end of the novel (p. 245). Therefore, the objection that his love precludes the possibility of a desire for revenge does not stand up to close scrutiny.

If one asks what offense Stendhal wanted to avenge in his novel, the first answer that presents itself is the injury to his self-love, or narcissism, inflicted on him by Countess Curial. This view is corroborated by a remark made by Stendhal a few years after *Armance* was published:

In thirteen days two years. When love meurt vraiment, on se rappelle toutes les actions *of* Menti offensantes pour la vanité, et la Vanité à l'usage du Monde qui dormait à l'époque de ces actions de Menti s'occupe à les sentir pour la première fois.[17]

In light of the above discussion it may be assumed that this vanity was not quite as dormant as Stendhal later supposed and that, in fact, it found expression in his novel. He compensates for these wounds in two ways, by having Armance suffer from the ending of their relationship, and by giving himself, or rather his representative, Octave, the initiative. In other words, what he originally experienced passively, the loss of love, he now relives actively in his phantasy.

This last consideration brings out the second discrepancy between the real situation and the novel, namely, that Octave commits suicide whereas Stendhal contented himself with writing a novel. Ever since Freud's *Beyond the Pleasure Principle,* it has been well established that one of the primary functions of play, and certain other phantasy productions, is to enable the individual's ego to come to terms with a painful event experienced passively, by repeating that event with the individual taking the active, rather than the passive role. Thus the child, after a visit to the dentist, plays that he is the dentist and someone else, a playmate, toy, or imaginary person, is the patient. I am suggesting that the writing of *Armance* served a similar purpose for Stendhal, both because Octave takes the initiative in breaking off with Armance, and because Stendhal has his hero do what he himself had contemplated doing, kill himself. Of course the analogy breaks down in the latter use, since it is not a question of an event actually experienced by Stendhal but only an intention. The difference, however, resides in the time element rather than in the nature of the event; both are feared because of the mental pain involved, but in the former case it has actually been experienced; in the latter it is merely anticipated. The phantasy, then, represents the active "trying out" of this unpleasant possibility. Thus Stendhal was able to use suicide as a means of avenging himself without having to suffer the consequences. By dealing with this possibility in imagination, he could avoid it in reality.

Having established with some degree of certainty the presence of revenge as a strong motive for writing the novel, I am now in a position to suggest that one reason for its title is that it is directed toward Armance, or rather Countess Curial and the other objects of Stendhal's unhappy love affairs. Yet this suggestion, however tempting it might at first appear, is immediately beset with difficulties; there are still no solid grounds (in spite of her role in the novel) for considering her to be the major character, as would be expected from the title. Shall I then conclude that this whole path of inquiry has been nothing more than a blind alley?

But suppose that Armance *is*, in a sense, the main character! This suggestion is not as nonsensical as it may seem at first glance. In his biographical essay on Stendhal, Dr. Edmund Bergler identifies unconscious homosexuality as one of Beyle's dominant character traits. Bergler's point of departure is Stendhal's famous declaration of love for his mother in Chapter 3 of *La Vie de Henry Brulard*:

> Ma mère, Mme Henriette Gagnon, était une femme charmante et j'étais amoureux de ma mère.
>
> Je me hâte d'ajouter que je la perdis quand j'avais sept ans.
>
> En l'aimant à six ans peut-être, 1789, j'avais absolument le même caractère qu'en 1828 en aimant à la fureur Alberthe de Rubempré. Ma manière d'aller à la chasse du bonheur n'avait au fond nullement changé, il n'y a que cette seule exception: j'étais pour ce qui constitue le physique de l'amour comme César serait s'il revenait au monde pour l'usage du canon et des petites armes. Je l'eusse bien vite appris et cela n'eût rien changé au fond de ma tactique.
>
> Je voulais couvrir ma mère de baisers et qu'il n'y eût pas de vêtements. Elle m'aimait à la passion et m'embrassait souvent, je lui rendais ses baisers avec un tel feu qu'elle était souvent obligée de s'en aller. J'abhorrais mon père quand il venait interrompre nos baisers, je voulais toujours les lui donner à la gorge. Qu'on daigne se rappeler que je la perdis par une couche quand à peine j'avais sept ans.[18]

Confronted with these texts, Bergler asks himself the following question: *"How is it that Stendhal had not repressed his Oedipus complex, but had retained it in consciousness?"*[19] For, although every child has these feelings at one stage of his development, normally they are repressed and can never again become conscious in the adult.

Bergler lists in *Stendhal* four possible sources of knowledge of one's own Oedipus complex: (1) psychological genius, (2) schizophrenic psychosis, (3) moral insanity, (4) observation of others and use of this observation for masochistic purposes on one's self. He concludes that none of these fit Stendhal's situation. Although Stendhal had a great deal of psychological insight, to call him a genius and let it go at that would be to give up any hopes of an explanation. He was not schizophrenic, nor did he suffer from moral insanity. And he observed the Oedipus complex in himself first, not in others (p. 79).

These considerations lead Bergler to a fifth possibility:

Apparently there is still a *fifth possibility* which could explain the discovery of the positive Oedipus complex in one's self: namely, if the *negative component of the Oedipus complex were of overwhelming strength,* there might exist, in a situation dangerous to the unconscious part of the ego, the tendency to compromise *by surrendering content that is less unpleasant in order to retain content that is more important but consciously still more embarrassing.* In that case the *unconscious homosexual tendency must have been one of the decisive drives in Stendhal's psyche,* and his ego must have striven to maintain it by every means at its disposal, even including the most farreaching renunciation of repressions. [pp. 79–80]

An example of Stendhal's unconscious homosexuality is his cult of energy:

Thus Stendhal's "deification of energy," in part a compensation for his timidity and potency disturbance . . . , can be reduced to unconscious phantasies of being raped, in which Stendhal again takes both roles unconsciously, that of the aggressive man of action and,

above all, that of the overpowered victim enjoying passive masochistic pleasure. [p. 85]

.   .   .   .   .

How far this unconscious feminine identification went with Stendhal, is proved by the juxtaposition of the following statements. He
says of his *alter ego* Julien Sorel (in *Rouge et Noir*): "His com-
plexion was so fair, his eyes so soft, that Mme de Rênal, with her
somewhat romantic inclinations, in the first moment took him for a
young girl in disguise." And in *Henry Brulard*, Stendhal reports
about himself: "I have much too delicate skin, veritable woman's
skin. Later I always got a blister on my hand, when I had held my
sword for an hour. The slightest scrape is enough to rub the skin
from my fingers, in a word, the outer covering of my body is that
of a woman." [p. 86]

.   .   .   .   .

Last but not least, the diagnosis of homosexuality is supported by
Stendhal's paranoid traits. [p. 87]

Thus it is not at all unlikely that Stendhal should identify with
the female lead as well as the male. In Chapter 5, I will show
that this was the case in his last novel, *Lamiel*. That this is also
true with *Armance* will become clear from the following considerations.

Octave de Malivert seems to be a youthful version of Stendhal. This fact has, of course, been recognized by virtually all
the critics. Any remaining skepticism on this issue can be dispelled by a perusal of the notes prepared by Martineau for the
Garnier edition, in which he points out how many of Stendhal's
experiences, character traits, and personal tastes are given to
Octave. What the critics have not noticed, or at least not stated
explicitly, is the extraordinary similarity between Octave and
Armance. Blin does note that they both are extremely proud
and at the same time feel inferior: "Comme tous les maîtres

d'orgueil . . . Octave est frappé d'un complexe d'infériorité, sinon d'une véritable manie de la persécution. Armance, qui fait montre par ailleurs d'une égale fierté, souffre du même mal."[20] This trait is objectified in their relationship to their society, from which they feel excluded and which they judge haughtily; Octave is estranged because of his malady and bizarre ideas, Armance because of her lowly position, due to her poverty, as maid in waiting. They both have the same over-scrupulous sense of duty; they both subject themselves to painful and purposeless self-analysis; and they both conceive of love as a kind of platonic ideal. Even more striking are the similarities in their stories. Octave invents the idea that he cannot marry until the age of twenty-six; Armance invents a mysterious fiancé. Octave comes into a fortune at the beginning of the novel; Armance inherits a large amount of money later on. Finally, when their love is exposed to themselves and the others, they have the identical reaction: they heap reproaches upon themselves as though they had committed an infamous crime, undergo hysterical fits, and decide to withdraw from society, Armance to a convent, and Octave to America (Chaps. 7 and 17). Furthermore, each is convinced he possesses a "fatal secret." Octave speaks of his constantly, but it is worth emphasizing that Armance does the same: "Quoi! se dit-elle, après quelques moments, si tranquille, si heureuse même, malgré mon fatal secret, il y a une demi-heure, et perdue maintenant!" (p. 67).

All of this shows that Armance, no less than Octave, is a representative of Stendhal himself; they are actually two halves of the same character. The final proof is provided by Stendhal's comments referring to the passage which describes Armance's "fever" when she thinks Octave has found out about her love. Of "Bientôt Armance se vit religieuse" Stendhal remarks:

"Dispositions morales de l'animal *when he was making* Olivier. . . ."[21] Again, when Armance exclaims: "Ah! il faut arracher de mon coeur cette passion affreuse," Stendhal says, "Le désespoir de l'auteur *in making this.* . . ." (p. 284). He attributes to Armance not the feelings of Countess Curial or some other woman he has observed, but his own. In short, he identifies with her.

The entire love story of Octave and Armance could be read as a bisexual phantasy, in which Stendhal plays both roles. The two characters alternate in playing now the active, now the passive role, but there is no essential difference between them. If this analysis is correct, then it should be possible to find evidence indicating the sado-masochistic origin of the phantasy. And, indeed, such evidence is near at hand. I have already cited an instance of Octave's cruelty to Armance and have suggested that his suicide is partially motivated by a similar intention.

The element of psychic masochism can be seen throughout the novel in the various forms of torture that Octave and Armance gratuitously inflict upon themselves and upon each other, but it reveals itself most clearly in one particular sequence of events. In Chapter 23, Octave finally brings himself to admit his love for Armance unequivocally. This confession is followed by the only period during which they are both happy. The reason for this unique time of happiness is not, as one might have expected, some fortunate occurrence that changed their lives for the better. On the contrary, when such an event does take place, as, for example, when Octave and Armance inherit large sums of money, they tend to belittle its importance or ignore it completely. No, what has happened is that Octave has fought a senseless duel with the Marquis de Crêveroche, killed him without the slightest compunction, been wounded himself, and believes that he is about to die from a case of typhoid fever caused by the infection of his wounds. In other words, it is a typical case of self-punishment, willingly paid as the price for even momentary happiness. As Reik has shown, one of the essential factors in masochism of any sort is the time element: the individual must suffer "punishment" in order to have his pleasure, so that the former always precedes the latter in time.[22] This should not be confused with the sequence of events often seen in literature, especially tragedy, in which the hero must die in order to expiate his guilt.

At this point one might object: Of course they are happy for the first time; they have finally declared their love and live together on terms of intimacy and mutual agreement. And this just a few days after Octave had expected to be separated from Armance forever! Indeed, Stendhal indicates that the thought of putting off his trip for a while occurred to Octave as he was trying to goad the marquis into continuing their duel: "Tout en parlant, Octave était peut-être plus heureux qu'il ne l'avait été de sa vie entière. Je ne sais quel espoir vague et criminel il fondait sur sa blessure qui allait le retenir quelques jours chez sa mère, et par conséquent pas fort loin d'Armance" (p. 160).

However, this last statement actually supports the claim made above, namely, that Octave wanted to use his suffering, i.e., his wound, in order to procure himself a pleasure—staying with Armance (and also his mother). And why should he have needed any excuse to stay with her? It was he and no one else who had decided he must leave, and this for no apparent reason. It is natural that his declaration of love should bring on a period of relative happiness for them both, but it is natural that he should need the threat of death to loosen his tongue? Once this danger is no longer imminent his relations with Armance rapidly deteriorate to their former level. The parallel with the final events of the novel are, once again, quite striking, for then too he can make his "confession" only when he is sure that he is soon to die. The point is that Octave feels not merely embarrassment at his impotence, but guilt, which has to be alleviated by some sort of punishment prior to any aggressive action or pleasure. As Blin puts it: "On voit bien que dans tout ce comportement, célant, couvrant, dérobant, taisant, même des actes ou des projets innocents, il ne prétend qu'à dissimuler un *défaut* dont il garde conscience comme d'une *faute*."[23]

Which brings up the central problem of the novel, the question of Octave's impotence. The most searching analysis of the problem to date is that of G. Blin in his Introduction to the Revue de la Fontaine edition of *Armance*. In his effort to prove that Octave's impotence must be due to physiological causes, Blin makes the following statement:

Ces indications nous éloignent de rapporter l'impuissance d'Octave, comme une psychanalyse imprudente pourrait le faire, à une censure de respect. Les manuels nous enseignent en effet que l'inhibition génésique correspond le plus souvent à une faute incestueuse non liquidée. Le *fiasco* se produit généralement quand toute femme rappelle par fixation inconsciente la mère ou la sœur idéalisées. Mais les données nous manquent pour que nous puissions parler dans le cas d'Octave "d'idées libidinales d'ordre parental refoulées."[24]

However, a close reading of the text provides several indications of Octave's fixation to his mother:

Une fois qu'Octave se fut assuré que tel était le désir constant d'un père qu'il respectait et *de sa mère qu'il aimait avec une sorte de passion*. . . . [p. 5, italics mine]

"Je t'aime trop pour te remercier encore," dit Octave en prenant la main de Mme de Malivert et la pressant contre ses lèvres. . . . [p. 11]

"Excepté dans les moments où je jouis du bonheur d'être seul avec toi, mon unique plaisir consiste à vivre isolé. . . ." [p. 12]

Ce soir-là Octave resta chez sa mère jusqu'à une heure. Vainement l'avait-elle pressé d'aller dans le monde ou du moins au spectacle. "Je reste où je suis le plus heureux," disait Octave. . . . "Hélas! chère maman, la vue de tous les hommes m'attriste également; je n'aime que toi au monde. . . ." [p. 14]

"Ma chère cousine, je viens de recevoir deux blessures qui peuvent me retenir à la maison quinze jours chacune. Comme vous êtes, après ma mère, ce que je révère le plus au monde. . . ." [p. 163, Octave to Armance]

As noted above, his first thought, after he is wounded, is that he will be able to spend a few days with his mother, and therefore with Armance.

Confronted by so many direct statements of Octave's love for his mother, one may begin to wonder why they were not censored by Stendhal's conscience as he wrote the novel. The reason is that none of these statements, however exaggerated they may appear, has an overt sexual connotation, and consequently they can all be subsumed under the heading of normal filial love by the reader's (and author's) conscious mind. That the relationship has a less innocent undercurrent can nevertheless be perceived in the scenes early in the novel in which Mme de Malivert tries to give her son a beautiful horse and then the revenue from the sale of her most precious jewels. In the chapter on dream symbolism in his *Introduction to Psychoanalysis*[25] Freud says:

Yet another noteworthy symbol of the female genital organ is a *Jewel case*, whilst 'jewel' and 'treasure' are used also in dreams to represent the beloved person. [p. 139]

Special representations of sexual intercourse are less frequent in dreams than we should expect after all this, but we may mention in this connection rhythmical activities such as *dancing, riding* and *climbing*. [p. 140]

In her analysis of "Metzengerstein," a story by Edgar Allan Poe, Marie Bonaparte finds a similar meaning behind the ideas of horses and horseback riding:

Edgar devait [le] souhaiter au quinquagénaire [John Allan, Edgar's foster-father], resté vigoureux d'esprit, mais haï, qui avait gardé jusqu'à la fin sa passion pour les chevaux réels et pour les 'chevaux' et la 'chasse' symboliques qui signifient, dans l'inconscient, les *femmes* et leur *chevauchement*.[26]

The symbolic meaning of the horse was acknowledged by Stendhal himself. In Chapter 17 of *La Chartreuse de Parme*, Count Mosca says to Gina:

"Nous n'aurons que vingt mille livres de rente," lui dit-il, "pour vivre tous trois à Naples, Fabrice, vous et moi. Fabrice et moi nous aurons un cheval de selle à nous deux."[27]

Martineau mentions in a note to these lines: "Stendhal voit que sa phrase prête à 'plaisanterie basse,' aussi, note-t-il sur l'exemplaire Chaper, d'ôter cette ligne.[28] Again, in *Lucien Leuwen*, Stendhal has Mme Grandet compare herself to a horse: "Le voilà [M. Grandet] qui parle de ma réputation comme il parlerait des bonnes qualités de son cheval."[29]

In the language of unconscious symbolism, then, the horse represents a woman, Octave's mother, and the jewels represent her genitals—her most precious treasure. Her offer of them to Octave can thus be seen as a representation of the adolescent's wish that his mother initiate him into adult sexual life herself. Octave of course rejects these offers because of the guilt and fear attached to this wish.

It is thus quite evident that Blin is wrong, that Octave's impotence is caused, at least in part, by his fixation on his mother. Nevertheless, recognition of this fact does not resolve the entire enigma of the novel, for there are many other works of fiction based on similar material in which the hero is not actually impotent, the *Rouge* and the *Chartreuse*, for instance. The question still remains, therefore, of establishing the precise nature of Octave's illness.

In the novel itself no mention is made of the true nature of Octave's malady. However, it is frequently alluded to as the subject of a great "confession" that he is to make. Characteristically he can never quite bring himself to do so. One is tempted to explain this reticence on the grounds that such an admission would understandably be a terrible blow to Octave's ego and would make life unbearable for him with those who knew his secret. This explanation is acceptable, however, only at the cost of ignoring one highly important fact. Octave constantly feels himself obliged to *reveal* this secret. Indeed, he makes three different attempts to do so. Once he confesses that he was a kleptomaniac in his childhood. A second time he writes the truth in a letter but does not mail it. The third time, on his death bed, he finally sends Armance the letter.

That this whole affair was the result of an irrational compulsion, entirely outside of his conscious control, is shown by the episode of the letter. After consulting a friend of the family, Octave goes to a cafe and writes his letter:

En sortant du café, il chercha des yeux une boîte aux lettres, le hasard voulut qu'il n'en vît pas. Bientôt un reste de ce sentiment pénible qui le portait à retarder un tel aveu le plus possible, vint lui persuader qu'une lettre de cette importance ne devait pas être confiée à la poste, qu'il était mieux de la placer lui-même dans la caisse d'oranger du jardin d'Andilly. Octave n'eut pas l'esprit de reconnaître dans l'idée de ce retard une dernière illusion d'une passion à peine vaincue. [p. 22]

And Stendhal has arranged things so that Octave, incensed by the false letter planted by his uncle, tears up his own instead of leaving it for Armance to read.

It is interesting to note that Stendhal himself had the same difficulty as Octave. Try as he might, he could not find a way of informing his readers that Octave was impotent. Yet without this bit of information the reader was bound to look on the novel as more an inept attempt at mystification than anything else. Stendhal makes several remarks, in his letters and marginal comments, which show that he was acutely aware of the necessity of imparting this fact to his readers, but he claimed that "good taste" would not allow him to do so. Martineau, who agrees that this omission was a great error, seems to accept Stendhal's reason for it:

Jamais livre n'eut plus besoin de préface. On ne le comprend pas sans explication. L'auteur y parle sans cesse d'un secret qu'il ne révèle jamais, afin de raconter honnêtement une histoire assez scabreuse. Il se félicitait de sa décence, mais il l'exagéra à tel point qu'elle apparaît comme un défaut dans une oeuvre à d'autres égards pleine d'intérêt. [p. i]

But if Stendhal was so concerned about offending the public, why did he choose such a topic in the first place, especially since La Touche's novel on the same topic had so recently caused a great scandal? As with Octave, I think we are safe in concluding that Stendhal was under a compulsion to reveal this secret and to keep it hidden at the same time. This claim is further supported by the fact that Stendhal, in his *avant-propos* and later on in the novel, keeps assuring the reader that he is not responsible for its content and that this very content might give the reader a bad opinion of him. In other words he feels guilty about and tries to rid himself of this feeling by disclaiming any responsibility for it. It is true that these disclaimers are made with reference to the social and political views propounded in the novel; however, Stendhal made no secret of these views in real life; he expressed them openly to his friends and even published them in his various writings. Why then should he suddenly be ashamed of them in a novel, where he could invoke the right of poetic license to defend himself against reproaches? The problem is easily resolved as a matter of displacement. The feelings that Stendhal expresses in relation to the social and political ideas of the novel have been transferred from their real object, its unconscious content. By putting these feelings back into their proper context, we are able to discover the kernel of truth hidden in them. Stendhal is right, in a sense, in saying that he is not responsible for these contents, because they originate in his unconscious, without his conscious knowledge. The guilt he feels pertains to the forbidden nature of the unconscious phantasies, all of which ultimately deal with incest. His compulsion to reveal and hide simultaneously Octave's "secret" would then pertain, in reality, to his own "secret," namely, the unconscious phantasies expressed in the novel.

Applying these conclusions to Octave makes it possible to explain the situation so beautifully summed up by Blin when he called Octave's impotence "un *défaut* dont il garde conscience comme d'une *faute*." The source of the guilt which transforms the defect into a fault, in Octave's own eyes, is the unconscious wish, or wishes, which he acts out in the novel. The guilt feeling reaches his consciousness only after it has been displaced from its true origin onto a resultant product.

All that remains, therefore, is to undo the work of displacement in order to trace the feelings back to their origin. This might seem difficult, if not impossible, without Stendhal's associations to guide us. Fortunately, there is a more convenient method at our disposal, in the novel itself. In these last paragraphs I have been maintaining that Stendhal and his alter ego Octave were trying to confess and conceal something, but that this something, Octave's (and Stendhal's?) impotence, was not the real object of their exertions. It was the very fact that they wanted to do both at the same time which drew attention to the subterfuge involved. The form of the disguise revealed the presence of what was to be hidden from view, as so often happens with the compromise formations that result from unconscious wishes. It is therefore to be expected that what is actually confessed will, in like manner, indicate the latent content.

At the beginning of the novel Octave is described as a very withdrawn young man. Time and again the narrator or the other characters of the book, especially Mme de Malivert, remark on his excessive penchant for daydreaming, on his apparent lack of involvement with other people and external reality: "Mme de Malivert observait constamment que la vie réelle, loin d'être une source d'émotions pour son fils, n'avait d'autre effet que de l'impatienter, comme si elle fût venue le distraire et l'arracher d'une façon importune à sa chère rêverie" (p. 16). This rejection of the outside world, along with his immensely exaggerated sense of duty, is often cited by the other characters of the novel as proof of Octave's demoniacal character. Since it is the cause of his condemnation by others and a source of self-reproach, it must in some way be related to his sense of guilt, to his crime, as he calls it. That Octave's pangs of conscience are directly related to sexual matters is betrayed by a seemingly casual statement later in the novel, when Octave is debating, for no apparent reason, whether he should marry Armance: "La voix du devoir qui commençait à se faire entendre prescrivait à Octave de fuir Mlle de Zohiloff à l'instant . . ." (p. 133).

Octave's conscience thus interposes itself between him and Armance in much the same way that "reality" intervenes between him and his daydreams. One concrete element of this vague "reality" can be deduced from Mme de Malivert's observations. In making a kind of balance sheet of her son's good and bad qualities, she happens to think of his tendency toward dissimulation. "This cruel reality" Stendhal goes on to say, destroyed her dreams of Octave's happiness. As an example of this supposedly wicked trait the author tells us that Octave hated to play chess with his uncle, Commander Soubirane, but that he pretended to like it! The absurdity of basing such dark forebodings on so banal a fact is patent. Indeed, it is so blatant that I am led to wonder what could have prompted Stendhal to have used this example. The answer can be deduced from an analogy from the psychology of the obsessional neuroses. If an obsessional is asked to give an example of the thing he fears, his "example" will in fact reveal the real source of his fear.[30] In like manner, it is safe to assume that Stendhal's "example" contains the true obstacle to Octave's dreams of happiness. The cruel reality is, namely, none other than the commander himself. If one bears in mind that it is the latter who, by means of a forged letter and other tactics, does all in his power to prevent Octave's marriage to Armance, this conclusion will be deprived of its apparently fanciful character.

If one further recalls the scorn heaped on the commander (who is in any case Octave's *uncle*), by Stendhal and his hero, it will require no great imagination to see in M. de Soubirane a representation of the "bad father," who opposes the gratification of his son's wishes.

But what is this gratification, the source of such great guilt feeling? As already noted, Octave is reputed to have an evil character because of his excessive indulgence in phantasies and his consequent lack of interest in the real world. In order to remedy this condition, his mother urges him to frequent the salon of his cousin, Mme de Bonnivet. The curious thing about the relationship between Octave and this cousin is that it consists almost entirely in the latter's attempts to convert him to a new, quasi-mystical religion, that is, to save his soul. In fact, he states that his love for Armance dates from these discussions with her protector: "J'aime Armance, et je l'aime depuis que je me suis soumis à entendre les dissertations de Mme de Bonnivet sur la philosophie allemande" (p. 132). Furthermore, the author insinuates that, without realizing it, Octave is also in love with Mme de Bonnivet:

Durant cette absence cruelle, Octave ne put qu'adresser à Mme de Bonnivet deux ou trois lettres fort jolies; mais d'un ton singulier. Si un homme étranger à cette société les avait vues, il eût pensé qu'Octave était amoureux fou de Mme de Bonnivet et n'osait lui avouer son amour. [p. 196]

Now, taking all these facts together, one can distinguish in them a pattern in conformity with a universal phantasy described by Freud in the second part of his article, "Dostoyevsky and Parricide." In it, apropos of a novella by Stefan Zweig, he traces such stories of salvation back to the adolescent's desire that his mother should "save" him from the evils he imagines consequent to the sin of onanism by initiating him into the mystery of adult sexuality with her own body.[31] To be sure, the version in *Armance* shows a high degree of sublimation, but Octave's sarcastic remarks about Mme de Bonnivet's attempts to convert him show, on one level, that this type of sublimation was impossible for him.[32] That is why he is more interested in the more substantial possibilities offered by a liaison with the coquette, Mme d'Aumale, although there, too, his inhibitions win out.

On one level, then, Octave's crime is onanism. However, as Freud points out in the article cited, the adolescent, or the adult neurotic, is in a sense mistaken in attaching his guilt feeling to this practice. For it is not onanism itself, but the phantasies which regularly accompany it that form the deepest source of guilt, and these phantasies have their roots in early childhood. In the novel, however, these roots are revealed in the confessions made by Octave.

In particular, Octave admits to two "crimes," visiting prostitutes and kleptomania. As regards the latter, Martineau notes:

M. Georges Blin, dans la préface de son édition d'*Armance,* a fait remarquer que le vol morbide et les perversions sexuelles, au dire de quelques auteurs, se trouvent assez souvent associés. Encore faut-il remarquer qu'ici l'aveu d'Octave ne saurait guère être retenu, car Stendhal ignorant tout de ces théories récentes, il doit falloir voir en lui un simple alibi destiné à égarer Armance.[33]

The fact that Stendhal was, of necessity, unaware of "these modern theories" does not render this admission valueless, as Martineau supposes. For he fails to explain why Stendhal chose to have Octave admit to this particular "crime" as an alibi rather than any other. The association between compulsive stealing and the perversions, mentioned by Blin, points to a common source in infantile sexuality. And, indeed, analytic experience has shown that such activities represent to the child "stealing mother's love." Kleptomania is thus a symptom of an ambivalence conflict in the child's feelings for its mother. It feels cheated of this love, for some reason or other, and is therefore angry at mother, and at the same time it wants and needs her love, that is, it loves her. Stendhal did not need to be acquainted with a theoretical presentation of this meaning, because he unconsciously knew it already, probably from his own childhood experiences.

Octave's other "crime" is that of visiting prostitutes. As is well known, Stendhal was guilty of the same offense in real life. But once again I must ask why he lent Octave this particular facet of his own life. The origin and significance of this behavior have been discussed in some detail in an article by Freud, "A Special Type of Choice of Object by Men:"

Investigation then leads us back to the period in the boy's life at which he first obtained more or less detailed knowledge of the sexual relations between adults, somewhere in the years before puberty. The secret of sexual life is revealed to him then in coarse language, undisguisedly derogatory and hostile in intent. . . . The greatest impression on the child who is being initiated is made by the relation the information bears to his own parents. . . . Along with this piece of "sexual enlightenment" there seldom fails to go, as a corollary, a further one about the existence of certain women who practice sexual intercourse as a means of livelihood and are universally despised in consequence. . . . When he cannot any longer maintain the doubt that claims exception for his own parents from the ugly sexual behavior of the rest of the world, he says to himself with cynical logic that the difference between his mother and a whore is after all not so very great, since at bottom they both do the same thing.[34]

To the unconscious, then, having relations with the prostitute may be equated with having them with the mother. What distinguishes this aspect of the mother complex from many others is the strong element of ambivalence present. The child evidently feels a great deal of resentment toward his mother for doing such "ugly" things with his father.

In addition to the two crimes that Octave admits to, stealing and visiting prostitutes, mention is made of a third possibility. To be sure, Armance, not Octave, makes this suggestion, but it is Stendhal who puts the words into her mouth: "Il devint bientôt évident pour [Armance] qu'Octave avait commis quelque grand crime . . . et en honnête homme il ne voulait pas permettre qu'elle liât son sort à celui *d'un assassin* peut-être . . ." (pp. 225–226, italics mine). So she thinks he might be a murderer! Then whom did he kill? Of course, in the novel he does not kill anyone; but then he never stole anything either. Once again Octave's crime is dealing with a phantasy, in this case a thought murder. The question then becomes, "Whom did he wish to kill?" Since I have already shown that his other crimes were, at bottom, the desire to possess his mother, his murder must be the concomitant desire to do away with his father. And in fact this wish is fulfilled in the novel. The only death that occurs in it, apart from Octave's own, is related in the very last sentence: "Peu après, *le marquis de Malivert étant mort*" (p. 245, italics mine).

The marquis' death, like the fulfillment of Octave's other aggressive and sexual wishes, can take place only after appropriate retribution has been exacted. After marrying Armance, Octave spends a short time with her in Marseilles and then embarks on a voyage to Greece, ostensibly to help fight the Turks. In fact, a few days after his departure, he commits suicide by poisoning himself. The primary reason for this act is that it is a punishment for his death wishes against his father, which, as just noted, are realized immediately thereafter.

The second factor can be deduced from the manner and circumstances of Octave's suicide. He carries out his intention by means of *drinking* poison. Furthermore, he does it after seeing Mount Kalos, which means "beautiful mountain," clearly symbolic of a breast, the more so since, apparently, no such mountain exists. Lastly, he dies on the sea, probably an indication of a rebirth phantasy. The beauty of this passage has been noted by more than one critic. They attribute its peculiar quality to the euphonious cadence of the sentence. Although there is no reason to deny this, I think its attraction is predominantly due to its meaning, a symbolic return to the mother. Its peculiar quality can thus be given a name that describes it perfectly—nostalgia.

Octave's suicide is thus both a punishment for his murderous impulses against his father and the fulfillment of his wish to be reunited with his mother in death, life after death being conceived as a return to the warmth and darkness of the womb. And although Mme de Malivert does not die, as do Mme de Rênal and La Sanseverina, both she and Armance are consigned to live in a convent, i.e., to retire from life.

At the deepest level, then, the suicide phantasy represents an oral ambivalence conflict, the desire to return to the warmth and comfort of early infancy coupled with a primitive attempt at revenge on the mother who deprived the baby of its paradise. This meaning is well documented by psychoanalytic experience, for example, Hanns Sachs' *Gemeinsame Tagträume*.[35] The positive or nostalgic side of these feelings is shown by Octave's desire for death as a release from all pain and trouble, repeated many times in the novel. The negative element could not, of course, be expressed so directly, since it would be much too shocking to be acknowledged. Nevertheless its presence is betrayed, first, by the various examples of ill feeling discussed above, and, second, in a way more directly related to suicide, by certain remarks and events. For example, in a note on the Bucci edition, Stendhal writes:

Comme [Octave] ne pouvait songer à atteindre à un certain bonheur qu'il se figurait extrême, son imagination ne voyait plus dans la vie aucun plaisir ni rien qui lui semblât valoir la peine de vivre. *Sans un extrême attachement pour sa mère, l'idée de son malheur l'eût conduit à mettre un terme (Sans son amour pour sa mère il eût terminé, mis un terme) à sa vie.* [p. 268, italics mine]

Stendhal's hesitation in choosing the best formulation for this thought is a fair indication of the importance its hidden meaning had for him, especially since he himself was surprised at the small number of alterations he had made in revising the text. From the passage cited it is clear that suicide meant "hurting his mother."

Another indication of this intention occurs in the final sentence of the novel in which not only Armance but also Mme de Malivert is consigned to living in a convent. The revenge motif previously spoken of in connection with Armance and Countess Curial thus applies equally well to Octave's mother. Finally, Octave's ability to express such excessive attachment to his mother can now be understood as, in part, an effort to mask the hostility he felt toward her. Since this hostility was undoubtedly even more threatening to him than his attachment to her, he was able to make the attachment manifest in word and deed as a defensive measure against his negative feelings.[36]

The objection might be raised that I am making too much of Octave's suicide which is, after all, merely a natural way of getting him out of his predicament and ending the novel. The fact remains, however, that it is not an isolated incident used to furnish a convenient denouement, but rather a phantasy which is repeated several times throughout the novel. Thus, after his first visit to Mme de Bonnivet's salon and the first appearance of Armance in the novel, he has a narrow escape from being crushed by a carriage and then indulges in a long daydream about suicide (pp. 24–25). Here again, as in the scene depicting his mental torment after discovering that he is in love with Armance, the main theme of his musing is suicide. Interestingly enough, his encounter with the carriage is immediately preceded by a daydream of falling in love. Again, Octave smiles at the possibility of death when his doctor informs him that his chances for recovering from his tetanus infection are not very good (p. 170). The conclusion is inescapable that suicide is the dominant theme of the novel as well as its end.

It is now time to bring together a few loose ends left dangling in the previous discussion. I suggested two possible explanations for the unusual title of the novel. According to the first, Armance represents Countess Curial, and secondarily Stendhal's other loves, on whom he wanted to avenge himself. Thus it was her story because it was directed against her. In the second, I maintained that Armance and Octave were equivalent, because of Stendhal's unconscious feminine identification. These two views can be reconciled by recognizing the first as Stendhal's conscious or preconscious train of thought while writing the novel. It must be assumed that his ideas of disappointment and vengeance toward Countess Curial reawakened the memory not only of his earlier unfortunate love affairs but also of his infantile feelings of love and resentment toward his parents. The powerful impression made upon him by his current contradictory feelings toward Countess Curial mobilized the two basic ambivalence conflicts of his childhood, preserved in his unconscious. The title thus derives from the surface level of thought and the deeper conflicts; his desire and revenge are aimed first at the countess, but ultimately at his mother.

Several psychologists and sociologists have asserted that "the germ of all subsequent development of social relations"[37] can be found in the original mother-child relationship. The motif of revenge against the mother might thus be the unconscious source of the social criticism in *Armance* (see above pp. 25–28). The infant's helpless rage against its seemingly all-powerful mother later becomes the young man's hostility towards his society; society also is capable of frustrating the individual's wishes and is also relatively impervious to the individual's attacks. Stendhal's and Octave's sarcastic attacks on Restoration society are thus derivatives of Beyle's childhood aggression towards his mother. Their content, which is the supposed inadequacy and despair of Restoration nobility, is a projection of Beyle's own feelings of impotent rage and consequent suicidal depression.

Unable to integrate this aggression which threatens to destroy his love object, yet desiring and needing to preserve it as well, to be able to love, Stendhal (and Octave) reaches a curious compromise solution, the so-called double denouement analyzed by Prévost:

Ce besoin de progression [in the plot] fait que Stendhal et son lecteur, au lieu de porter à Octave un intérêt de plus en plus vif, s'intéressent au contraire de plus en plus à Armance, ou plutôt à l'impossible mariage entre les deux jeunes gens. Cette antithèse entre la trame traditionnelle d'un roman d'amour, qui mène vers le mariage, et la donnée du livre, déconcerte le lecteur.

Il faudra qu'il y ait deux dénouements.

1. D'abord, comme dans tous les romans, les obstacles sociaux à la conclusion du mariage seront levés.

2. Quand le mariage aura lieu, Octave, pour fuir cette union impossible, se tuera.

Ainsi le second dénouement, la mort, est d'accord avec la donnée première du livre et en désaccord avec le développement heureux avant le second dénouement, celui-là tragique. Nous retrouverons cette antinomie dans le *Rouge et le Noir*. Et le double dénouement, si singulier à première vue, sera une des plus constantes habitudes de Stendhal.[38]

The observation is certainly just, but Prévost's explanation for it is belied by his own remark that Stendhal uses the double ending in *Le Rouge et le Noir* and other novels, *La Chartreuse de Parme* in particular. For in these two novels there is no *donnée,* comparable to Octave's impotence in *Armance, to* warrant Julien's de facto suicide or Fabrice's retreat to the charterhouse as logical denouements of their plots. In each case this unusual arrangement can be traced back to the presence of these two related unconscious tendencies: first, the hero's desires toward his mother are fulfilled; then his guilt toward father and mother, stemming from his conflicting feelings of hostility and affection for them, wins out. Each of Stendhal's heroes was doomed to end in withdrawal from the world, and failure.

In each case the young hero, Stendhal's current alter ego, is described as he attempts to make the crucial step from adolescence to maturity. Broadly speaking, this involves two major areas of life, sexuality and love, and finding a career. In all three novels the career definitely takes second place to love. Octave abandons his career as an artillery officer to stay with his family and never seriously tries to find another profession. Fabrice allows himself to be made into an archbishop but obviously he takes no real interest in that occupation; his real occupation is his preoccupation with his love life or the lack of it. And even Julien, who devotes so much time and energy to securing himself a place in society, shows by his senseless attack on Mme de Rênal that his career was after all only of secondary importance to him. The real story of each hero concerns his attempt to experience mature love, and this involves detaching his libido from its early incestuous objects. But this striving is limited by Beyle's unintegrated rage. Each of his heroes regresses first to the negative oedipal level, and when each realizes that this type of love does not fulfill his desires, he falls back into despair. The resulting death or withdrawal from the world in defeat is also a gratification of the wishes of Stendhal's heroes for self-punishment. They cannot bear to succeed, or rather, punishment is their greatest success.

Happiness' End

On September 8, 1829, while leafing through the daily news-paper, Beyle came upon the announcement of the death of Pierre Daru, his cousin and protector. Beyle had been planning to leave Paris at that time but immediately went to offer his condolences to the Daru family. Unfortunately, there was no one at home but the servants. Although the funeral was to be held three days later, Beyle decided to leave for Italy that very evening. As he puts it, in his *Souvenirs d'Egotisme:*

Je me trouvais bien ingrat. Je mis le comble à mon ingratitude en partant le soir même pour l'Italie, je crois, j'avançais mon départ, je serais mort de douleur en entrant dans sa maison. Là aussi il y avait un peu de la folie qui me rendait si baroque en 1821.[1]

In fact, he did not go to Italy but undertook a lengthy, rambling voyage through southern France—Toulouse, Carcas-sonne, Perpignan—to Barcelona. Returning to France, he passed through Montpellier on his way to Grenoble, his first visit to his home town since the death of his father, ten years earlier. After spending some time in Grenoble, he returned to southern France, to Marseilles, where he had lived, almost twenty-five years earlier, with one of the first mistresses of his youth, the actress Mélanie Guilbert. It was there, during the night of the twenty-fifth of October 1829, that he first had the idea of writing a novel based on the story of one Antoine Berthet, whom he had heard about in a recent conversation.

Who was this Berthet? The son of a poor worker from the town of Brangues, a village in the same department as Grenoble (l'Isère), he had started to prepare himself for an ecclesiastical career by entering a theological seminary. For reasons still not fully understood, he soon left the seminary. Generally, it is believed that his departure was due to illness, but it is possible that he was asked to leave because of "dangerous reading" or some other transgression. In any event, he soon became the tutor of the children of a M. Michoud de La Tour, also of Brangues. This career was also rather short-lived. The reason this time was certainly not illness. Berthet claimed that he had become the lover of Mme Michoud. However, this claim was not proved, and it is possible that it was based more on his phantasy than on reality. Aided by the influence of his priest, he managed to be admitted to the seminary in Grenoble. Once again he was dismissed, and once again he became a tutor, this time in the household of a M. de Cordon. Apparently chastened by his earlier experience, he made no advances to Mme de Cordon; instead he started an affair with Cordon's daughter. Upon losing this position, he swore to avenge himself, and on July 22, 1827, he shot Mme Michoud in a church at Brangues, where she had been attending mass. Condemned to death by the court, he was guillotined February 23, 1829.

The proceedings of Berthet's trial had been published in the *Gazette des Tribunaux* toward the end of 1827. In all probability Beyle did not read these accounts when they first came out, but it is known that he had obtained copies of them before or while he was in Marseilles in 1829. And so, on the night of October 25, he began to read or reread them. Within a few weeks, he had completed the first draft of what was to become *Le Rouge et le Noir*.

Such are the facts that have been painstakingly assembled by various Stendhal scholars and summarized by Henri Martineau in his introduction to the novel and his biography of the author. Virtually every moment of Beyle's life during these months has been accounted for, and yet the facts do not seem to gel. How can the vicissitudes of his journey be explained? Why did he leave Paris before Daru's funeral? Most important, what is the relationship between Daru's death, or rather the impact of this event on Beyle, and the story of Berthet? It must be remembered that recently Beyle had heard of a similar case, that of Laffargue, which he spoke of at length in the *Promenades dans Rome,* yet it had not inspired him to write a novel.

Since the whole process seems to have been set off by the news of Pierre Daru's death, I will begin by examining Beyle's relationship with him. When Beyle first arrived in Paris in 1799, a youth scarcely seventeen years old, he intended to take the entrance examination for the Ecole Polytechnique. For reasons unknown he failed to take this test and soon fell violently ill. Alone in the big city, almost without friends, and separated from his family for the first time in his life, he lay feverish in his room. Then his cousin Daru arrived on the scene, had the youth moved to his own home, and procured the services of a doctor for him. When Beyle recovered, it was Daru who found him a job in the offices of the War Ministry. Since office work was not to Beyle's liking, Daru once again used his influence to obtain for him a commission as second lieutenant in the French armies in Italy. Indeed, as long as Napoleon remained in power, Daru, despite several quarrels with his young cousin, made sure that the latter received various jobs connected with the army. Then, in 1814 when Beyle's career in government was reaching its zenith, Napoleon fell. After trying unsuccessfully to obtain a position from the new Bourbon regime, Beyle left for a long stay in Italy, which lasted until 1821. Soon after his return to France, he renewed his applications to the Restoration government, still counting on the influence of Daru to see him through. Indeed, just before the latter's death, he was taking measures to see that Beyle's request would be successful.

How did Beyle show his gratitude to Daru for thirty years of protection? Although he often showed remarkable skill in carrying out his assignments, equally often he shirked his duties, went on extended leaves of absence without permission, and indulged in various types of misconduct, all of which caused Daru a great deal of embarrassment. Several times Daru refused to protect his cousin any longer because of this.

Beyle's other means of showing his gratitude was still less laudable. He fell in love with Mme Daru, while they were both in Austria during the Napoleonic wars, tried without success to seduce her (see "Consultation pour Banti" in *Oeuvres Intimes*). I am reminded of Berthet's behavior in the family of his benefactor, M. Michoud.

Reviewing all these facts, I may suggest that for Beyle, Pierre Daru, older cousin, protector, and sexual competitor, was a second incarnation of his father. This conclusion is all the more probable because Beyle himself twice makes the same connection, though indirectly. In his diary entry of January 20, 1812, he writes: "Quand je vais chez *moth*[er]."[2] In note 2 Martineau explains: "Chez Mme Daru mère."[3] The second allusion is to the passage cited at the beginning of this chapter in which

Beyle emphasizes two things: his feeling of ingratitude toward Daru, and the fact that he acted at the time in the same mad fashion as in 1821.

The *Souvenirs d'Egotisme,* in which this citation appears, was an attempt on the author's part to come to terms with the most tormented period of his life. On his return to Paris in 1821, he suffered a severe attack of depression, a veritable mental crisis which lasted several months. Beyle and his biographers attribute this crisis to the frustration of his love for Mathilde Dembowska, whom he had courted unsuccessfully for almost three years in Italy. He had already written one book inspired by this unhappy affair, *De l'Amour.* Yet both he and his biographers overlook the fact that this was neither the first nor the last such affair in his love life; hence this explanation fails to account for the special significance this particular one admittedly held for him.

Now there is no question that Beyle was madly in love with Mathilde, as early as the spring of 1818, but there is considerable room for doubt that the frustration of this love had such a strong and lasting effect on him. It is usually true that for an external frustration to have such devastating effects on a person's psyche, it must in some way become linked to a preexisting, internal mental conflict. The source of this conflict lies near at hand: toward the end of July, 1819, shortly after being rebuffed by his lady, Beyle received the news of his father's death. As Freud has said, the death of a man's father is generally the most important event in his life, for it revives all the powerful infantile desires and fears concerned with that personage.

When Beyle alluded to his madness of 1821, he was thus referring to his state of mind that resulted from his father's death, the memory of which was naturally revived by the death of Daru, who had for so long played the role of father toward him. Beyle was stricken with guilt because his prehistoric wish for his father's death had once again come true. Since the belief in the "omnipotence of thought" lurked deep within him, he felt responsible for the realization of this wish. But, according to the law of the talion which governs unconscious morality, as punishment he too would have to die, to die of grief as he put it.

His next reaction was thus to flee from Paris, as far and as fast as possible. But as a piece of iron is drawn to a magnet, so was he inexorably led back to Grenoble, for the death of his "father" represented to his unconscious the golden opportunity to fulfill that other prehistoric desire—to possess his mother. Of course, in reality she had been dead some forty years, but her powerful image lived on in his mind, as is amply proved by his novels. In the same way ten years earlier, after attending his father's funeral in Grenoble, he went to Paris at first, but, despite his knowledge of the futility of his effort, soon returned to Italy and Mathilde one last time.

Undoubtedly his inner torment, caused by the battle between his incestuous desires, his guilt and love for his father, was only increased by his stay in Grenoble. When it reached unbearable proportions, he once again took flight, this time to Marseilles. The persistence of his wishes can be deduced from the fact that he chose as refuge the city in which he had actually lived with a woman for the only time in his life. There he finally arrived at the solution of his troubles which, although far from satisfactory, was to serve him the rest of his life. He wrote his first great novel, *Le Rouge et le Noir*.

In it Stendhal directly transposed the story of Berthet into that of Julien Sorel. Mme Michoud becomes Mme de Rênal, the seminary is transported from Grenoble to Besançon, and the Cordon family is replaced by the La Moles. Stendhal then divided the novel into four sections corresponding to the stages of Berthet-Julien's career (each pair of sections constituting one of the two Books of the novel): (1) Verrières, the story of Julien's love for Mme de Rênal; (2) Besançon, his stay in the seminary; (3) Paris, his affair with Mathilde de La Mole; (4) Prison, Julien's attempted murder of Mme de Rênal, and his last days.

In the first part of the novel, Stendhal describes Julien as entirely different, both physically and mentally, from his two older brothers and his father. Whereas the latter are large, strong, coarse, and uneducated, he is small, thin, and studious. He is much more like the son of a cultivated bourgeois or noble family than that of the nouveau-riche peasant Sorel. Moreover, his awareness of this difference causes him to fear the other members of his family, but at the same time gives him a feeling of superiority over them. In the course of the novel this vague feeling of difference takes on a more precise form. In Chapter 7, when Julien grows indignant at the hypocrisy of M. Valenod, one of the leaders of Verrières society who runs the local poorhouse and orphanage, he cries: "Ah! monstres! monstres! Et moi aussi, je suis une sorte d'enfant trouvé, haï de mon père, de mes frères, de toute ma famille."[4] His sympathy for the supposedly mistreated orphans of Verrières stems from his own feeling that he is a kind of foundling, since his own father hates him. (Incidentally, it is surprising that Julien adds, "by my whole family," since his father and brothers apparently are his whole family.)

As the story progresses, the idea that Julien might not be his father's son comes more and more to the fore. Curiously enough it is not only Julien who entertains this phantasy. At the very end of Book 1 Abbé Pirard recommends Julien to the Marquis de La Mole in these terms: "On le dit fils d'un charpentier de nos montagnes, mais je le croirais plutôt fils naturel de quelque homme riche. Je lui ai vu recevoir une lettre anonyme ou pseudonyme avec une lettre de change de cinq cents francs" (p. 211). Some twenty pages later, Pirard, struck by Julien's extraordinary honesty, thinks: "Serait-ce la force du sang?" and, after a moment of hesitation, goes on to say: "Ce qu'il y a de singulier . . . c'est que le marquis vous [Julien] connaît" (p. 233). He refers here to the fact that the marquis correctly identified Julien as the young seminary student whom Pirard was proposing to him as personal secretary merely on the basis of his description. The marquis' knowledge had naturally given the priest a shock.

But was his astonishment, in fact, completely natural? On the contrary, his reaction seems quite absurd in light of the events that led the marquis (for it was he) to send the anonymous letter with the check to Julien:

Sans cesse en correspondance avec l'abbé Pirard, pour une affaire qu'ils suivaient tous les deux avec passion, le marquis finit par goûter le genre d'esprit de l'abbé . . . L'abbé Pirard disait au marquis qu'on voulait l'obliger, à force d'avanies, à donner sa démission. Dans la colère que lui inspira le stategème infâme, suivant lui, employé contre Julien, *il conta son histoire au marquis.* [p. 202]

So it was Pirard himself who told Julien's story to the marquis! This, then, is one of the points in the novel where, as in a dream, the work of secondary elaboration has failed to unite the dream elements into a coherent whole. And, as in a dream, a study of it should lead to one of the important phantasies underlying the manifest content of the novel.

The next expression of this theme is made neither by the abbé nor by Julien, but by a minor character, the Chevalier de Beauvoisis. The latter, who has just fought a rather ridiculous duel with Julien, is appalled by the humble social position of his adversary, for he fears that it will put him in a bad light in high society. In order to forestall any possible ridicule on this account, he spreads the rumor that Julien is the illegitimate son of an intimate friend of the Marquis de La Mole (p. 270).

The marquis himself soon gets wind of this rumor and, far from being angered by it, feels that it is in his interest to give it credence in Parisian society. He even goes so far as to embellish it somewhat, for he states that Julien is supposedly the illegitimate son of a rich nobleman from Franche-Comté (p. 270). This last detail was omitted by the good chevalier.

It can scarcely be attributed to chance that in the very next chapter, the marquis, suffering from an attack of the gout, hits upon the idea of conferring upon his secretary a kind of second personality: "Permettez, mon cher Sorel, que je vous fasse cadeau d'un habit bleu: quand il vous conviendra de la prendre et de venir chez moi, vous serez, à mes yeux, le frère cadet du comte de Chaulnes, c'est-à-dire le fils de mon ami le vieux duc" (p. 272).

Once this idea has been explicitly expressed, it seems, like a contagious disease, to take on an independent life of its own. The epidemic attacks not only Julien, Pirard, Beauvoisis, and the marquis, but also Mathilde. One day, while speaking to the young gentlemen of her society, her brother Norbert, the Marquis de Croisenois, Messrs. de Caylus and de Luz, she becomes indignant at their apparent scorn for the low-born Julien. In order to emphasize the greatness of the latter's individual worth, she invents the following hypothesis:

"Que demain quelque hobereau des montagnes de la Franche-Comté," dit-elle à M. de Caylus, "s'aperçoive que Julien est son fils naturel, et lui donne un nom et quelques milliers de francs, dans six semaines il a des moustaches comme vous, messieurs . . . Mais que vous restera-t-il si j'ai la malice de donner pour père à Julien un duc espagnol, prisonnier de guerre à Besançon du temps de Napoléon, et qui, par scrupule de conscience, le reconnaît à son lit de mort?" [p. 314]

Finally, after the marquis has actually given Julien a fortune, a commission in the army and a title of nobility, and is apparently willing to allow Julien to marry Mathilde, the young man almost comes to believe in the literal truth of this phantasy:

Serait-il bien possible, se disait-il, que je fusse le fils naturel de quelque grand seigneur exilé dans nos montagnes par le terrible Napoléon? A chaque instant cette idée lui semblaït moins improbable . . . Ma haine pour mon père serait une preuve . . . Je ne serais plus un monstre! [p. 446]

The fact that this phantasy is put into the mouths of various characters who seem to have arrived at it more or less independently should not be misleading as to its true source. For in each case it is formulated in essentially the same terms. In the last analysis, this idea, like everything else in the novel, can be traced back to the mind of the author, Stendhal.

Now what is the true identity of this man who is supposed to be Julien's real father? Is he merely some vaguely defined "rich gentleman?" Close scrutiny of the various statements of the phantasy shows rather that there are two more or less distinct candidates for this high honor. Both, of course, are rich and of noble lineage, but the first is said to be an old friend of the Marquis de La Mole, the Duke of Chaulnes; the second has no name, but he is of Spanish extraction, an enemy of Napoleon, and comes from Franche-Comté.

The Duke of Chaulnes, aside from the passage cited above, is mentioned only twice in the novel. The first time, Abbé

Pirard is describing the members of the La Mole family to Julien, shortly after his arrival in Paris. (How Pirard knows all this is another mystery, since until shortly before that time he had never even met the marquis!) He explains that Mme de La Mole, the marquis' wife, is the daughter of the old Duke of Chaulnes. Thus, the latter is not simply the friend of the marquis, but his father-in-law. The second mention of the duke is even more revealing, because it is obviously an "error" on Stendhal's part, one of those little lapses of everyday mental life whose meaning is often portentous. In order to emphasize Mathilde's unusual character, Stendhal describes her extraordinary boldness:

Elle avait trouvé quelque bonheur en se permettant d'écrire à quelques jeunes gens de la société. Cette hardiesse si inconvenante, si imprudente chez une jeune fille, pouvait la déshonorer aux yeux de M. de Croisenois, *du duc de Chaulnes son père* [p. 535], et de tout l'hôtel de Chaulnes, qui voyant se rompre le mariage projeté, aurait voulu savoir pourquoi. [p. 328, italics mine]

According to this passage, the duke is Mathilde's *father!*[5] In other words, he is another representation of the marquis himself.

This interpretation is supported by several other facts. When sending the anonymous letter to Julien, the marquis signed it "Paul Sorel," as though it had come from Julien's father. When Pirard thinks "Serait-ce la force du sang?" and then continues by telling Julien that the marquis knew his name, clearly he thinks in the interval, represented by three dots in the text, that the marquis must be Julien's real father. What other bridge could there be between the two thoughts? Finally, after giving his secretary the famous blue suit, the marquis thinks: "Je le traite *comme un fils;* eh bien! où est l'inconvénient?" (p. 276).

The second candidate is no less interesting. In the very first chapter of the novel a man is introduced who is noble and rich, who lives in one of the most beautiful towns of Franche-Comté (p. 3), who is a sworn enemy of everything having to do with the great Napoleon, and who is of Spanish extraction (p. 5). The town is Verrières, and the man—M. de Rênal.

In the context of the plot outline of the novel, these conclusions can be summarized in the following reconstructed story: Julien is the illegitimate son of M. de Rênal or of the Marquis de La Mole. He has been raised by a man of humble origins, the peasant Sorel. During his adolescence he returns, without knowing it, to the home of his real father(s), first as a preceptor in the Rênal household, then as private secretary to the marquis. Finally, he is recognized for what he is and receives the advantages due him because of his exalted origins: riches, a commission in the army, a title of nobility, and, last but not least, the daughter of the house, Mathilde. It is at this point that Julien utters his famous statement: "Après tout, mon roman est fini, et à moi seul tout le mérite" (p. 444).

Is this a striking, new, original story? Not at all. It is as old as the human race itself. The earliest known version was written about 2800 B.C. in Babylonia. The hero's name is Sargon, not Julien Sorel, but the plot is virtually the same. Otto Rank, in his book, *The Myth of the Birth of the Hero,*[6] lists more than a score of such hero myths, including such famous names as Moses and Abraham, Oedipus and Hercules, Judas and Jesus, Siegfried and Lohengrin. If the list were expanded to include the heroes of fairy tales, novels, and romances as well as those of mythology, it could be increased almost at will.

It is one of the beauties of psychoanalysis that quite often its methods and results make it possible to trace what seem to be quite disparate thoughts back to the same emotional source. The literary critic is especially grateful for such insights, since they afford him one way of seeing the hidden connections behind the often bewildering plethora of events, ideas, feelings and phantasies that make up a long novel. Fortunately, the phantasy of illegitimate birth has been discussed at length by Freud in an article called "Family Romances," quoted by Rank:

The detachment of the growing individual from the authority of the parents is one of the most necessary, but also one of the most painful achievements of evolution. . . . For the young child, the parents are, in the first place, the sole authority and the source of all faith. . . . From the psychology of the neurosis, we have learned that very intense emotions of sexual rivalry are also involved in this connection. The causative factor evidently is the feeling of being neglected. Opportunities arise only too frequently when the child is neglected, or at least feels himself neglected, when he misses the entire love of the parents, or at least regrets having to share this with the other children of the family. The feeling that one's own inclinations are not entirely reciprocated seeks its relief in the idea—often consciously remembered from very early years—of being a stepchild, or an adopted child. . . . Accurate observation of these daydreams shows that they serve for the fulfillment of wishes, for the righting of life, and that they have two essential objects, one erotic, the other of an ambitious nature (usually with the erotic factor concealed therein). About the time in question [prepuberty], the child's imagination is engaged upon the task of getting rid of the parents, who are now despised and are as a rule to be supplanted by others of a higher social rank. . . . With the added knowledge of the manifold sexual relations of father and mother—with the child's realization of the fact that the father is always uncertain, whereas the mother is very certain—the family romance undergoes a peculiar restriction: it is satisfied with ennobling the father, while the descent from the mother is no longer questioned, but accepted as an unalterable fact. This second (or sexual) stage of the family romance is moreover supported by another motive, which did not exist in the first (or asexual) stage. Knowledge of sexual matters gives rise to the tendency to picture erotic situations and relations, impelled by the pleasurable emotion of placing the mother, who[7] is the subject of the greatest sexual curiosity, in the situation of secret unfaithfulness and clandestine love affairs.

.   .   .   .   .

The discovery will be made that these new and high-born parents are invested throughout with the qualities which are derived from real memories of the true lowly parents. . . . *The entire endeavor to replace the real father by a more distinguished one is merely the expression of the child's longing for the vanished happy time, when his father still appeared to be the strongest and greatest man, and the mother seemed the dearest and most beautiful woman.* [pp. 67–71]

It is not difficult to trace the extensive parallels between this typical phantasy and Julien's career. The parents of higher social position are the Rênals and the La Moles. Both are noble and rich; M. de Rênal is mayor of Verrières and the most powerful man of the town. The marquis is one of the most influential noblemen of Parisian society; moreover, he is the richest landowner of Franche-Comté (p. 10) and his ancestors were for a long time the governors of that province (p. 100). Yet, to anyone familiar with Beyle's life, it is evident that both share the outstanding traits of his father or his later representatives. M. de Rênal's most striking characteristic is his love of money, just like Chérubin Beyle, at least in the eyes of his son. He is excessively proud of the new house he has built, and it is well known that M. Beyle, much to Henri's chagrin, spent the last years of his life on the construction of a new house. M. de La Mole is much more like grandfather Gagnon in his eighteenth-century culture and urbanity, and like Pierre Daru in that he hires Julien as secretary (Beyle's first job was as secretary to

Daru) and obtains for him a commission in the army, as Daru did for the young Stendhal in 1800; his name is modeled on that of Count Molé who assumed Daru's role as political protector of our author after his cousin's death.

The original situation that gives rise to the phantasy, the feeling of neglect by one's parents and the consequent hostility, is also included in the novel. Both times that Julien states that he might be a foundling, he mentions his family's hatred toward him or his own hostility toward them.

The only point that seems to be lacking is the element of secret love affairs on the part of the mother, but it will be remembered that Mme de Rênal is courted by Valenod, although she does not actually have relations with him. This moralistic reversal of the phantasy is paralleled by a similar reversal of another theme studied by Rank in this connection, the so-called myth of exposure. In mythological versions, the hero is often set out to die soon after his birth, ostensibly because a dream or an oracle has warned his father that the new son will cause great damage. This motif corresponds to the practice at one time common among some ancient peoples of leaving babies out to die or of driving the sons of the family away from home when they reached sexual maturity, both motivated in part by the father's fear of his sons' reprisals. Instead of being exposed as a baby or driven out forcibly as an adolescent, Julien himself violently desires to leave his home (p. 23). This reversal, commonly found in fairy tales, seems to indicate a higher level of morality, in that the son tries to avoid the dangers of the Oedipus situation of his own free will.[8] In the last analysis, nevertheless, nothing is gained, for Julien's new environment is merely a representation of the home he fled.

The one clear-cut difference between the scheme given by Freud under the title "family romance" and the novel under examination is the existence in the latter of two distinct "fathers" in each of whose homes Julien acts out his "family romance." The explanation for this circumstance is near at hand. For, if M. de Rênal represents Julien's father, then Mme de Rênal is his mother; and if the Marquis de La Mole is his father, then Mathilde is his sister. In light of these facts, it is evident that the bipartite structure of *Le Rouge et le Noir,* as well as that of *La Chartreuse de Parme,* corresponds to the dual fixation of Beyle on his mother and sister Pauline.

There is ample evidence for this claim in the novel. In the first place, like Sorel, the Rênals have three sons. The intention hidden by this seeming coincidence is the identification of the two families. The reason for this identification is that discussed above in connection with the "family romance:" Julien thus becomes the son of the Rênals. There are various allusions to this aspect of the relationship between Julien and the Rênals, but perhaps none is clearer than the following one:

[Mme de Rênal] se permettait avec [Julien] les mêmes gestes intimes qu'avec ses enfants. C'est qu'il y avait des jours où elle avait l'illusion de l'aimer comme son enfant. Sans cesse n'avait-elle pas à répondre à ses questions naïves sur mille choses simples qu'un enfant bien-né n'ignore pas à quinze ans? [p. 97]

Indeed, Mme de Rênal is the ideal mother from the child's point of view. She is beautiful, kindly, innocent and, above all, she does not really love her husband but cares only for her children. The last sentence of the passage cited gives one of the fundamental motives of the phantasy. The adolescent boy imagines that his first love will initiate him into the secrets of adult life, especially sexual life, exactly as he wished his mother would do when he was a child. The future situation is thus built up out of early memories and wishes; the phantasy thus seeks in reality to restore the old situation. That is why Julien's flight from his home amounts only to a return home.

The obstacle to the fulfillment of these wishes is, of course, M. de Rênal, just as in childhood the boy is barred from carrying out his desires by the presence of his father. This situation regularly gives rise within the boy to the wish that his father should "go away." Being absent is the child's first conception of the word death, before he understands the difference between mere temporary absence and the permanent departure of death. In *Le Rouge et le Noir,* the desired death of M. de Rênal is expressed several times by his absence, always when Julien becomes intimate with Mme de Rênal. Their affair actually begins in the country at Vergy, while M. de Rênal is away, in Verrières. For the first time in his life, so he says, Julien feels completely happy in the mountains of Vergy: "C'est sur les sommets de ces rochers coupés à pic que Julien, heureux, libre, et même quelque chose de plus, *roi de la maison . . .*" (p. 50, italics mine). He is happy because he has taken the place of M. de Rênal and has become the king of the house. However, when M. de Rênal returns unexpectedly, he is furious about the "changes made in his property without his permission" (an expression of Julien's guilt and fear of reprisals). The whole episode is a symbolic representation of the actual seduction scenes, which also take place at Vergy, but several chapters later.

Shortly before the end of this first part of the novel, which ends with Julien's forced departure from Verrières, there is another repetition of this episode. Julien is with Mme de Rênal and the children, and all are enjoying themselves immensely until the sudden arrival of M. de Rênal makes everyone feel uncomfortable: "Je suis de trop dans ma famille, à ce que je puis voir! dit-il en entrant" (p. 147). Once again Julien has, for a brief moment, taken over the family of his employer, only to be removed from this position by the return of his feared rival. The guilt attendant upon the fulfillment, real or symbolic, of these forbidden wishes, is expressed in various ways. First, M. de Rênal returns several times and puts fear into the heart of his employee. Secondly, Julien must fight a terrible inner battle in order to carry out his seduction of Mme de Rênal (cf., the famous hand-holding scene at Vergy and his hesitation before keeping his rendezvous in her bedroom at two in the morning), and is prevented from enjoying the fruits of his victory (n'est-ce que ça?) by his guilt feeling. The most forceful expression, however, comes in a slightly different context. After the seduction, Julien seems to be relatively unconcerned about the consequences of his action; Mme de Rênal, on the other hand, is tormented by an enormous sense of sinfulness. This feeling culminates in the powerful scene in which her youngest son, Stanislas-Xavier, is stricken by a terrible fever. She fears that he will die and that his death is God's retribution for her sinful deeds. She decides that, in order to save her son, she must henceforth "hate" Julien. This conviction seems absurd, but, like all irrational beliefs, it is not without meaning. The effect produced by these scenes on the reader is proof that on some level, Mme de Rênal's reaction makes sense.

The absurdity results from her feeling that little Stanislas-Xavier, who after all is totally innocent, should have to pay with his life for his mother's crime. It would be understandable if she felt that, because of her sin, she herself must be punished, must even die. But why her youngest son? Now, in the unconscious, the moral code is dominated by the Law of the Talion. Hence, if a child must die, it is because he himself has killed, at least in phantasy. In addition, an important finding of psychoanalysis states that the result of an unconsciously determined action always reveals one of its main intentions. The result of the scene in question is that Julien is forced to leave the house with the possibility that he may never return (pp. 115–16). Thus it is Julien who "dies" (absence); little Stanislas is merely a substitute for Julien, who is the youngest of Sorel's three sons just as Stanislas is the youngest of the Rênal boys. Furthermore, Mme de Rênal repeatedly thinks of Julien as her child. The crime which merits this harsh punishment must be the intended or symbolic murder of M. de Rênal. Convincing evidence of this deduction is to be found in Mme de Rênal's anguished cry to Julien during this scene: "O mon unique ami! ô pourquoi n'est-tu pas le père de Stanislas! Alors ce ne serait pas un horrible péché de t'aimer mieux que ton fils" (p. 115). The last part of the puzzle now falls neatly into place: Stendhal presents so much of Mme de Rênal's guilt feeling and so little of Julien's because the former represents the latter. Mme de Rênal's oppression is a projection of Julien's own guilt; hence it is perfectly comprehensible that the punishment should fall on Stanislas, who is here simply a doublet of Julien. The son must die, for it is he who has wished to kill his father.

The first part of Book 2, which I have entitled "Paris," is almost an exact replica of "Verrières." I have already shown at some length that the Marquis de La Mole represents Julien's father. Hence, Mathilde would be his sister. The continual variations in their feelings toward each other are, as in the case of Mme de Rênal, a measure of the inner conflict resulting from incestuous wishes. The role of the injured third party is now taken by Mathilde's fiancé, the Marquis de Croisenois. Incidentally, if the passage about the Duke of Chaulnes (p. 328) is interpreted to mean that the latter is Croisenois' father, the result is still an incestuous relationship, for that would make Croisenois Mathilde's uncle, since the duke is Mme de La Mole's father.

The most striking difference between the two sections is the large role played by Mme de Fervaques in "Paris" which does not seem to have a counterpart in "Varrières." The first time this lady appears, Julien is deeply impressed:

La brillante maréchale de Fervaques entra en faisant des excuses sur l'heure tardive. Il était plus de minuit; elle alla prendre place auprès de la marquise. Julien fut profondément ému; elle avait les yeux et le regard de Mme de Rênal. [p. 260]

When Julien, following his friend Korasoff's advice, decides to pay suit to the maréchale in order to win back Mathilde's love, he consoles himself with the thought of her beautiful eyes that remind him of Mme de Rênal. Mme de Fervaques even makes a contribution of a sort to Julien's "family romance." Because he is not an ordained priest, she hesitates to acknowledge his suit; she fears that: "Quelque amie maligne peut supposer et même répandre que c'est un petit cousin subalterne, parent de mon père, quelque marchand décoré par la garde nationale" (p. 415).

Mme de Fervaques, leader of the devout society of Paris, believer in the new German mysticism, with a physical resemblance to Mme de Rênal and perhaps a relative of Julien—all these traits remind us of Mme de Bonnivet in *Armance*. Both these ladies, who try to convert the heroes, represent the mother in competition with the sister. It is Julien (Octave) who is divided by his love for both mother and sister. The result is that, when he is with Mme de Rênal, he thinks of the beauties of Parisian society; when with Mathilde, he thinks of Mme de Rênal. Mme de Fervaques is a more concrete representation of this same inner conflict. As is to be expected, when Julien is in prison, nothing more is said about the maréchale, for now Mme de Rênal herself comes back into the story.

If Mme de Fervaques represents the mother in competition

with the sister (Mathilde), then her counterpart in the first
section of the novel must stand for the sister in opposition to the
mother (Mme de Rênal). It is Mlle Elisa, Mme de Rênal's
maid, whose offer of marriage Julien haughtily refuses, and
who, by colluding with Valenod, causes Julien to be sent away
from Verrières. It will be remembered that Mathilde, too, takes
the first step by announcing her love to Julien. Furthermore, it
is Mme de Rênal's letter which definitively separates Julien
and Mathilde, just as Elisa's letter had done earlier.[9]

The similarity between the two parts of the novel extends to
the fate of the male characters also, although the fulfillment of
Julien's death wishes toward them is hidden so deftly as almost
to escape notice. Nevertheless, they are there. Five pages from
the end of the novel Stendhal states:

Mlle de la Mole apprit la mort du marquis de Croisenois. M. de
Thaler, cet homme si riche, s'était permis des propos désagréables
sur la disparition de Mathilde. . . .

. . . Ivre de colère et de malheur, M. de Croisenois exigea des
réparations tellement fortes, que le millionaire préféra un duel. La
sottise triompha; et l'un des hommes de Paris les plus dignes d'être
aimés, trouva la mort à moins de 24 ans. [p. 503]

How many times had Julien imagined that he would be victorious in a duel with Croisenois!

The Marquis de La Mole meets his end in a different way.
After he has received Mme de Rênal's letter, and he has forbidden Mathilde to marry Julien, she tells her lover: "Tout est
perdu; *mon père,* craignant mes larmes, *est parti* dans la nuit de
jeudi. Pour où? personne ne le sait" (p. 447, italics mine). This
mysterious departure to an unknown destination, which has
only the flimsiest of conscious motivations (could the marquis
really have been that much afraid of his daughter's tears?),

represents a departure of another sort, death. And, in fact, from this page to the end of the novel, there is no mention made of the marquis. He has really disappeared.

To conclude this part of the analysis, I may assert that, on one level, the novel illustrates fulfillment of the masculine desire to take the place of the father in order to possess mother and sister, and portrays the conflict between these two loves. On another level it has quite a different meaning, a homosexual rather than a heterosexual one. From the very beginning Julien's weakness and delicateness, in contrast to the strength and virility of the other members of his family, are emphasized. Mme de Rênal's first impression is even more explicit: "Le teint de ce petit paysan était si blanc, ses yeux si doux, que l'esprit un peu romanesque de Mme de Rênal eut d'abord l'idée que ce pouvait être une jeune fille déguisée . . . (p. 26). Later on in this first interview she is again struck by Julien's femininity: "Ce fut en ce moment seulement, quand son inquiétude pour ses enfants fut tout à fait dissipée, que Mme de Rênal fut frappée de l'extrême beauté de Julien. La forme presque féminine de ses traits et son air d'embarras . . ." (p. 28).

This same femininity explains Sorel's exaggerated hatred and brutal treatment of Julien. If the only force behind the novel were the positive oedipal wishes, this enmity would have been attenuated or disguised in some fashion. It can be expressed so openly here because it is also used as a defense against Julien's deeper, homosexual wishes.

Since the fulfillment of these wishes mitigates Julien's guilt feeling for his masculine desires, they must precede the latter in time. Thus the novel begins with his presence in the all-male Sorel family. And one of the first incidents after he has become preceptor to the Rênal children is the episode in which he is beaten senseless by his brothers. Stendhal contrives matters so that Mme de Rênal finds him lying on the ground, unconscious and covered with blood, in a little woods that overlooks the Cours de la Fidélité. Her fear and pity for him are the same as when, earlier in the story, she had seen her son romping on the wall of that same promenade. Indeed, given the identification between Julien and her sons, it is easy to recognize the one scene as simply a repetition of the other, the more so since the fear of falling is generally an expression of femininity[10] (e.g., the expression "a fallen woman").

Julien's extreme sensitivity to M. de Rênal's continual "persecutions" has the same basis. Likewise, his doubt as to whether he should accept his friend Fouqué's offer to work for him is an expression of his hesitation between man and woman as objects of sexual attraction.[11] Finally, Julien's repeated insistence on his poverty, echoed in M. de Rênal's scorn and cause of Mme de Rênal's pity, is the regressive expression of his lack of masculinity, i.e., femininity, as is so often the case in novels. (Balzac is the prime example in French literature, e.g., Lucien de Rubempré in *Les Illusions Perdues*.)

Despite these varied manifestations, homosexuality plays a secondary role in "Verrières," whereas, in "Besançon," the concluding section of Book 1, it is the dominant tendency. In "Besançon," Stendhal recounts Julien's stay at the seminary and dwells particularly on his relationship to Abbé Pirard. The overwhelming impression made by Julien's entrance into the seminary is that of a descent into Hades.[12] As he approaches the gate, he thinks: "Voilà cet enfer sur la terre, dont je ne pourrai sortir!" (p. 168). As in the classical legends, this hell too has a monster as guardian of the gate:

Un homme pâle, vêtu de noir, vint lui ouvrir. Julien le regardait et aussitôt baissa les yeux. Ce portier avait une physionomie singulière. La pupille saillante et verte de ses yeux s'arrondissait comme

celle d'un chat; les contours immobiles de ses paupières annon-
çaient l'impossibilité de toute sympathie. . . . [p. 168]

And so the description continues for several more lines. When
Julien informs this apparition of his desire to see Pirard, he does
not utter a word but merely signals the young man to follow
him. The staircase is old and rickety as in a haunted house.
Above the entrance of the room they are about to enter is a
cemetery cross painted black. The room is dark and low; in it
the two paintings on the walls are blackened with time. A
deathly silence reigns in the whole building. When the gatekeeper returns, he again motions silently to Julien. When
Pirard looks at Julien, the latter "restait encore immobile comme
frappé à mort . . ." (p. 169). Pirard is described as having a
forehead of mortal pallor, beady black eyes and pitch black
hair. In short, the whole scene suggests terror and death; all is
silence, immobility, pallor, and blackness. Eventually Julien's
emotion overcomes his control and he faints. Pirard calls this fit
an attack of epilepsy.

Considering the context of this masterful passage, coming as
it does immediately after Julien's expulsion from Verrières due
to his adulterous relationship with Mme de Rênal, it is not hard
to see that his terrible anxiety is motivated by his fear of reprisals from his father, here represented by the priest Pirard.
The meaning of hysterical fainting, which forms the climax
of this episode, has been studied by Freud in his article, "Dostoyevsky and Parricide."[13] There he describes this symptom as
the resultant of overpowerful ambivalent feelings towards one's
father. The individual wants to get rid of his father in order to
have his mother to himself; however, because he also has great
affection for his father, he feels guilty and deserving of punishment. The result is that he identifies with his father (takes his

place), but his dead father; i.e., he faints, thus gratifying his wish to be his father and simultaneously punishing himself for this wish.

Now from a knowledge of dream symbolism as well as the context of this episode, it seems clear that the above explanation is applicable to Julien. The continual references to blackness, climbing the old staircase, the description of the room to which Julien is led, all of these factors constitute a symbolic presentation of coitus, the very sin of which Julien is guilty. His terror of the place and of the gatekeeper represent his fear of punishment—death—for his crime. His falling unconscious marks the turning point in his emotional situation. Henceforth his conscience is victorious, he gives up his incestuous aims.

The justness of these interpretations is shown by Julien's later feelings toward Pirard. He performs a complete about-face, going from stark hatred and abject fear to violent love. When Pirard announces Julien's promotion to preceptor:

Julien, transporté de reconnaissance, eut bien l'idée de se jeter à genoux et de remercier Dieu; mais il céda à un mouvement plus vrai. Il s'approcha de l'abbé Pirard et lui prit sa main, qu'il porta à ses lèvres.

.   .   .   .   .

[Pirard, surprised at first, admits his affection for Julien.]

.   .   .   .   .

Il y avait si longtemps que Julien n'avait entendu une voix amie, qu'il faut lui pardonner une faiblesse; il fondit en larmes. L'abbé Pirard lui ouvrit les bras; ce moment fut bien doux pour tous les deux. [pp. 196–197]

The same scene is repeated almost verbatim when Pirard is about to leave Julien to fend for himself at the Hôtel de La Mole. The only difference, and it is a noteworthy one, is Julien's final speech: "J'ai été haï de mon père depuis le berceau; c'était un de mes grands malheurs; mais je ne me plaindrai plus du hasard , j'ai retrouvé un père en vous, monsieur" (p. 236).

In other words, the conflict between his love and his hatred for his father has been resolved, at least temporarily, by the victory of his love and the repression of his hatred. However, Julien, like anyone else, cannot simply abandon all sexual gratification. Therefore, when he gives up his desire for his mother, the homosexual tendency in his character is enormously reinforced, that is, his love for his father becomes resexualized. This transformation is accomplished by his substituting identification with his mother for the former attempt to take her as love object. Then his conscience acts toward him the way he imagined his father did toward his mother—he becomes masochistic. Thus, there are no women in this whole section of the novel, with the exception of the cafe scene preceding his entrance into the seminary and his fleeting glimpse of Mme de Rênal in church. For the same reason, he constantly feels that he is the victim of persecutions on the part of the priests and other seminary students.

Book 2 is basically a repetition of Book 1 but with Mathilde, the sister, in the place of Mme de Rênal, the mother. The symmetry of the two parts is quite striking in the homosexual aspect as well as the heterosexual. Indeed, each episode seems to have its counterpart. In both parts Julien submits to a kind of ordeal, a test of his knowledge of Latin, shortly after his arrival in his new home. In the first section he is beaten by his brothers, which arouses Mme de Rênal's pity and eventually her love; in the second, he goes riding with Mathilde's brother, Norbert, and falls off his horse. When this outing is mentioned at the table, Norbert tries to hush up the story of Julien's misfortune, but the latter insists on telling it to everyone, to the infinite delight of Mathilde.

Julien's reaction to his first night with Mathilde is the same as that after his conquest of Mme de Rênal, the famous "N'est-ce que ça," which reveals his inhibited potency. But this time the reason is made more clear. After heroically climbing the ladder to Mathilde's room (a repeat performance of his last visit to Mme de Rênal, and a symbol of intercourse with its attendant dangers), he does not feel the slightest bit of sexual excitement. In order to arouse his desire, he has to remind himself that he is triumphing over M. de Croisenois; indeed, he tries to convince himself that Croisenois has already enjoyed Mathilde's favors (pp. 338–339). But this need to share a woman with another man is a disguised expression of homosexual desire for the man. Most probably Stendhal himself often needed to have recourse to similar phantasies to avoid the dread fiasco of which he spoke so often.

The same instinctual desires explain Julien's exaggerated fear that Mathilde's declaration of love is the result of a conspiracy of the young aristocrats of her society, as well as his enjoyment of the mental torture inflicted on him by Mathilde. A few days after this first love scene, she takes great pleasure in arousing his jealousy of her other suitors:

O combien étaient punis, en cet instant, les mouvements d'orgueil qui avaient porté Julien à se préférer aux Caylus, aux Croisenois! Avec quel malheur intime et senti *il s'exagérait leurs plus petits avantages!* Avec quelle bonne foi ardente il se méprisait lui-même!

Mathilde lui semblait adorable, toute parole est faible pour exprimer l'excès de son admiration. En se promenant à côté d'elle, il regardait à la dérobée ses mains, ses bras, son port de reine. Il était sur le point de tomber à ses pieds, *anéanti d'amour et de malheur,* et en criant: "Pitié." [p. 350, italics mine]

Julien revels in self-abasement and even becomes sexually excited as is shown by his admiring glances at Mathilde.

Despite all this, Julien almost succeeds in fulfilling the primary wishes of the "family romance." It requires no special analytic insight to see that Julien's story, in so far as it concerns ego interests, is precisely the history of his attempts to "grow up," to free himself from his attachment to his parents and to take his place as an independent adult in society. As stated in the study of *Armance*, Stendhal wrote and rewrote the same novel, the story of a young man's attempt to reach maturity. Now, when Julien is about to marry Mathilde, he has attained his aims. He is ready to begin a career as an officer in the army. He has become a nobleman. He has found a wife and has made her pregnant. In short, he has become a Father.

This victory is short-lived. The denouement of the novel appears all the more surprising since Julien has just fulfilled some of the deepest and most powerful desires of childhood. I am thus confronted with the task of trying to shed some light on this puzzling ending. It has seemed problematic to readers ever since the book was published, and according to one report, it even bothered Stendhal. Its most forceful condemnation was formulated by Faguet, some seventy years ago.[14] He argued that Stendhal had betrayed Julien's character in having him shoot Mme de Rênal. Until that point Julien had been a clever schemer who took advantage of the opportunities that came his way in order to fulfill his grandiose ambitions. Shooting Mme de Rênal could only ruin his chances for success, whereas, if he had waited and played his cards correctly, he would have retained the upper hand. Stendhal made this error because the murder attempt was part of Berthet's story, which he took as the model of his novel.

Rambaud claims that Stendhal was at a loss to explain Julien's action, and therefore he described the sequence very rapidly, without any of the customary peeks into the inner workings of Julien's mind. Prévost, on the other hand, admires this last trait because by it Stendhal conveys to the reader Julien's abnormal mental state, a state well known to psychiatric science. He too, however, is forced to conclude that Stendhal did not make the murder probable in the context of the novel, but included it because it had taken place in real life.

Martineau shows that Julien is not a crafty schemer, but rather an impulsive character, whose very impulses often ruin his plans. He agrees that the rapidity of Stendhal's description of the events immediately preceding the shots is a masterful piece of artistry, in accord with the psychological situation. And he points out that Stendhal was by no means a slave to the models he chose for his fiction. If the ending of the real story had not pleased him, he certainly would have altered it as he did so many other parts.

Henriette Bibas agrees with Martineau in most respects, but she notes that he neglected to determine the precise nature of the shock which caused Julien to enter this abnormal state. She argues that he was outraged not because Mme de Rênal's letter revealed that he had seduced a woman, but because he made a habit of doing so for personal gain; he was a professional seducer, so to speak. Furthermore, the image of Julien contained in the letter and accepted by the Marquis was too close to the truth for him to react to it unemotionally.

There is one thread which runs through the discussions of these critics and of many others, e.g., Thibaudet, Léon Blum, Alain. It is the simple fact that all of them experience a certain malaise when confronted with this crime; each feels that its relation to the rest of the novel is a problem that must be explained, no matter whether they finally decide that it is fitting or inappropriate.

What Julien has done is tantamount to matricide. That Julien's love for Mme de Rênal is at bottom incestuous has already been established. Moreover, in their past relations, Mme de Rênal had shown nothing but love for Julien. Surely one letter, no matter what its content, should not have been enough to obliterate all of that from Julien's memory. Why, then, does he do it?

It must be conceded that, in the main, Martineau's arguments are valid. Julien is certainly an impulsive character, as is shown time and again by his actions and as is stated repeatedly by Stendhal. The suppression of any commentary during Julien's flight to Verrières is justifiable on psychological and artistic grounds. And the argument that Stendhal inserted these events into his novel merely because they took place in his model is really no explanation at all. Not only does it fail to take into account Stendhal's prerogative as a creative writer to alter these events, a prerogative he exercised liberally in other places, as Martineau points out; but also, and above all, it does not answer the question of why Berthet's story appealed so strongly to Stendhal's imagination.

Bibas comes closer to the heart of the matter in trying to determine what it was in the letter that caused such a great shock in Julien. But her answer, although to a great extent correct, does not provide a complete explanation. She can explain why Julien feels hurt so deeply, but she is unable to say why he felt compelled to perform the specific act in question—shooting Mme de Rênal. Here are the key words of the letter:

En conscience, je suis contrainte de penser qu'un de ses moyens pour réussir dans une maison, c'est de chercher à *séduire la femme* qui a le principal crédit. Couvert par une apparence de désintéressement et par des phrases de roman, son grand et unique objet est de parvenir à *disposer du maître de la maison et de sa fortune.* [pp. 448–449, italics mine]

In the light of the previous analysis, it is not hard to recognize in these accusations a description of oedipal wishes. The desire to control the "master of the house" and his fortune ordinarily represents the child's desire to have his father's sexual potency, in order to supplant him with his mother. The cause and effect relationship has thus been reversed in the letter. He desires this power in order to "seduce" his mother, not vice-versa. On reading the letter, Julien unconsciously translates these statements back to their true meaning. Since these desires were the deepest motives of his actions in the first part of the novel, he is profoundly shocked to see them formulated openly as an accusation against him. As Bibas puts it: "C'est une chose horrible que d'apercevoir tout à coup, entretenue de soi chez autrui, une image repoussante, et qu'un cortège d'actes, bien réellement accompli, atteste fidèle . . . (p. 26).

But why go out and murder Mme de Rênal as a result of this shock? The motive of revenge is in itself insufficient, for two reasons. If Julien were angry because his future was threatened by this letter, then he would have proceeded in the manner outlined by Faguet, in an effort to maintain his position. More important, whatever feelings of hostility were aroused by this letter, they had to compete against even stronger feelings of love, as is evident from the first part of the novel and from the scenes in the prison. Furthermore, if the oedipal wishes discussed above were the decisive factor in his action, he would have sought his revenge against the person who had deprived him of his desire, his father or some substitute figure. But it is surely unthinkable that he would carry out a symbolic murder, whose real object was his father, against Mme de Rênal whom he loved so much! The answer must be sought elsewhere.

I will now turn back to the one point on which all the critics seemed to agree, that this ending seems to be an intrusion whose presence needs justification. Looking at the circumstances surrounding the letter episode, I notice several rather surprising facts. Why does the marquis request information about Julien's character from Mme de Rênal? His reason at first seems plausible enough: he does not want his daughter to marry an adventurer who loves her money and name, not herself. Yet Mathilde has already told him that it was she who first declared her love to Julien. And no matter what Julien's past actions and motives had been, henceforth he would be in no position to do any adventuring, since he would owe everything to the marquis' protection. What about the baby? Mathilde refused to have an abortion or to keep its birth a secret. Dismissing Julien as an adventurer would not solve that problem. Nevertheless, the marquis' concern would seem justified as the natural desire of a father to protect his daughter from future unhappiness, if it were not for one fact. His immediate reaction on hearing of Mathilde's plans is not, "I fear that my daughter has been taken in by a lowly schemer," but "I want my daughter to marry a duke!" Not once during the weeks that he vacillates does it enter his mind that Mathilde's future happiness might be in danger! And why should it? Her love for Julien is obviously very strong. When the marquis suddenly decides to write to Mme de Rênal, the decision has all the earmarks of a last resort, the only possible excuse for delaying or canceling a marriage he opposes.

Thus far I have been questioning the marquis' motives in *writing* to Mme de Rênal. Now I feel it necessary to ask another question, or rather the same one with a different emphasis. Why does he write to *Mme* de Rênal. Why not M. de Rênal? In nineteenth-century France the ordinary course would be to write to the head of the household for such information. If someone, for instance, wanted to find out about Julien's character while he was in Paris, he would naturally question the marquis, not his wife! I submit that the only reason no one (to my knowledge) has ever questioned this circumstance is that the readers already know that Mme de Rênal is in a better position than her husband to supply such information, but the marquis could not possibly have known it.

Finally, how can Mme de Rênal bring herself to write such a letter? Nothing at any point in the novel indicates that she has the slightest bit of vindictiveness in her character, and certainly none against Julien. Is Stendhal's explanation, that she was completely under the influence of her confessor, acceptable? Of course, it is true that religion played a great part in her life, and that anyone carrying a burden of guilt as great as hers could be made to do strange things under the guidance of a clever manipulator. And yet it is hard to believe that she would have done such a thing without some other motive. In the past her guilt had made her fear terrible things for herself, it had imposed severe penance upon her; but never was it directed to someone else's harm, least of all Julien's.

All these signs point in the direction of a single conclusion: this ending is in fact an intrusion, a bit of foreign matter that has somehow forced its way into the novel of its own accord, so to speak, against or beyond Stendhal's will. And yet, at the same time, it is quite clear that this ending was in Stendhal's mind before he wrote the book. Indeed, paradoxical as it sounds, the whole novel was constructed with the precise intention of preparing this denouement. As Martineau shows, the plot structure and the principal events of the novel are taken directly from the case history of Antoine Berthet. What he neglects to point out is that the other story which inspired Stendhal's imagination, the story of Laffargue,[15] has only one point in common with that of Berthet: each murdered his former mistress. When it is remembered that the same event recurs several times in the *Chroniques Italiennes*, that Mathilde tells Julien a similar story, although with the roles reversed, and Julien himself once almost stabs Mathilde in a blind fury, the conclusion becomes inescapable that it was this murder which acted as the main impetus for Stendhal's writing.

How can this apparent paradox be reconciled? The solution may be found by following the results to their logical conclusion. If the denouement presents itself as a piece of foreign material that has intruded on the rest of the novel, and if the novel is the expression in phantasy of the basic conflicts in Stendhal's personality, it follows that this denouement must represent an early splitting of his ego, one that had catastrophic consequences for the rest of his development. The fact that all his novels have similar double endings supports this thesis.

Now, continuing this train of thought in the same direction, I am led to search for the origin and meaning of this ending, not in the novel itself, but outside it, in Beyle's own past.

This task would probably be an impossibility if it were not for Beyle's constant search for self-knowledge which led him to write his incomparable autobiography, *La Vie de Henry Brulard*. In the third chapter of that book Beyle recounts his earliest memories:

Mon premier souvenir est d'avoir mordu à la joue ou au front Mme Pison du Galland, ma cousine. . . . Je la vois encore, une femme de vingt-cinq ans qui avait de l'embonpoint et beaucoup de rouge. . . .

"Embrasse-moi, Henri," me disait-elle. Je ne voulus pas, elle se fâcha, je mordis ferme. Je vois la scène, mais sans doute parce que sur-le-champ on m'en fit un crime et que sans cesse on m'en parlait.

Ce glacis de la porte de Bonne était couvert de marguerites. C'est une jolie petite fleur dont je faisais un bouquet. Ce pré de 1786 se trouve sans doute aujourd'hui au milieu de la ville, au sud de l'église du collège.

Ma tante Séraphie déclara que j'étais un monstre et que j'avais un caractère atroce.

.   .   .   .   .

Le second trait de caractère fut bien autrement noir.

J'avais fait une collection de joncs, toujours sur le glacis de la porte de Bonne. . . .

On m'avait ramené à la maison dont une fenêtre au premier étage donnait sur la Grande Rue à l'angle de la Place Grenette. Je faisais un jardin en coupant ces joncs en bouts de deux pouces de long. . . . Le couteau de cuisine dont je me servais m'échappa et tomba dans la rue, c'est-à-dire d'une douzaine de pieds, près d'une madame Chenavaz ou sur cette madame. C'était la plus méchante femme de toute la ville. . . .

Ma tante Séraphie dit que j'avais voulu tuer Mme Chenavaz; je fus déclaré pourvu d'un caractère atroce. . . .

Je me révoltai, je pouvais avoir quatre ans. De cette époque date mon horreur pour la religion, horreur que ma raison a pu à grand'-peine réduire à de justes dimensions, et cela tout nouvellement, il n'y a pas six ans. Presque en même temps prit sa première naissance mon amour filial instinctif, forcené dans ces temps-là, pour la république.

Je n'avais pas plus de cinq ans. [pp. 55–56]

At this point the reader may well be wondering why I chose to reproduce this particular passage, when my supposed goal is to explain the origin and meaning of the denouement of *Le Rouge et le Noir*. Perhaps a short narration of how I came to connect the two phenomena will make the transition seem less abrupt. When I first read *Henry Brulard,* this passage did not make much of an impression on me, at least not consciously. Several months later I began reading Goethe's autobiography, *Truth and Fiction*. I soon came to the passage in which he describes how, as a small boy, urged on by some friends, he threw a whole set of dishes out the window. I was immediately reminded of Beyle's description of his earliest memories, but could not figure out what the connection between them was. In the interim I had read Bergler's essay on Stendhal and had noted that he used these early memories merely to show that as a child, Beyle had had a great deal of aggression. This interpretation, although correct, obviously was too general to explain any of the details of the event. Furthermore, it seemed absurd to suppose that this incident was proof that Stendhal had had more aggression than other children of the same age. Then, while looking for an article on a totally different subject, I happened to come upon Freud's essay: "A Childhood Recollection from Goethe's *Truth and Fiction*."[16] As I shall try to show, this essay gives an interpretation of Goethe's memory which can be applied to those of Beyle; from this result one can deduce the importance of certain childhood experiences of Beyle and their later effect on his life and his fiction.

Freud's point of departure is the conviction, gained from analytic experience, that a person's earliest memories escape the general amnesia of early childhood because they refer to events which had special emotional importance for the child. These "screen memories" must be interpreted in order for their true significance to be understood. Usually the first memory recounted by the patient is "the very one that holds the key to his mental life" (p. 113). Freud goes on to relate that a patient of his had reacted to the birth of a little brother when he was about four years old, by throwing "all the crockery he could

lay his hands on out of the window of the villa into the road—
the very same thing that Goethe relates of his childhood in
Dichtung und Wahrheit!" (p. 114):

We might thus form the opinion that throwing crockery out of the
window is a symbolic action, or, let us say more correctly, a magical
action, by which a child (both Goethe as well as my patient) violently expresses his wish to get rid of a disturbing intruder. . . . This
"Out with it!" seems to be an essential part of the magic action and
to arise directly from its hidden meaning. The new baby must be
thrown out, through the window, perhaps because he came through
the window. [p. 117]

He adds that the analogy between his patient's memory and
Goethe's might be deemed insufficient proof of the identity of
their meanings. However, he soon found that many people
have similar memories with the identical significance. He cites
three more examples in support of his thesis that such memories
are typical occurrences. In one of these cases the child was only
two and one-half years old. In the other the child's anger was
first directed toward the mother herself before the newcomer's
birth. Both of these additional points will enter into my discussion of Beyle.

The second of his memories will be considered first, since it
has the greatest similarity to the scenes analyzed by Freud.
Beyle relates that he was playing on the balcony of a window
that faced the Grande-Rue at the corner of Grenette square,
when he "accidentally" dropped his knife onto the street, on or
near a Mme Chenevaz, the "meanest woman of the city." He
claims that it was an accident, but does not explain why he was
scolded not only by his aunt Séraphie, who, he feels, bore him
ill will, but also by the members of his family who loved him
most, his grandfather and his great-aunt Elisabeth. Clearly

they thought he had done it on purpose. His manner of introducing the episode shows that, at least in retrospect, he felt guilty about it: "Le second trait de caractère fut bien autrement noir." In any case, it is more than likely that he did it "on purpose," that is, as a result of a powerful impulse, but then disowned his action, denying his "responsibility" not only to others but also to himself. This happens often enough with adults; how much more understandable in a five or six-year-old child. Again, if it had been just an accident, it would be hard to understand why it remained in Stendhal's memory so vividly, unless it had taken over the meaning of another event of importance to Stendhal's emotional development. In either case, then, it can be taken as a screen memory.

Its hidden content is not hard to divine. Once again there is an object (the knife) thrown from the window onto the street, i.e., getting rid of the baby. In addition, the expression of hostility toward his mother comes out, not only in a general act of naughtiness, but as a direct attack against a woman. It takes no great imagination to see that Mme Chenavaz, the meanest woman in the whole city, is a substitute for Beyle's own mother. The meanness is, of course, the result of a projection of his own hostility onto his mother, and her evil desire to give him a rival for her affection. I agree with his aunt Séraphie, that he wanted to kill Mme Chenevaz, that is, his mother. If this seems like a harsh judgment, it would be well to recall that he wanted to "kill" her precisely because he loved her so much that he could not bear to share her love with anyone else. The unconscious does not bother itself with trifling considerations such as the obvious conclusion that the death of his mother would automatically deprive him of the very thing he wanted to protect—her love. Once again I am reminded of the famous dictum that contradictory wishes concerning the same person can exist side by side without ever colliding with each other. It should also be borne in mind that the unconscious knows no half-measures; any hostility is immediately translated on that level as a death wish.

This whole interpretation is, of course, acceptable only if I can establish to a fair degree of certainty that this memory refers to the time when a newcomer was about to make its appearance in the Beyle household, or had just done so. Beyle says: "Je me révoltai, je pouvais avoir quatre ans." Then, just before going on to another subject, he revises his estimate in a one-line paragraph: "Je n'avais pas plus de cinq ans." It is not surprising that he should have difficulty in remembering the exact date of an event that took place some forty-five years before the passage was written, especially since it happened during his early childhood. Yet this haziness in his memory is in sharp contrast to the vividness of his description of the event itself. This in itself would not be sufficient evidence that he was, unconsciously, confusing the issue on purpose. However, my suspicions on this account are fully confirmed by another fact. In describing his first memory Stendhal does not even try to determine his age at that time. Yet he states without the least hesitation that the woman he hit was twenty-five years old at the time. Why does he remember this apparently irrelevant fact so clearly? This is especially puzzling since it is extremely unlikely that a small child would know the age of an adult and remember it. My surprise only increases when I realize that he has betrayed his own age in a remark that seems to have an entirely different purpose. When describing the meadow where he was playing, he says: "Ce pré de 1786 se trouve sans doute aujourd'hui au milieu de la ville, au sud de l'église du collège." Since Beyle was born January 23, 1783, he must have been about three years old when he bit Mme Pison du Galland's cheek. He mentions that the meadow was covered with daisies, which bloom between May and October. In Grenoble's climate, the most probable season would be June or July. That would put Beyle's age at three and one-half years—the same age as Goethe and Freud's patients!

Beyle had two younger sisters: Pauline, born March 21, 1786, and Zénaïde-Caroline, born October 10, 1788. Therefore, the first memory refers to the time shortly after Pauline's birth. It is easy to see that his refusal to kiss his cousin's cheek and the bite he inflicts on her are childish expressions of his anger at his mother for giving him Pauline as a rival. Again, the mechanism of displacement is in operation, but this time the object of his attack is a relative who resembles his mother physically—her "embonpoint," and in age—his mother was twenty-nine years old in 1786.

If Beyle knew quite well the date of a memory from his third year, it certainly cannot be the great distance in time which "confuses" him about his age when the second event occurred. Rather I must consider this confusion a deliberate, although unconscious, attempt to camouflage the meaning of his attack on Mme Chenavaz. (A similar intention can be discerned as the motive for his mentioning the date, 1786, in a context that leads the reader to assume it refers more to the meadow than to Beyle.) As so often happens, the camouflage used reveals the very fact it was supposed to conceal, for Beyle ends up by naming his true age—five years. The date was thus 1788, and, as Martineau points out in his *Calendrier de Stendhal,* since the rushes were in season, it must have been during the summer of that year.[17] Zénaïde was born in October of that year, so little Henri's resentment was provoked this time by his awareness of his mother's pregnancy, i.e., by the expectation of another baby.

In *Henry Brulard* there is a theme which dominates the first chapters, a leitmotiv to which Beyle returns again and again, as though even at the age of fifty he had not yet succeeded in assimilating it—the death of his mother. After a long description of his grandfather, Beyle tells of his first Latin lessons, sometime in 1789. He remarks: "Ici commencent mes malheurs" (p. 60). Then, as though he were starting a new train of thought, he leaves out any account of these lessons and says:

Mais je diffère depuis longtemps un récit nécessaire, un des deux ou trois peut-être qui me feront jeter ces mémoires au feu.

Ma mère, Mme Henriette Gagnon, était une femme charmante et j'étais amoureux de ma mère.

Je me hâte d'ajouter que je la perdis quand j'avais sept ans.

En l'aimant à six ans peut-être, 1789. . . . [p. 60]

Then follows the famous description of his desire for his mother and irritation at his father. What interests me here is the repetition of the date, 1789. I begin to suspect that his "malheurs" pertain to matters of greater importance than learning Latin. What looked like a new series of thoughts, "Mais je diffère depuis longtemps . . . ," is really a continuation, and indeed the explanation, of his statement: "Ici commencent mes malheurs."

He ends the description of his passion for his mother by saying: "Qu'on daigne se rappeler que je la perdis par une couche quand à peine j'avais sept ans" (p. 60). A few lines later he states: "Elle périt . . . en 1790, elle pouvait avoir vingt-huit ou trente ans. Là commence ma vie morale" (p. 61).

In Chapter 4 he repeats: "C'est-à-dire: j'ignore absolument les détails, elle était morte en couches apparemment par la maladresse d'un chirurgien nommé Hérault" (p. 63). This whole chapter is devoted to his mother's death. I shall quote a few highly significant passages from it:

"Mon ami, ceci vient de Dieu," dit enfin l'abbé [Rey]; et ce mot, dit par un homme que je haïssais à un autre que je n'aimais guère, me fit réfléchir profondément.

On me croira insensible, je n'étais encore qu'étonné de la mort de ma mère. Je ne comprenais pas ce mot. Oserai-je écrire ce que Marion [the maid] m'a souvent répété depuis en forme de reproche? Je me mis à dire du mal de *God*. [p. 66]

... il se trouva qu'avec ma mère finit toute la joie de mon enfance. [p. 69]

In Beyle's own opinion, then, the death of his mother was the most significant event in his life. Moreover, the nature of this significance was clear to him; her death put an end to the happiness of his childhood. From the passages cited above it can be seen that the two statements, "Là commencent mes malheurs" and "Là commence ma vie morale," are really equivalent in his mind; they both refer to his unhappiness after his mother's death.

An examination of Beyle's account of the circumstances of his mother's death and his feelings at the time reveals two facts that we have neglected until now. Twice he mentions that his mother died "en couches," that is, in childbirth. And her death is attributed to the stupidity of the doctor, and thus indirectly to that member of his family who chose him; later, God himself is made the villain who is to blame for it.

To take the second fact first. To a child, who can scarcely comprehend the meaning of the word death in any case, there is no such thing as a natural death, or death due to illness. If someone dies, it must be due to the operation of some malevolent agency which killed the person for a purpose, whether it be punishment, revenge, or some other end. This attitude toward death is just one part of the animistic world view common to children and primitive peoples. Its two basic premises are the belief that all nature is composed of beings like ourselves, i.e., the failure to distinguish between organic and inorganic, human, animal and plant; and the belief in the omnipotence of thought, i.e., that merely wishing a thing will make it happen.

In the passages quoted, Beyle shows two examples of how these tenacious beliefs still subsist in modern, civilized adults. First he blames the doctor for his mother's death. This seems to have been his true opinion at the time he wrote *Henry Brulard,* although it is based on nothing more than hearsay and on the fact that an acquaintance of his, a Mme Petit, died for similar reasons. In fact, he begins the paragraph with a clear admission of his ignorance: "C'est-à-dire, j'ignore absolument les détails." He blames the doctor because he must blame someone; his beloved mother could not have just died in childbirth as so many thousands of other women have done through no fault of anyone.

The second example is Abbé Rey's statement that "this comes from God." Here, the infantile nature of this belief is even more obvious. If something happens, it is because God wills it so. Unfortunately, children are not as foolish as adults in these matters; they do not let themselves be beguiled by pious assertions that it is all part of a wise plan whose purpose is benevolent. To little Henri it was clear that if God took his mother away, as everyone agreed, then God was evil and deserved to be abused and hated. This is one of the bases of Beyle's later views on religion which the "Raillane tyranny" merely increased.

But for the unconscious, doctor and God are equated with the original authority in the child's life, his father. I will not be far from the truth, then, in supposing that both of these explanations of the cause of his mother's death are really attempts to blame it on his father. Indeed, it is the father who first comes between the child and his mother and, in the child's self-centered view of things, takes mother away from him. It is thus an easy step to the conviction that his mother's definitive removal through death was the result of his father's evil intention to deprive him of his mother. Strange as this reasoning may seem, there can be no doubt, judging from Beyle's own statements, that this remained his unconscious belief throughout his life.

But Beyle had an even more powerful motive for wanting to blame her death on his father. Twice he mentions that his mother died in childbirth. I have already shown that he reacted with great hostility toward his mother on the occasion of the birth of his sisters, once after the baby had arrived and once during his mother's pregnancy. Now, if he was aware of the meaning of pregnancy at the ages of three and five, he could not but have known it at the age of seven. It seems likely that he reacted to the situation in the same manner as on the two previous occasions, namely, with feelings of hostility toward his mother. As stated above, this hostility was translated as a death wish against her. It is a terrible thing for such a wish to become a reality, because of the belief in the omnipotence of thought. The inescapable conclusion is that Beyle was convinced that he had killed his mother!

There are several indications in *Henry Brulard* that he associated the births of his two sisters, his mother's third pregnancy, and his violent, ambivalent feelings toward his mother. When describing his passion for his mother, he says: "Je voulais couvrir ma mère de baisers et qu'il n'y eût pas de vêtements. Elle m'aimait à la passion et m'embrassait souvent." The paragraph ends with the statement that she died when he was seven years old, just as the first mention of his love for her is immediately followed by the announcement that she died when he was seven. Yet, on the very next page he denies that she loved him! "D'ailleurs, elle n'a participé en rien à cet amour. . . . Quant à moi, j'étais aussi criminel que possible, j'aimais ses charmes avec fureur" (p. 61). When a person emphatically asserts an idea and immediately there-after denies the very same idea, one begins to suspect that this idea is serving as a cover for another, related to it but still more important to that person's emotional life. I would suggest that the hidden idea is in this case Stendhal's hatred of his mother. He was "as criminal as possible," not because of his excessive love, but because of his hidden resentment. This resentment found expression in his remark that his mother did not love him, ostensibly said as protection of her memory but really meant as a reproach. How else can the fact be explained that each time he mentions his love, he immediately "excuses" it on the grounds that she died when he was seven? Is the reader sup-posed to believe that as a boy of six he knew that his mother was going to die the next year, so that he was justified in loving her excessively to make it up to her? Perhaps Beyle expected his readers to believe the excuse, but its real content can be found only by making a few transpositions. It is the fifty-year-old Beyle who is speaking, not the six-year-old Henri. His justi-fication is: "I could not have killed mother, I loved her so much." The meaning of these first chapters of *Henry Brulard* might be summed up as follows: "Despite my great love for my mother, she abandoned me twice, and when she threatened to do it a third time, I killed her for it."

The effect of little Henri's trauma was that, until his death, he carried with him an almost intolerable burden of guilt based on his unconscious conviction that he had murdered his mother.

Needless to say, he used all the energy at his command to maintain the repression of this idea. The severity of his depressions and his frequent suicidal phantasies give some indication of the strength of the emotion attached to it. Yet, at least once, it broke through to consciousness in almost undisguised form—in the denouement of *Le Rouge et le Noir*. When Julien rode off to Verrières to shoot Mme de Rênal, he was only repeating what Henri Beyle imagined he had done in Grenoble some forty years earlier.

The paradox of this ending can now be resolved. It presents itself as an intrusion because the sudden death of Beyle's mother put an equally abrupt end to the romance of his childhood. All his phantasies of reconquering his mother's love and of doing away with his rival had become complete impossibilities once he realized that she was irrevocably gone. His only chance to be reunited with her was by following her in death—hence his suicidal phantasies. However, her death not only ruined his chances for future happiness by making his childhood fixation to her definitive, thus barring the normal transfer of his love and desire during puberty onto another woman; it also set up within him a compulsion to repeat her "murder," a desire that was undoubtedly reinforced by his strong instinctual sadism. Hence his double attraction for stories in which a man killed his mistress; and hence the fact that it was this very ending, planned from the outset, which gave rise to his creative efforts in writing *Le Rouge et le Noir*. The only two avenues of libidinal gratification open to him were the sadistic murder of his love object or the masochistic reversal of this same desire, death at her hands or suicide, due to his guilt feeling. Both of these conditions find their optimum satisfaction in the denouement of *Le Rouge et le Noir,* where Julien murders Mme de Rênal and is executed because of this crime.

The obvious artificiality of this denouement, first noticed by Faguet and emphasized earlier in this essay, can be explained in part by the suddenness with which the actual event intruded on Beyle's life. But it has another motivation. When the manifest context of a dream shows marked absurdities, this is always a sign that the dreamer himself violently rejects its latent content: in this case, Beyle's judgment that his mother deserted him and that he killed her for it would therefore appear ridiculous to him on a conscious level and would support the numerous absurdities surrounding the episode of Mme de Rênal's letter and Julien's subsequent behavior. Unfortunately, his rational knowledge, that such an interpretation of his mother's death in childbirth was wholly unwarranted, was helpless in the face of his much stronger unconscious conviction that this is what had happened.

It might be argued that Julien does not really kill Mme de Rênal, since she recovers from the bullet wounds. Julien himself would disagree. In his speech before the court, he says specifically:

J'ai pu attenter aux jours de la femme la plus digne de tous les respects, de tous les hommages. Mme de Rênal avait été pour moi *comme une mère*. Mon crime est atroce, et il fut *prémédité*. J'ai donc mérité la mort. . . . [p. 482, first italics mine]

And M. Valenod's declaration of the verdict reached by the jury is quite emphatic on this point: "Valenod toussa, puis déclara qu'en son âme et conscience la déclaration unanime du jury était coupable de meurtre, et de meurtre avec préméditation" (p. 483). In fact, Mme de Rênal does die of a broken heart soon after Julien's execution. In the last analysis, Julien is the cause of her death. Her temporary recovery and eventual demise are an expression of Beyle's own reluctance to believe that he had actually killed his mother and an unsuccessful attempt to exculpate himself.

This hesitation is a direct parallel of Henri's state of mind when his mother died, as can be seen from the description in *La Vie de Henry Brulard* (pp. 64–69). Even after he had seen her in her coffin, he still did not really understand the meaning of death since he was convinced that she might be injured by the dirt thrown onto her in the grave. This conviction was, of course, based on the secret but all-powerful wish that she might come back to life, that is, come back to Henri. This wish is partially fulfilled in *Le Rouge et le Noir* when Mme de Rênal not only "comes back to life," i.e., recovers from the bullet wounds, but also literally comes back to Julien, in prison.

Once again Beyle's preconscious judgment of this wish fulfillment is manifested in the absurdity of the circumstances of Mme de Rênal's visits, pointed out by H. Bibas:

Rien de bizarre comme de voir le *Rouge* prendre cet aspect d'Allégorie morale, avec cette couronne octroyée en raison du bon combat [referring to the victory of "love" over "ambition" and the "spirit of domination" in Julien's soul, and the prize, seeing Mme de Rênal again]. Elle n'est pas sans être décernée contre le cours naturel des événements, la vraisemblance s'en accommode comme elle peut. . . . Tous les obstacles qui s'interposeraient pour empêcher l'intimité des amants sont levés comme par l'action d'une baguette magique. Aucune démarche de la part de M. de Rênal.[18]

Indeed, it is surprising that Bibas did not penetrate the hidden meaning of these scenes, since she emphasizes both the too convenient disappearance of Messrs. de Rênal and de La Mole and Julien's sudden recovery from his state of abnormal excitation on learning that Mme de Rênal is not going to die.[19] He can then cease punishing himself since, with Mme de Rênal still alive, his guilt has been removed. In like manner, if

Henriette Gagnon had returned from her coffin, Henri Beyle would have been exonerated. But the truth has an unpleasant habit of asserting itself against all wishful thinking, and so Henri eventually was forced to recognize that his mother's death was real and irreversible, just as Mme de Rênal finally dies because of Julien.

This phantasy, as is generally the case, is built around a kernel of remembered reality preserved in Stendhal's unconscious. The description in *Henry Brulard* shows that he was most impressed by the sight of his mother in her coffin. Since he still persisted in believing that she was alive, his nostalgia for his mother must have taken the form of a desire to join her in the coffin. In the novel, their situations are reversed, so that Julien is inside the prison, which represents the coffin, and Mme de Rênal comes to visit him. The end result is the same— their reunion, a prefiguration of their ultimate reunion at the very end of the novel, in death.

The marked fondness that Stendhal's heroes, particularly Julien and Fabrice, display for prisons can be traced back to this phantasy of reunion with the mother in death. What gives these scenes their emotional appeal to readers who have not had similar experiences is another, more profound unconscious determinant, already mentioned in the study of *Armance;* the unconscious conception of death as a return to the mother's body, to the womb. This idea, which also connotes that of intercourse, is given plastic expression in the phantasy of entering prison. I shall examine this point in greater detail in my analysis of *La Chartreuse de Parme.*

I embarked on this lengthy discussion of the denouement of *Le Rouge et le Noir* in the hopes of finding an answer to the puzzling question of why Julien destroys all his chances for success precisely at the moment when he has realized his deepest wishes as expressed in his phantasy of illegitimacy, when he has become a Father. And, indeed, my expectations have been confirmed. It will be recalled that Freud's concluding statement in his essay on "family romances" reads: "The entire endeavor to replace the real father by a more distinguished one is merely the expression of the child's longing for the vanished happy time, when his father still appeared to be the strongest and greatest man, and the mother seemed the dearest and most beautiful woman." And so it is with Julien. The strength of his ego drive toward independent adulthood is more than counterbalanced by his nostalgia for the dependence and security of infancy, conditioned as he is by the death of Stendhal's mother with all the heavy psychological consequences of that event. The sudden intervention of Mme de Rênal to block Julien's marriage with Mathilde thus represents the victory, in his own mind, of his earlier love for his mother over that for his sister; just as the jealousy of the two women is an expression of his own love for both.

I have already mentioned that the primary significance of the prison scenes is a reunion with his mother, as well as a punishment for his crime against her. A detailed analysis of this last section of the novel would show the step-by-step progress of Julien's return to childhood. I shall content myself with a limited number of examples, designed merely to prove the more general thesis. Before Julien's trial, and therefore several days before Mme de Rênal's first visit to his cell, he reacts to Mathilde's visit by withdrawing into a kind of revery:

Dans le fait, il en était éperdument amoureux [de Mme de Rênal]. Il trouvait un bonheur singulier quand, laissé absolument seul et sans crainte d'être interrompu, il pouvait se livrer tout entier au souvenir des journées heureuses qu'il avait passées jadis à Verrières ou à Vergy. [p. 471]

Even without the knowledge that Mme de Rênal represents
Beyle's mother and that Verrières is a substitute for Grenoble,
no reader could overlook the emotional tone of nostalgia that
everyone harbors in the depths of his heart for the carefree days
of his childhood, when every event, however insignificant, was
colored with the supreme knowledge that he was loved by his
mother. The fact, noticed by many Stendhal critics, that
Julien's love for each woman is impaired by his desire for another finds its explanation in the fixation on sister and mother.
He always is drawn to remain faithful to the latter's image,
conserved in his memory, and yet he cannot possess her without the accompanying anxiety imposed by the barrier against
incest. When Mme de Rênal first visits Julien in prison and he
tells her: "Sache que je t'ai toujours aimée, que je n'ai aimé
que toi" (p. 491), he speaks the truth. Neither Mathilde nor
any other woman could destroy his inner fidelity to the mother
of his childhood.

Thus far I have spoken almost exclusively of the mother-son
relationship as it concerns the denouement and the final scenes
of the novel. But I have not forgotten the great importance of
Stendhal's relationship to his father. He, too, makes his appearance in Julien's prison cell, although wearing several disguises. Twice Julien receives visits from father figures, the
Abbé Chélan, and his real father, the carpenter Sorel. Each of
these visits has profound emotional effects on him. In the first
case, he is horrified by Chélan's mental and physical decrepi-
tude, a sure sign that he is soon to die. Appropriately enough,
this fear for Chélan's life is quickly transformed into fear of his
own death. Indeed, only the idea of his own death could have
caused Julien's reaction, in which despair and depression out-
weigh pity. This fear of death is natural enough under the
circumstances; he is in prison waiting to be tried for murder.

Yet it is not hard to discern behind this "natural" motivation a deeper, unconscious determinant, quite similar to the process of Julien's fainting spell in Abbé Pirard's office. He fears that he must pay with his life for his desire to kill his father, embodied by the dying Abbé Chélan in this scene. This death wish is implied by his aggression against his "mother" which, in accordance with Stendhal's sadistic sexuality, has the unconscious meaning of intercourse.

Julien's reaction to old Sorel's visit is still more revealing. When he finds out that his father is there to see him, he thinks:

. . . ce matin-là il éprouvait vivement le remords de ne pas aimer son père.

Le hasard nous a placés l'un près de l'autre sur la terre, se disait-il . . . et nous nous sommes fait à peu près tout le mal possible. Il vient au moment de ma mort me donner le dernier coup. [p. 496]

What evil deeds has Julien committed against his father? As far as the manifest content of the novel is concerned, the answer is none. In fact, from the time he enters the Rênal household as tutor until the time Pirard arranges for Sorel and his other sons to receive a pension from the marquis, Julien has no dealings of any kind with his father. His self-reproaches—not loving his father enough, having harmed him as much as possible—can only refer to his secret wishes which have been carried out against others but were always directed against Sorel in thought.

The actual scene that takes place between them fully confirms this view:

". . . si vous voulez mourir en bon chrétien, il convient de payer vos dettes. Il y a encore les frais de votre nourriture et de votre éducation que j'ai avancés. . . ."

"Voilà donc l'amour de père!" se répétait Julien l'âme navrée, lorsque enfin il fut seul. [p. 497]

As so often happens, his unconscious guilt feeling finds concrete expression in the form of a debt.[20] Actually, Julien's feeling of guilt is conscious, but the real reason for this feeling (his parricidal wishes) is hidden from him. Stendhal therefore supplies him with a reason, Sorel's claim that Julien owes him money. In an effort to alleviate his guilt feeling Julien can repudiate this demand as the unjustified claim of an old miser, thus turning his reproaches against himself into the ironic reproach against his father: "Voilà donc l'amour de père!"

That this reversal cannot free Julien from his deep-seated guilt feeling can be seen from the pages that follow. He sinks into a state of depression the severity of which is greater than that of any other period of his imprisonment, ostensibly because of the stories of the two prisoners whom he invites into his cell. His thoughts, appropriately enough, take on the form of obsessive meditations about God:

> Ah! s'il y avait une vraie religion. . . . Mon âme le comprendrait, mon âme en a besoin. . . .
>
> Mais un vrai prêtre, un Massillon, un Fénelon. . . . Alors les âmes tendres auraient un point de réunion dans le monde. . . . Ce bon prêtre nous parlerait de Dieu. Mais quel Dieu? Non celui de la Bible, petit despote cruel et plein de la soif de se venger . . . mais le Dieu de Voltaire, juste, bon, infini. . . . [p. 500]

The reader of *Henry Brulard* will remember that Voltaire's God meant more to Beyle than a mere vague idea of some benevolent, impersonal principle guiding the universe:

> Dans le fait j'ai été exclusivement élevé par mon excellent grand-père, M. Henri Gagnon. Cet homme rare avait fait un pèlerinage à Ferney pour voir Voltaire et en avait été reçu avec distinction. Il avait un petit buste de Voltaire, gros comme le poing, monté sur un pied de bois d'ébène de six pouces de haut. [p. 57]

To little Henri the image of Voltaire had become inextricably mixed with that of his grandfather, and his grandfather remained throughout his life the image of the "good father," the father who dispenses love and protection freely to his children. One might say that Stendhal transferred all his positive feelings onto Henri Gagnon, while his hostility remained toward Chérubin Beyle. This same splitting mechanism is behind the various father pairs that appear in the novel and whose highest embodiment is in the two Gods, the despotic, vengeful God of the Bible, and the good God of Voltaire. The visit of old Sorel, the bad father, is thus compensated for by Julien's vision of the several good religious fathers—Massillon, Fénelon, Voltaire. This vision is the expression of his nostalgia for the happy days of his childhood when he was protected by his father.

In his meditation Julien soon approaches the real source of his feelings:

Hélas! Mme de Rênal est absente; peut-être son mari ne la laissera plus revenir à Besançon. . . .

Voilà ce qui m'isole, et non l'absence d'un Dieu juste, bon, tout-puissant, point méchant, point avide de vengeance.

Ah! s'il existait . . . Hélas! je tomberais à ses pieds. J'ai mérité la mort, lui dirais-je, mais grand Dieu, Dieu bon, Dieu indulgent, rends-moi celle que j'aime! [p. 501]

In the first sentence he forgets God for a moment and lays the blame for his separation from Mme de Rênal where it belongs, on her husband. Thus Henri blamed his father, as do all boys, for separating him from his mother. In the second sentence he shies away from the painful truth and blames his isolation once more on God—did not Abbé Rey say that the death of Beyle's mother was God's doing? Here Julien uses a familiar mechanism by means of which repressed material can reach consciousness provided it arrives with a negative sign, as a denial.

If the absence of a benevolent God did not bother him, why would he make such an extensive list of his qualities? Finally Julien, the latent homosexual and psychic masochist, makes an ultimate act of submission and self-abasement to God. No one with even a superficial knowledge of children can fail to see the infantile nature of this pleading. A free translation of the passage would be: "Please, Daddy, I'll do anything you say; you can do anything you want to me, but give me back my Mommy!" It is impossible to say whether or not these thoughts reached Henri's consciousness in this form when he was seven years old; but there can be no doubt that Stendhal was haunted by similar phantasies throughout his life and that these phantasies drew their emotional strength from his oedipal feelings and the death of his mother.

One further proof of the above contention, if more evidence be needed, is Julien's reaction when he learns that Mme de Rênal will recover from the bullet wounds: "Grand Dieu! elle n'est pas morte! s'écria Julien; et il tomba à genoux, pleurant à chaudes larmes. Dans ce moment suprême il était croyant" (p. 455).

This entire last section of the novel, "Prison," is an exact parallel of the second part, "Besançon." Again there is the entrance into the forbidding building, symbolizing intercourse and the return to the mother's body, and again Julien's crisis ends in masochistic submission to his father. Stendhal himself was at least obscurely aware of the equivalence of these two parts of the novel, for when Julien is about to enter the seminary for the first time, he thinks: "Pour un pauvre diable comme moi . . . sans protecteurs et sans argent, il n'y aura pas grande différence entre un séminaire et une prison . . ." (p. 166).

Julien's story ends, as it must, with his execution. His punishment is the classical talion of the Oedipus complex, both death and castration—the guillotine. Mathilde, the epitome of the castrating woman, has her final triumph after the execution; she carries off Julien's head, symbolic of his sexual organ. This scene contains the whole novel in miniature. Stendhal turns Julien's defeat into a masochistic victory, just as in real life, the author accepted punishment for his desires, making it a source of pleasure. By his death, Julien appeases his father, the law, and gains an outlet for his libido, Mathilde's love. But more important, he pays for his thought crimes against both parents and rejoins his mother: "Mme de Rênal fut fidèle à sa promesse. Elle ne chercha en aucune manière à attenter à sa vie; mais trois jours après Julien, elle mourut en embrassant ses enfants" (p. 508).

One may then summarize the manifest content of *Le Rouge et le Noir* as follows: it is the story of Beyle's life, in which reality and wishful phantasies are liberally mixed; his early childhood days in Grenoble are represented by the first section of the novel, Julien's stay with the Rênals in Verrières; the period of depression after his mother's death, the Raillane tyranny and his school days are symbolized by Julien's stay at the seminary in Besançon; later, Beyle left Grenoble for Paris, where he lived with his relatives, the Darus, corresponding to Julien's life in Paris with the La Moles; the final section of the novel leaves the realm of reality entirely and represents the logical conclusion of those elements of the novel which are based on Beyle's phantasy rather than on the events of his life; it is purely a psychic possibility he discovered within himself. The latent content is the story of the child within the adult who, far from participating in the maturing process, remains fixated to those earliest experiences before his mother's death, repeating them in various covert ways *ad infinitum,* or rather *ad mortem.*

III

Unfinished Symphony

Dans l'embryon, la colonne vertébrale se forme d'abord, le reste
s'établit sur cette colonne. De même ici: d'abord l'intrigue d'amour,
puis les ridicules qui viennent encombrer l'amour, retarder ses
jouissances, comme dans une symphonie Haydn retarde les conclusions de la phrase.[1]

Stendhal always had a great interest in and appreciation for
music. The first books he published, largely plagiarized it is
true, dealt with the lives of Haydn and Mozart, two of the
greatest composers of the eighteenth century. Throughout his
life one of his sources of pleasure was listening to music,
especially opera. It is therefore not at all surprising that he
should think of his latest novel in terms of a musical composition; *Lucien Leuwen* was to be a great symphony, a symphony
of love.

The possible points of comparison between a symphony and
a novel are many: the rich harmonies and the extended development of individual themes and motifs, the opportunity to
introduce leitmotivs or the juxtaposition of separate movements

having different forms and tones and which, nevertheless, work together in some mysterious way to form a whole. Modern literature and literary criticism have brought to light a host of such analogies. Music, being pure form which develops in time, is perfectly suited to furnishing terms to describe the formal characteristics of other works of art in which the time dimension is crucial.

Yet Stendhal was concerned with none of this. For him, the *tertium comparationis* was the element of *retardation*. As Haydn delays the final cadence of his symphony, so Stendhal will hold off the final resolution of his plot, the moment when Lucien can enjoy the pleasures of love with Mme de Chasteller. In place of the deceptive cadences of the symphony or the last-minute resuscitation of motifs which seemed forever buried, he provides the internal and external obstacles which forestall the consummation of Lucien's love. (How right was Aldous Huxley in naming his essay on *Armance* "Obstacle Race," a title just as appropriate for *Lucien Leuwen*.[2])

On the night of May 8, 1834, in a sudden inspiration Stendhal conceived the broad outline of his novel:

L'histoire qu'il écrit ne sera pas seulement un épisode d'une vie de lieutenant de province,[3] le héros sera ensuite successivement secrétaire d'un ministre à Paris, puis attaché d'ambassade à Rome. A la fin du livre il se mariera avec la femme qu'il a tant aimée aux premiers chapitres.[4]

There can be no doubt then that the resolution of the book was to be Lucien's marriage to Mme de Chasteller.

Beyle's attitude toward marriage was always rather ambivalent, as is shown by the fiction he created as well as by his life. Octave de Malivert commits suicide shortly after his mar-

riage to Armance; Julien Sorel is about to marry Mathilde de La
Mole when the fatal letter from Mme de Rênal puts an end to
his plans; Fabrice del Dongo never seems to think of asking
Clélia to marry him (after the love scene in prison, she marries
the Marquis Crescenzi), and in *Lamiel* there is no mention of
marriage except in Dr. Sansfin's phantasy.[5] In his youth, Beyle
toyed with the idea of marrying his mistress, Mélanie Guilbert,
but nothing came of it.[6] At the time of writing *Lucien Leuwen,*
however, marriage was very much on his mind.

In 1827 Beyle noticed a young Italian woman named Giulia
Rinieri. It is possible that he met her from time to time in
Parisian society during the ensuing years. In any case, she
suddenly declared that she loved him in 1830 and they soon
became lovers. The day before his departure for Italy, where
he was to take up his duties as consul, Beyle asked her to marry
him but was refused by her guardian. Even so, he continued
to see her in Siena and Rome, hoping that she might eventually
marry him. So great was her attraction for him that, although
he constantly complained of having to stay in Civitavecchia
and was longing to return to his beloved Paris, it seems that he
refused a leave of absence offered him, in order to remain near
Giulia. Finally, in April 1833, she terminated the relationship
and soon married someone else. After returning from a short
visit to Paris, Beyle was still thinking of marriage. He proposed
to a Mlle Vidau of Civitavecchia, but once again failed to receive the approval of the lady's family. These events took place
in 1834 and 1835, the very years when *Lucien Leuwen* was
written.[7]

What effect these rebuffs had on Beyle can only be surmised.
Furthermore, there is so little direct evidence about these affairs that it is difficult to tell whether his failures were really
caused by the intervention of his intended's male relatives (an

uncle in each case) as Beyle claims, or rather to the lack of interest of the women themselves. If Beyle's assessment of the situations was correct, one might still wonder whether a more energetic suitor might have overcome or circumvented the obstacles placed in his way. Be that as it may, the fact remains that the "ridicules qui viennent encombrer l'amour" did not simply delay the conclusion; in Beyle's life they *prevented* it.

In his extraordinarily perceptive essay on the modern novel, "Ideas sobre la novela" (Madrid, 1963), Ortega takes *Lucien Leuwen* as a classical example of a novel which is immensely captivating and yet has virtually no plot:

> Para mí ha sido siempre un ejemplo clásico de la independencia en que el placer novelesco se halla de la trama, una obra que Stendhal deja apenas medida y se ha publicado con títulos diversos: *Luciano Leuwen, El cazador verde,* etc. La porción existente alcanza una abundante copia de páginas. Sin embargo, allí no pasa nada. . . . Assistimos únicamente a la minuciosa germinación del delectable sentimiento en uno y otro ser; nada más. Cuando la acción va a enredarse, lo escrito termina, pero quedamos con la impresión de que hubiéramos podido seguir indefinadamente leyendo páginas y páginas en que se nos hablase de aquel rincón francés, de aquella dama legitimista, de aquel militar con uniforme de color amaranto. [pp. 174–75]

Apparently Ortega is speaking only of the first volume of *Lucien Leuwen,* which takes place in Nancy and deals almost exclusively with Lucien's affair with Mme de Chasteller. The point I want to bring out is Ortega's impression that one could go on reading about this affair indefinitely. As is evident from the rest of his essay, he feels that this is possible because Stendhal has succeeded in arousing such intense interest in the psychological processes of his characters that their actions seem unimportant. Each change of mood, each thought or feeling becomes an object of our concern. In short, it is the state of being in love, in all its various aspects, that occupies the reader's attention, not the ultimate outcome of that love.

But this evaluation of the reader's involvement in the novel overlooks one important fact: there is a progression in the feelings of both Lucien and Mme de Chasteller. Despite the many sudden reversals in their attitudes towards each other, there is a general drift in their feelings which tends to bring them ever closer together. Yet reading about the affair could go on indefinitely only if the affair actually lasted indefinitely, a condition which, in turn, would be based on an indefinite delay of the final union of the two lovers.

In a sense this infinite delay was realized by Stendhal. When it seems as though the two must soon become lovers, Beyle causes Dr. Du Poirier to intervene in such a way as to send Lucien fleeing back home to Paris and his mother:

"Je ne puis plus aimer Bathilde!" se disait-il tout haut de temps en temps. . . . Toutes les choses du monde avaient perdu leur importance à ses yeux, deux objets surnageaient seuls: sa mère et Mme de Chasteller. [pp. 1063–64][8]

Sometime during Lucien's stay in Paris, Mme de Chasteller was to arrive, but this eventuality never materialized, although there are a few chapters which lay the groundwork for her trip (Chaps. 40 and 41). Most significant is the fact that Stendhal was unable to complete the novel. It cannot be that he thought it was unimportant. He had spent the better part of eighteen months working on this novel (May 1834, to November 1835) and had written over six hundred pages of it.[9] He gave up the idea of a third volume in April 1835 and ceased work on the novel entirely in November of that year in order to devote himself to the writing of *Henry Brulard*.[10] In other words, instead of completing the forward-looking portion of the novel, the one that would lead his hero to some kind of adjustment, Stendhal once again turned his eyes backward, toward even earlier periods of his childhood.[11] The end result is that, unlike a Haydn symphony, the resolution never comes. The delay has become permanent; as Ortega says, "Allí no pasa nada."

Theodor Reik has discussed this type of situation at length in his book, *Masochism in Modern Man*.[12] In it he shows that what is in essence a necessary and valuable stratagem of the ego —learning to delay a pleasure until the proper time for its gratification—becomes distorted in the masochistic character. The pleasure is delayed longer and longer, until finally it is put off indefinitely, or rather until some point in an imagined, and never realized, future.

The counterpart of this "Final Victory" theory of life is the "Flight Forward" in which the individual hurries to be punished before the gratification, often inflicting some disgrace or displeasure on himself, if fate or other people do not do it for him. In the second chapter of the novel, when Lucien is imagining what his future life as an officer in Nancy will be like, he has phantasies of just this sort:

Il se figurait la guerre d'après les exercices du canon au bois de Vincennes.

Peut-être une blessure! mais alors il se voyait transporté dans une chaumière de Souabe ou d'Italie; une jeune fille charmante, dont il n'entendait pas le langage, lui donnait des soins, d'abord par humanité, et ensuite . . . Quand l'imagination de vingt ans avait épuisé le bonheur d'aimer une naïve et fraîche paysanne, c'était une jeune femme de la cour. [p. 774]

(It is interesting to note that this very phantasy becomes a reality in the *Chartreuse*. In Chapter 5 the Flemish girls who take care of Fabrice's wounds seem quite taken with him as well. In like manner Julien's seduction of Mme de Rênal is preceded by the episode in which she finds him lying senseless on the ground, beaten by his brothers.) The pattern is clear: first the wound, then a woman to take care of him, then love.

Lucien almost manages to convert these phantasies into reality. Of course there is no war at the time, so a wound in battle cannot be arranged. The alternative is slightly less dramatic but equally revealing. On Lucien's arrival in Nancy, while his squadron of Lancers is promenading through the town, he notices a fascinating personage looking down from her window:

C'était une jeune femme blonde qui avait des cheveux magnifiques et l'air dédaigneux: elle venait voir défiler le régiment. Toutes les idées tristes de Lucien s'envolèrent à l'aspect de cette jolie figure; son âme en fut ranimée. [p. 794]

The impact of this lovely vision on Lucien can be truly measured only if we bear in mind the gloomy, even disgusting first impression made by Nancy on the young Lancer. Entranced in his thoughts and in the process of gazing at the window, Lucien is caught unprepared when the squadron begins to move again:

Le second escadron, dont Lucien faisait partie, se remit en mouvement tout à coup; Lucien, les yeux fixés sur la fenêtre vert perroquet, donna un coup d'éperon à son cheval, qui glissa, tomba et le jeta par terre. . . .

. . . Lucien remarqua que la dame aux cheveux d'un blond cendré souriait encore, que déjà il était remonté. [p. 794]

Despite this demonstration of affection on Lucien's part, it is not until nine chapters and several months later that he begins thinking seriously about Mme de Chasteller (the young lady at the window). One day, as he is riding down the Rue de la Pompe past her house, he notices that her shutters are open and begins to show off his riding prowess:

> . . . Il était évident que quelqu'un regardait. C'était, en effet, Mme de Chasteller. . . .
> Enfin, Lucien eut cette mortification extrême, que son petit cheval hongrois le jeta par terre à dix pas peut-être de l'endroit où il était tombé le jour de l'arrivée du régiment. [p. 895]

After making himself look foolish a second time, Lucien is now able to meet Mme de Chasteller in society and to pursue her. The imagined wound is now caused by falling off a horse, the battle is horseback riding, but the total effect is the same. Once Lucien has received his self-inflicted punishment, he is more or less free to follow his real desires, to become active in his suit of Mme de Chasteller.

The same procedure is evident in the longest episode of Book 2. Lucien has been entrusted with an important mission concerning the upcoming elections to the Chamber of Deputies. He must help the prefects of two towns make sure that the governmental candidate will be elected. Although his high sense of morality makes him regard this mission with a feeling bordering on loathing, he nevertheless feels that it is a good opportunity to prove himself in action.

Before he has a chance to do anything, fate takes on the role that Lucien has played toward himself in Book 1. He and his friend Coffe arrive at Blois and decide to stop there for dinner. While they are eating they hear a great commotion; the proprietor of the inn urges them to escape. Once outside Lucien confronts an angry group of people who shout at him:

> "A bas l'espion, à bas le commissaire de police!"
> Rouge comme un coq, il prit sur lui de ne pas répondre et voulut

s'approcher de sa voiture. La foule s'écarta un peu. Comme il ouvrait la portière, une énorme pelletée de boue tomba sur sa figure, et de là sur sa cravate. Comme il parlait à M. Coffe dans ce moment, la boue entra même dans sa bouche. [p. 1189]

Once he has been subjected to this disgrace, Lucien is free to give himself over to energetic action. He goes through a period of self-reproach, of disgust with himself and his job, but when the time comes to act, he forgets these torturing thoughts and concentrates on the business at hand—getting his men elected. Despite his inexperience and his fears of being inadequate, he works so well that the enemy of the juste-milieu in Caen, a M. Mairobert, is almost defeated. Indeed the reason for Lucien's failure—by only one vote—to prevent Mairobert's election was the procrastination of the minister of the interior in sending him the money he needed.

Nevertheless, as with Mme de Chasteller, Lucien does fail in this mission. The ignominy of this failure is emphasized by the contrasting fortunes of Lucien's father and Dr. Du Poirier, both of whom are elected without too much difficulty. Lucien's attitude toward Du Poirier, the political chief of the Carlist party in Nancy, is that of son to father:

Mais Leuwen ne pouvait rompre avec Du Poirier. . . . Ne rompant pas avec un homme aussi actif, aussi entrant, aussi facile à piquer, il fallait le traiter en ami intime, *en père*. [pp. 952–953, italics mine]

It is as though Lucien has been competing against rivals of infinitely greater strength than himself. Whereas page after page has been devoted to Lucien's efforts to prevent Mairobert's election (pp. 1216–1267), the news of M. Leuwen's and Du Poirier's success is given in a few paragraphs, thus making it seem as though their campaigns required little effort.

Lucien's relationship with his father is quite unique among Stendhal's novels, provided the word "father" is taken literally. The actual fathers of Stendhal's other heroes are either cruel boors, as M. Sorel and the Marquis del Dongo, or of little importance, as M. de Malivert, or nonexistent as in the case of the orphan Lamiel; but in each of these novels except *Armance*, there is a substitute father—the Marquis de La Mole, Count Mosca, Dr. Sansfin—whose role is similar to that of M. Leuwen.

The reader's first impression of M. Leuwen is rather agreeable:

[Lucien] passait très bien son temps chez son père, homme de plaisir et riche banquier, lequel avait à Paris une maison fort agréable.

M. Leuwen père . . . ne redoutait au monde que deux choses, les ennuyeux et l'air humide. Il n'avait point d'humeur, ne prenait jamais le ton sérieux avec son fils et lui avait proposé, à la sortie de l'école, de travailler au comptoir un seul jour de la semaine. . . . [Chap. 1, p. 768]

Although Lucien is well paid for his day's work, from time to time the wealthy father must pay his son's debts. He says jokingly: "Un fils est un créancier donné par la nature" (p. 768). When Lucien desires to be an officer in the army, M. Leuwen uses the influence of his powerful friends to get him a commission (reminiscent of the Marquis de La Mole). Little is heard of M. Leuwen throughout the rest of Book 1 because Lucien is away from home in Nancy. Occasionally M. Leuwen sends his son money or advice, or attempts to smoothe his way in the army by speaking to the right people in the government. That is all.

It is only in Book 2, after Lucien's return to Paris, that his father starts to play a prominent role in the novel. Lucien, who has just beaten an ignominious retreat from Mme de Chasteller and army life, is in great need of moral support. M. Leuwen, in his easygoing way, is ready to help him:

"Je ne veux point abuser de mon titre de père pour vous contrarier; soyez libre, mon fils. . . . Vous connaissez la vie de régiment, vous connaissez la province; préférez-vous la vie de Paris? Donnez vos ordres, mon prince. Il n'y a qu'une chose à laquelle on ne consentira pas: c'est le mariage."

"Il n'en est pas question, mon père." [Book 2, Chap. 1, p. 1069. Note that Stendhal is well aware of the equation: prince = son.]

True to his word, M. Leuwen arranges for Lucien to become *maître des requêtes*, acting as confidential secretary to the Minister of the Interior, M. de Vaize, an unheard-of advancement for so young a man. Lucien, whose confidence had been badly shaken by his recent experiences in Nancy, is filled with anxiety at the prospect of undertaking this new venture:

A quoi bon choisir un état pour la troisième fois? Puisque je n'ai pas su plaire à Mme de Chasteller, que saurai-je jamais. Quand on possède une âme comme la mienne, à la fois faible et impossible à contenter, on va se jeter à la Trappe. [p. 1076]

After much hesitation, Lucien decides to take the job; in order to overcome his son's last scruples, M. Leuwen gives him the typical Stendhalian indoctrination speech:

"Voici le principe: tout gouvernement, même celui des Etats-Unis, ment toujours et en tout; quand il ne peut pas mentir au fond, il ment sur les détails." [p. 1080; he continues in this vein for several paragraphs.]

Beneath his joking, his cynicism, and his apparently laissez-faire attitude toward Lucien's future, M. Leuwen gives proof of a deeper and more realistic concern for his son's welfare. Not only does he get him a demanding job, but he also urges Lucien to spend his evenings at the opera so that his days will be fully occupied. Like a human version of divine providence, M. Leu-wen not only guides his son's life, but has hidden reasons for asking him to do seemingly unpleasant things, and all for Lucien's own good. M. Leuwen's solicitude is so great that he even forces him to acquire a mistress. When Lucien at first greets this plan rather coolly, his father has a long, emotional talk with him in what is probably the key scene of Book 2:

"Je vous aime, et par conséquent vous me rendez malheureux; car la première des duperies, c'est d'aimer. . . . Dans ma longue carrière, je n'ai connu qu'une exception, mais aussi elle est unique. J'aime votre mère, elle est nécessaire à ma vie, et elle ne m'a jamais donné un grain de malheur. *Au lieu de vous regarder comme mon rival dans son coeur, je me suis avisé de vous aimer,* c'est un ridicule dans lequel je m'étais bien juré de ne jamais tomber, et vous m'empêchez de dormir." [p. 1156, italics mine]

M. Leuwen becomes very angry and forces his son to take 12,000 francs that he is to spend on a mistress: "Il faut que le public sache que tu as une maîtresse" (p. 1156). At this point even Lucien begins to suspect that it is possible to get too much of a good thing. When his father threatens to be angry if Lucien does not accept the 12,000 francs: "Le sujet de la querelle serait neuf, dit Lucien en souriant. *Les rôles sont renversés*" (p. 1156, italics mine).

The roles are reversed; everything is just the opposite of what one might have expected: M. Leuwen does not look on Lucien as a rival; M. Leuwen does not want to use his authority to deprive his son of his freedom; M. Leuwen does not wish to be repaid for the things he gives his son. Yet in terms of what actually happens, as opposed to what is said, a very different picture emerges. M. Leuwen decides that Lucien should not marry Mme de Chasteller; Lucien does not marry her. (It was of course Du Poirier, that other father figure, who actually prevented the marriage in the first place.) M. Leuwen suggests that Lucien work for M. de Vaize, and Lucien becomes de Vaize's secretary; his father urges him to go to the opera, and Lucien attends the opera; and upon Leuwen's suggestion that he become, or pretend to become, Mme Grandet's lover, Lucien does just that. In fact, when it seems as though Lucien might not be able to make this conquest alone, M. Leuwen makes a deal with Mme Grandet: if she will sleep with Lucien, her husband will become a minister in the new government.

If M. Leuwen is a realistic character, then he is obviously a mass of reaction formations. His lordship doth protest so much that it is evident that these negations of rivalry and authority are a defense against the opposite, hostile impulses, for, as pointed out above, the end result is always the opposite of the conscious intention.

On the other hand, M. Leuwen can be considered as a construct shaped to fit the needs of the main character, Lucien, with whom Stendhal identified most closely. Then M. Leuwen becomes the embodiment of Lucien's conflicting feelings towards his father, his conscience, authority in general. In part, M. Leuwen fulfills the role of the "good" father, the protector, helper, who is just such a model of divine providence as was mentioned earlier. Above all, Lucien's deep longing for dependence, symbolized by his return home after defeat in Nancy, is expressed in the passive way in which he lets himself be guided and protected by his father.

But Lucien has other feelings as well. The first lines of the novel inform us that Lucien was expelled from the Ecole Polytechnique for taking part in an attempt to overthrow the king (p. 768). Despondent after the mud is thrown in his face during the electoral campaign, he thinks:

Que devenir? Manger le bien gagné par mon père, ne rien faire, n'être bon à rien! Attendre ainsi la vieillesse en me méprisant moi-même, et en m'écriant: "Que je suis heureux d'avoir eu un père qui valut mieux que moi!" [p. 1199]

The final blow to his pride is the revelation of M. Leuwen's role in Mme Grandet's sudden passionate interest in Lucien:

Oui, mon père est comme tous les pères, ce que je n'avais pas su voir jusqu'ici avec infiniment plus d'esprit et même de sentiment qu'un autre, il n'en veut pas moins me rendre heureux *à sa façon* et non à la mienne. [p. 1355]

In a desperate attempt to flee his parents, Lucien takes a room in a hotel:

Ici je serai, se disait-il en [se] promenant avec délices, je serai tout à fait à l'abri de la sollicitude paternelle, maternelle, sempiternelle! [p. 1359]

Sensing how dependent he really is, Lucien develops a need for independence which becomes a violent passion, one that was supposed to be strong enough to detach him from his parents and take him to Madrid or Rome. (Stendhal, however, did not have the heart to write the third book of the novel, which would have dealt with Lucien's experiences there.) In Chapter 65 of Book 2 Lucien wants to visit Mme de Chasteller in Nancy, but cannot:

Le souvenir vif et imprévu de madame de Chasteller avait fait révolution dans le coeur de Lucien. Mais il était enchaîné à Paris par la vive amitié qu'il avait pour ses parents. [p. 1360]

If normal methods are not successful, sometimes it is necessary to have recourse to extraordinary ones. Since Lucien seems unable to free himself from his parents' influence while his father is alive, there is only one solution: M. Leuwen must die. Chapter 48, the last one completed by the author, begins with these surprising words: "Après la mort subite de M. Leuwen, Lucien revint à Paris" (p. 1378). No preparation, no hint of an illness, no suggestion that an accident took place—M. Leuwen just dies. There is little doubt that if Stendhal had ever revised the novel for publication, he would have given this event some preparation, but the very crudeness of the presentation here shows that it is the basic idea in the raw. The analogy with the Marquis de Malivert's sudden, inexplicable death at the end of *Armance* and the Marquis de La Mole's mysterious disappearance at the end of the "Paris" section of *Le Rouge et le Noir* is clear. Wish fulfillment has broken through to the surface in the same way that it did when Julien Sorel suddenly rode off to Verrières to kill Mme de Rênal. Only now, with M. Leuwen out of the way, is Lucien ready to leave Paris, to start a new life in another city.

Perhaps these two views of Lucien's relationship to his father might be united by saying that the youth suffers the consequences of being loved too much and in the wrong way—the exact opposite of Julien. This excessive love gives him so much protection that he is never able to try his own strength and thus develop that "curiosité de lutter avec le monde" of which M. Leuwen spoke (p. 1105). Lucien's deep sense of insecurity, his lack of ego strength, is emphasized in several of the passages just quoted, but it is most clearly expressed when he is trying to decide whether to become M. de Vaize's secretary:

Et il faut qu'avant demain matin, se disait-il avec terreur, je prenne une décision, *que j'aie foi en moi-même* . . . Est-il un être au monde dont j'estime aussi peu le jugement? [p. 1076]

The emotions and conflicts I have been discussing in terms of Lucien's relationship with his father are the same as those that are connected with the "family romance" in *Le Rouge et le Noir*.

It seems legitimate to ask why this could be done directly, that is, with the "real" father in *Lucien Leuwen* and only indirectly in *Le Rouge et le Noir*. I think that there are two principal reasons. First, since Lucien's relationship to his father is basically one of love, the existence of repressed hostility, which breaks out only at the end of the novel, does not seem so terrible. Second, and most important, there is no sexual competition between father and son in *Lucien Leuwen* as there is between Julien and his father substitutes. It is characteristic of *Lucien Leuwen* that the only mention of such competition is by way of denial (see p. 1156). The only other indication of such a possibility is also by way of reversal: M. Leuwen does not prevent Lucien from having the woman; he forces him to do so.

Aside from the affair with Mme Grandet, there is the hint of an additional "family romance" in Lucien's relationship to M. and Mme de Vaize. However, this situation is quickly suppressed. When Lucien is to meet his new employer for the first time, Stendhal describes his thoughts as follows:

Il se faisait une fête d'approcher M. le comte de Vaize, travailleur infatigable et le premier administrateur de France, disaient les journaux, *un homme qu'on comparait au comte Daru de l'Empereur.* [p. 1079, italics mine]

Daru had been Stendhal's own protector and employer many years before this was written, and Stendhal had entertained phantasies of seducing his wife.[13] Lucien's relationship to Mme de Vaize follows the same pattern. At first, when he has only known her a short while, he feels mildly attracted to her, but only as a friend (p. 1104).

Several chapters later, after Lucien's return from his mission to Caen, his feelings toward her have begun to change. Pleased that she has intervened on his behalf with her husband to obtain for Lucien a gratification for his services in the electoral campaign (even though the campaign was a failure), Lucien has a long conversation with her. He thinks:

"Je devrais faire la cour à cette femme timide; les grandeurs l'ennuient et lui pèsent, je serais sa consolation. Mon bureau n'est guère qu'à cinquante pas de sa chambre." [p. 1271]

During this conversation Lucien suddenly falls silent, and when gently reproached for this behavior, he excuses himself by saying:

"C'est que je suis sur le point d'éprouver pour vous, madame, un sentiment que je me reprochais."

Après cette petite coquinerie, Leuwen n'avait plus rien à dire à madame de Vaize. Il ajouta quelques mots polis, la laissa rouge comme du feu, et courut s'enfermer dans son bureau. [p. 1272]

Is it farfetched to hear in this turn of affairs a distant echo of the same pattern that was operative in the first part of the novel? After Lucien suffers a defeat, Mme de Vaize suddenly takes an interest in him, and his thoughts immediately turn to seduction.

The last scene of this little romance takes place when Mme de Vaize is afraid that M. Leuwen's political actions are going to cause her husband's ministry to fall:

"Je suis désolé de votre chagrin. Que ne puis-je vous consoler en vous donnant mon coeur! Mais vous savez bien qu'il est *vôtre* depuis longtemps. . . ."

La pauvre petite Mme de Vaize n'avait pas assez d'esprit pour voir la réponse à faire. . . . Elle se contenta de la sentir confusément. C'était à peu près:

"*Si j'étais parfaitement sûre que vous m'aimez, si j'avais pu prendre sur moi d'accepter votre hommage, le bonheur d'être à vous serait peut-être la seule consolation possible au malheur de perdre le ministère.*" [p. 1314]

The forbidden nature of the sentiments underlying this affair is shown by a strange passage, unique in this novel, which occurs on the very next page:

Lucien avait un grand remords à propos de son père. Il n'avait pas d'amitié pour lui, c'est ce qu'il se reprochait souvent sinon comme un crime, du moins comme un manquement de coeur. [p. 1315]

Everything in the novel up to this point has indicated, at least on the surface, that nothing but love existed between Lucien and his father. Nowhere had Lucien given any proof of insight into his other, hostile feelings. Remember that the revelation of M. Leuwen's complicity with Mme Grandet occurs only later. Nothing has happened between pages 1314 and 1315 to indicate such a change in feelings. And yet, there it is. Lucien speaks as though he had just stepped out of *Le Rouge et le Noir*. I think that it is reasonable to suppose that he becomes aware of these hostile feelings momentarily at this time because of the hidden rivalry implied in his amorous designs on Mme de Vaize.

"Allí no pasa nada," says Ortega of the first part of the novel, adding that the reader merely witnesses the "minuciosa germinación" of love in Lucien and Mme de Chasteller. For Ortega and many readers this detailed representation (I was going to say analysis, but although Stendhal's novel includes analysis, it is much more than that), this picture, is more than enough to give the true aesthetic pleasure we look for in a novel. As long as one means by plot ("trama") external actions and conflicts, i.e., those that occur among different individuals or between an individual and his society (and Ortega is careful to restrict his usage in his way), then Book 1 indeed has no plot. Even Lucien's conquest of Nancy's legitimist society is not a plot development in this sense, since it is not experienced by the

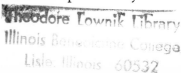

hero as a challenge of intrinsic interest so much as a stepping-stone toward his ultimate goal, Mme de Chasteller.

Yet, as was pointed out above, there is a growth, a movement, a progression in the feelings of the protagonists, so that the indefinite extension of this description could only be a theoretical idea or, if carried out in fact, a betrayal of the underlying laws governing the process taking place. Even Proust, Ortega's prime example of the plotless novelist, shows, by his portrayal of Swann in love with Odette and of Marcel in love with Albertine, that he was wiser than his critic. Stendhal also knew otherwise, as is manifest in the musical analogy placed at the head of this chapter and in the actual events which terminate Book 1.

Many critics have demonstrated the close analogy between the development of Lucien's love for Mme de Chasteller and Beyle's own experience with Mathilde Dembowska some twenty years earlier.[14] They have also shown that in *Lucien Leuwen*, as in Stendhal's other great novels, the steps in the evolution of romantic love are the same as those outlined in his treatise *De L'Amour*. This is to be expected since *De L'Amour* was written while Beyle was in love with Mathilde and is the result of his reflections on his own experience. But it is not enough simply to show the similarity between Lucien's feelings and those of Beyle, nor to point out that the novel serves in part as a compensation for life.[15]

The power and the beauty of the novel are to be found in the vividness and truthfulness of the picture Stendhal gives us of the dynamic process of love. More specifically, it is the exposure of those subtle feelings, and shifts in feeling, which ordinarily remain hidden in the more obscure recesses of the mind. Stendhal was more aware than most people of this underside of love, as he shows by the penetrating analyses in *De*

L'Amour, a book that has aroused the wonder and admiration of two twentieth-century psychologists, Edmund Bergler and Theodor Reik. Both evolved theories of love based on the observation of many other people, as well as themselves, and on the use of the psychoanalytic method; and both are amazed that only Stendhal, among all earlier authors on the subject, perceived essentially the same truths using only self-observation and the methods of Ideology.

In his biographical essay on Stendhal, Bergler describes his own theory as follows:

Without knowing Stendhal's book on love, L. Jekels and the author tried, in their article "Transference and Love" (*Imago* 1934, H. 1), to formulate more exactly the process of so-called object love. We maintained that all love consists of a *projection of one's own ego ideal onto the object,* with a subsequent, partial reintrojection of the ego ideal. The entire process is thus purely narcissistic and has the goal of wresting from the Daimonion its instrument of torture, the ego ideal, and of replacing the latter with an instrument better fitted for the battle against the Daimonion. The fact that the ego knows that it is loved by its ego ideal, and thus has found an antidote against guilt feeling, causes the euphoria [*hohes Glück*] of love. The downright mad overestimation of the object would result from the fact that behind the loved object one's own ego is hidden. All love would then be reduced, at the deepest level, to a desire to be loved. The 'hangover' which always follows love would again be the work of the Daimonion. . . . Thus, on the basis of analytic considerations, we come to results quite similar to those of Stendhal, whose insight into the narcissistic mechanism of love must inspire us with surprised admiration.[16]

The core of this theory is the idea that the love object temporarily takes the place of one's ego ideal; when love is returned it is experienced as love from the ego ideal and so the previous dissatisfaction with oneself disappears as if by magic. The analogy with Stendhal's concept of crystallization is clear:

On se plaît à orner de mille perfections une femme de l'amour de laquelle on est sûr; on se détaille tout son bonheur avec une complaisance infinie. . . . Ce que j'appelle cristallisation, c'est l'opération de l'esprit, qui tire de tout ce qui se présente la découverte que l'objet aimé a de nouvelles perfections.[17]

What Bergler calls the narcissistic mechanism of love is equivalent to Stendhal's idea that the perfections found in the loved person are supplied by the phantasy of the lover; they are not an intrinsic part of the love object any more than the salt crystals are a part of the branch around which they form. But in both cases an object of a specific nature is required in order to start the process of crystallization. The "perfections" of which Stendhal speaks are precisely those qualities that make up the image of the ego ideal (the "idealization" in romantic love).

Reik also puts Stendhal's book in a class by itself:

I assert that the last serious book which penetrated this secret domain was De L'Amour by Stendhal. It was written one hundred and thirty-five years ago—which is a long time when you consider the psychological import of the subject.[18]

Despite this disclaimer there is a great similarity between Reik's basic idea and Bergler's. Either Reik was unaware of Bergler's article or else he objected to the use of the concept of narcissism. In any case, the fundamental identity of their theories cannot be denied (as is clearly illustrated in Reik's Of Love and Lust):

What pushes us to love is thus an effort to escape from internal discontent. It takes the place of an original striving for self-perfection. . . . So far as I have been able to judge there is only one source

from which it [the internal discontent] comes . . . : it is the failure
to come up to the demands that we make on ourselves. [p. 34]

. . . . .

Thus love is really a second-best, a compensatory way for not ob-
taining the ego ideal state. Yet it is not self-love, as the theory of
narcissism makes out. As a matter of fact it is nearer to self-hate. It
is love for one's ego ideal, which will never be reached in oneself.
[p. 40]

. . . . .

In other words, loving means exchanging the ego ideal for an external object, for a person in whom are joined all the qualities that
we once desired for ourselves. [p. 41]

. . . . .

Deprived of the glory of love, the ego is where it stood before, or
almost there. He feels again unworthy. Again he is the prey of dis-
cord and depression. He belongs once again to the Have-nots of
the earth. [p. 88]

One of the conclusions Reik draws from his study of the
preconditions of love is that if the individual is to a large extent
satisfied with himself, he will not fall in love; he will not have
the incentive to transfer his ego ideal onto an external object. If
he is too dissatisfied with himself, he will not be able to rescue
himself through love, for his fear of total dependence on the
love object will be too great.

Lucien must obviously struggle against this latter problem.
I have already spoken of his insecurity as it appears in the
second part of the novel, after love has failed him, or he has
failed love (the "hangover" period of which Bergler speaks).
The depth of his despair at that time is a measure of the greatness of his need before he has met Mme de Chasteller. But I
need not content myself with such indirect evidence. It will be
recalled that Lucien falls off his horse in front of Mme de

Chasteller's window the day he comes to Nancy, in Chapter 4. The next day, after his official induction into the army, Lucien is angry and depressed because he feels that real war and heroism are no longer possible; being a soldier is thus either base or a sham. Stendhal comments:

N'eût-il mieux valu être fou de bonheur, comme l'eût été, dans la position de Lucien, un jeune homme de province, dont l'éducation n'eût pas coûté cent mille francs? Il y a donc une fausse civilisation! Nous ne sommes donc pas arrivés précisément à la perfection de la civilisation! [p. 814]

Unlike the literary critics, Stendhal is perfectly well aware that this lack of satisfaction, let alone enthusiasm, is characteristic of this one person and of a certain type of person, but *not* of everyone living in the 1830's. Stendhal attributes this feeling to a false civilization; today it would probably be called pseudo-sophistication. In the terms of the previous discussion, Lucien has an excessively high ego ideal. It is clear that this is not a reality problem, for several reasons. As Stendhal points out, not everyone would feel as Lucien. In any case, Lucien is obviously not at fault if times have changed the nature of military service; what is more, he is powerless to alter this condition. Finally, he knew all this before he accepted the commission. With his father's money and influence, and his own education and intelligence, he could certainly have chosen another career not so affected by contemporary historical conditions.

In Chapter 6 Lucien passes in review the various styles of life that he feels are open to him, the possibilities for his "chasse au bonheur." Naturally love and the conquest of women come into his thoughts:

". . . Mon mérite dépendra donc du jugement d'une femme, ou de cent femmes de bon ton! Quoi de plus ridicule! Que de mépris n'ai-je pas montré pour un homme amoureux, pour Edgar, mon cousin, qui fait dépendre son bonheur, et *bien plus son estime pour lui-même*, des opinions d'une jeune femme qui a passé toute sa matinée à discuter chez Victorine le mérite d'une robe, ou à se moquer d'un homme de mérite comme Monge, parce qu'il a l'air commun!" [p. 824, italics mine]

One could not hope for a clearer expression of the idea that the loved woman takes the place of the lover ego ideal, nor for a stronger statement of the fear of such dependency.

Lucien's statements about himself are then reinforced in Chapter 7 by Stendhal's description of his character:

Jeune, riche, heureux en apparence, il ne se livrait pas au plaisir avec feu: on eût dit un jeune protestant. L'abandon était rare chez lui; il se croyait obligé à beaucoup de prudence. "Si tu te jettes à la tête d'une femme, jamais elle n'aura de considération pour toi," lui avait dit son père. En un mot, la société qui donne si peu de plaisir au dix-neuvième siècle, lui faisait peur à chaque instant. [pp. 825–26]

Notice that protestantism, i.e., puritanism, Lucien's father, and society are all associated as the restraining forces of conscience. Their inordinate power over him is closely linked to the feminine nature of his qualms about the opposite sex. Whoever heard of a father telling his son that women will not respect him if he "throws himself at them?"

At this point of the story Lucien actually does get himself wounded, although it is not in battle as he had imagined, but rather in a duel. Instead of the young peasant girl or the rich lady's valet, it is Dr. Du Poirier who takes care of him. Nevertheless, it is through the doctor's good offices that Lucien is introduced to the noble society of Nancy, and eventually to Mme de Chasteller.

By Chapter 9, after his second fall, Lucien is actively preoccupied with Mme de Chasteller, her history, her appearance,
her ideas, her feelings. Above all, he wants to meet her and
spend some time with her. This project leads his thoughts
towards the possibility that she might be receptive to his court-
ing:

"Cette jeune femme est vexée par son père; elle doit être blessée de
l'attachement que celui-ci affiche pour sa fortune; la province
l'ennuie; il est tout simple qu'elle cherche des distractions dans
un peu de galanterie honnête." [p. 906]

In *De L'Amour* Stendhal outlines seven stages in the development of love:

    1. L'admiration
    2. On se dit: Quel plaisir de lui donner des baisers, d'en recevoir,
       etc.!
    3. L'espérance
    4. L'amour est né
    5. La première cristallisation commence
    6. Le doute naît
    7. Seconde cristallisation [pp. 8–11]

Reik has added a stage preceding the first one listed by Stendhal: Dissatisfaction with oneself. From the passages just
quoted it is evident that Lucien has reached the third step,
"l'espérance." Stendhal remarks that there might be only "un
clin d'oeil entre le no. 3 et le no. 4" (p. 15). Indeed, Lucien
soon realizes that he is in love:

Plus il insistait sur ce motif d'espérer, plus il devenait sombre.
"Aurais-je la sottise d'être amoureux?" se dit-il enfin à demi-haut;
et il s'arrêta comme frappé de la foudre, au milieu de la rue. . . . Le
soupçon d'aimer l'avait pénétré de honte, il se sentit dégradé. [p.
906]

Simultaneously with the realization that Lucien is in love comes a startling shift in emotion not foreseen in Stendhal's schema, although foreshadowed earlier in the novel. The idea of being in love is associated with shame and degradation. What strange beast is this, and where does it come from? Late in this same chapter Lucien's resistance to his new state becomes ever more violent:

Ce républicain, cet homme d'action . . . n'avait jamais songé à l'amour que comme à un précipice dangereux et méprisé, où il était sûr de ne pas tomber. . . . Il s'était étonné de tout ce qui lui arrivait, comme l'oiseau sauvage qui s'engage dans un filet et que l'on met en cage; ainsi que ce captif effrayé, il ne savait que se heurter la tête avec furie contre les barreaux de sa cage. [p. 909]

The imagery of these two passages seems to suggest an underlying phantasy based on common childhood fears concerning sexuality. The female organ is conceived as something enormous; this impression is not totally unjustified if it is the result of the child's observation of an adult and subsequent comparison with his own organ. From this conception can arise the fear of being held captive within the woman. Aside from this purely sexual source of anxiety, there appears to be another level of meaning in this phantasy. After all, Lucien is specifically afraid of love rather than sex. Thus his fear may stem from anticipation of the loss of separate identity implicit in the experience of love. Reik describes it this way:

To be oneself or not to be oneself, that is the question. The alternative here is similar to the doubt of the noble Dane: to bear those ills we have than to fly to others that we know not of. It is not the loss of freedom of action which the person fears, or if so it is only a reflex of a deeper fear, but the loss of individuality. [p. 140]

Actually there is no necessary contradiction between these

two levels of meaning; they might very well complement each other, and in Lucien's case this seems to be true.

It is in passages such as these that one can see the immense advantages of fictional presentation over analytic examination when one's object is the re-creation of an experience. Indeed, they show an advantage of narrative rather than scenic presentation in this particular case, for the fearful individual would most probably never allow these images into full consciousness, except perhaps for an occasional sudden flash of insight which would be immediately repressed. The narrator, by projecting the emotions onto a fictional character, can hold their psychic representatives in mind long enough to fix them in language. (I am thinking mainly of the second image—the bird in the cage. Many people might think of love as a precipice, as in the expression, "to fall in love," but then add that this is meant only figuratively. If they happen to be professors of literature, they probably say that it is part of a tradition.)

Lucien meets Mme de Chasteller several times, but each time he is overcome with anxiety and timidity. At a ball given for all of Nancy society his reaction is initially the same, until his mood suddenly changes:

Au mot que lui adressa madame de Chasteller, Lucien devint un autre homme. . . . Tout à coup il osa parler, et beaucoup. . . . Sans perdre rien de sa douceur et de son accent respectueux, la voix de Lucien s'éclaircit et prit de l'éclat. [p. 923]

Stendhal, that admirer of the *petit fait vrai*, is careful to point out that the very quality of Lucien's voice changes as he becomes animated. The simple fact of Lucien's change of mood takes on all the importance of a dramatic event, for the reader as well as the hero. This young "protestant," dominated by considerations of prudence, unable to give himself over to en-

joyment or enthusiasm, has suddenly become another person:
"C'était la première fois de sa vie que le succès le jetait dans une
telle ivresse" (p. 928).

This is not his first success in life, but it is the first time that
he is truly happy with his success. There are many ways of
trying to overcome the sense of disenchantment with oneself
designated by Reik as a necessary precondition of love: through
achievements, but Lucien does not value his army career; by
losing one's self in dope or drink, but Lucien's consolation from
the bottle is shortlived; through religion, but Lucien is a non-
believer; or through political involvement, but Lucien cannot
bring himself to join Gauthier and the Republicans. The last is
through love, and this seems to be the only path open to Lucien
at this time of his life. His intoxication with success, in inspiring
Mme de Chasteller to return his love, is thus not simply a victory of his impulses over his inhibitions, but of the prospect of
finding peace with himself through loving Bathilde. No amount
of success in the society of Nancy or with women for whom
he has no deeper feelings, such as Théodelinde de Serpierre or
Mme d'Hocquincourt, can compare with this emotion.

Like most Stendhalian heroes, Lucien suffers from a peculiar
form of jealousy. The apartment that he rents when he first
settles in Nancy belonged formerly to a certain M. de Busant
de Sicile, a lieutenant colonel once stationed in Nancy. Rumor
has it that the lieutenant colonel was in love with Mme de
Chasteller, and while Lucien was looking for reasons to hope
that he would be successful with Bathilde, he spent a great
deal of time trying to find out whether she had given herself to
Busant de Sicile (p. 902). Stendhal informs us that Lucien's
worries are unfounded:

Lucien n'arriva jamais à savoir la vérité sur M. de Busant. . . . Il
s'était porté amoureux de madame de Chasteller. Il avait constam-

ment ennuyé son père et elle de ses visites, et jamais elle n'avait pu parvenir à rendre ces visites moins fréquentes. [pp. 902–903]

In other words, there was never any question of her loving him, much less becoming his mistress. Yet Lucien continues to be preoccupied with M. de Busant so much that he even alludes indirectly to his suspicions at the ball. Mme de Chasteller is taken aback and begins to worry that she has done something that would make her unworthy of Lucien's love.

Jealousy is always a strange and unpleasant emotion, but Lucien's jealousy is of an especially peculiar type. It is retroactive; M. de Busant has left Nancy for good and is not a competitor for Bathilde's affection. Furthermore, Lucien is not jealous of the late M. de Chasteller, and yet the latter was Bathilde's husband. Even when Lucien gets to know Mme de Chasteller, sees her almost every day, and thus can be certain that there is no other man in her life, the tormenting thought of M. de Busant does not leave him. One has the impression that even if Lucien had found out what Stendhal is careful to hide from him, that Busant was never Bathilde's lover, he would not lose his jealousy.

In an article called "Certain Neurotic Mechanisms in Jealousy, Paranoia and Homosexuality," Freud analyses three types of jealousy:

The three layers or stages of jealousy may be described as (1) *competitive* or normal, (2) *projected,* and (3) *delusional* jealousy. There is not much to be said from the analytic point of view about normal jealousy.

.   .   .   .   .

The jealousy of the second layer, the *projected,* is derived in both men and women either from their own actual unfaithfulness or from impulses towards it which have succumbed to repression. . . .

This relief—more, absolution by his conscience—he achieves when he projects his own impulses of infidelity on to the partner to whom he owes faith.

.   .   .   .   .

The jealousy of the third layer, the true *delusional* type, is worse. It also has its origin in repressed impulses towards unfaithfulness— the object, however, in these cases is of the same sex as the subject. Delusional jealousy represents an acidulated homosexuality . . . As an attempt at defence against an unduly strong homosexual impulse it may, in a man, be described in the formula: "Indeed, I do not love him, *she* loves him!"[19]

Later in this paper Freud mentions that the third type is usually accompanied by elements of the other two.

In its first stages, Lucien's jealousy of Busant might belong to the class of normal competition. It persists, however, even when it no longer has any objective foundation. It is difficult to see how Lucien's jealousy could be of the projected sort, since he does not owe any fidelity to Bathilde when it is formed. But the workings of the mind are often obscure; Lucien might be attracted to Mlle de Serpierre and Mme d'Hocquincourt more than he admits to himself, and experience these temptations as transgressions of a faithfulness he ought to show to Bathilde because of his love for her. But it seems as though this jealousy is primarily of the third type. Otherwise it is hard to understand why Busant should occupy Lucien's thoughts as much as Mme de Chasteller (p. 902). Moreover, the persistence of this feeling in the face of contradictions from reality gives it something of the quality of a delusion. I hesitate to call it a delusion because the author does not allow Lucien to find out for a certainty that nothing ever happened between Busant and Bathilde. Yet he does inform the reader of this fact. It is as though Stendhal wants to reveal the delusional character of Lucien's jealousy without forcing the reader to look on him as being, in this respect, insane.

There are, however, other events in this part of the novel, which show that Lucien has to defend himself against unusually strong homosexual impulses. In Chapter 7 Lucien's commanding officer, Colonel Malher, suddenly acquires a great dislike of Lucien for the most trivial of reasons:

> Un matin, le colonel le fit appeler. . . .
>
> . . . On m'a fait rapport que vous mangez avec luxe chez vous, c'est ce que je ne puis souffrir. . . ."
>
> Le coeur de Lucien bondissait de rage; jamais personne n'avait pris ce ton avec lui. [p. 831]

The suddenness and ridiculous motivation of Malher's dislike is equalled only by the fury of Lucien's reaction, his defence against the temptation of passivity toward his superior.

He reacts in a similar way to a show of affection on the part of his protector, Lieutenant Colonel Filloteau, although here it is only a rapid flash of indignation:

> "Je viens passer l'inspection de votre quartier, mon cher camarade; car je vous sers d'*oncle*, comme on disait dans Berchiny, quand j'y étais brigadier, avant l'Egypte, ma foi! car je ne fus maréchal des logis qu'à Aboukir, sous Murat, et sous-lieutenant quinze jours apres."
>
> Mais tout ce détail était perdu pour Lucien; au mot d'*oncle* il avait tressailli; mais il se remit aussitôt. [p. 818]

This shiver at the word "uncle" shows that a profound inner chord has been struck. In light of Lucien's conflicts as they appear in Book 2, it is probable that here, too, it is fear of dependence on the older man that motivates Lucien's reaction.

All of this makes Lucien neither homosexual nor insane. It

does show one of the reasons for his insecurity, one of the internal obstacles to his love for Mme de Chasteller. The more energy he must expend in defending himself against homosexual impulses, the more he is driven to suspect Mme de Chasteller, and the less he can trust her and devote himself to the creative work of loving.

After the great ball scene, both protagonists go through periods of agonizing doubt, interrupted by moments of reconciliation. Lucien begins writing letters to her, then begins to visit her at home. Often he feels that he has fallen out of love, only to find the next day that he loves her more than before. It is only after months of this in-again, out-again, oscillation that he finally embraces her for the first time (Chap. 32). In the very next chapter Lucien suddenly falls from the good graces of Nancy society and soon a plot is formed to drive him out of town.

In a so-called Freudian analysis of a novel I ought, it seems, to be interested in tracing Lucien's love for Bathilde back to its source in infantile experience. There are only two indications of this source in the entire novel. The first is derived from chronology:

Mariée à dix-sept ans, veuve à vingt, rien de tout ce qu'elle [Mme de Chasteller] voyait à Nancy ne lui semblait agréable. [p. 939]

. . . . .

[M. de Pontlevé] se jeta dans la haute dévotion, et parvint ainsi, en 1828, à marier sa fille à un des maréchaux de camp attachés à la cour de Charles X. [p. 904]

M. de Chasteller died sometime soon after the July Revolution of 1830 (pp. 904–905). From these data I can conclude that Mme de Chasteller was born in 1810 or 1811.

Lucien's date of birth can be deduced from the following statements:

Lorsque, à quinze ans, il commença à lire les journaux, la mystification qui finit par la mort du colonel Caron était la dernière grande
action du gouvernement d'alors. [p. 875]

·   ·   ·   ·   ·

Le 3 juillet 1822 cet ancien lieutenant-colonel de dragons tomba
dans un abominable guet-apens préparé par le gouvernement.[20]

Lucien must have been born in 1807 or 1808. The difference
in ages between him and Bathilde is thus about three years—
the same difference that existed between Henri Beyle and his
sister Pauline.

The other hint, if I can call it that, is a statement made by
Bathilde when Lucien tries to kiss her hand:

"Je vous admets à une intimité dangereuse pour ma réputation et
dont vous auriez dû respecter les lois; . . . je vous traite *en frère.*"
[p. 1000, italics mine]

This evidence makes it likely that Bathilde is chosen after the
sister type, but its very flimsiness shows that this source is buried
away deep in the unconscious. In other words, it is not a pathological fixation but simply a normal path for Lucien's object
choice to follow.

The final scene of Book 1 is of a very different nature. Dr.
Du Poirier, the man whom Lucien has decided to treat "en
père," has taken it upon himself to drive Lucien out of Nancy
and away from Mme de Chasteller, by means of a farcical ruse:

Voici ce qui arriva: à huit heures et demie. . . . Anne-Marie fit
passer dans la cour Leuwen qui, deux minutes après, fut placé dans
un retranchement en bois peint qui occupait la moitié de l'antichambre de madame de Chasteller. De là, Leuwen voyait fort bien
ce qui se passait dans la pièce voisine et entendait presque tout ce
qui se disait dans l'appartement entier.

Tout à coup, il entendit les vagissements d'un enfant à peine né.

Il vit arriver dans l'antichambre le docteur essoufflé portant l'enfant dans un linge qui lui parut taché de sang.

"Votre pauvre maîtresse," dit-il en toute hâte à Anne-Marie, est enfin sauvée. L'accouchement a eu lieu sans accident." [p. 1061]

There is no need to dwell on the typical voyeur conditions, seeing without being seen (thus no fear of punishment), or on the characteristic association of giving a woman a baby and "saving" her. The irony and absurdity of the situation are equally obvious. Thus Stendhal emphasizes that the baby is not new-born but a month or two old (p. 1062). Several pages earlier, when Lucien was going through one of his periodic fits of jealousy of M. de Busant, the former remarks: "Eh bien, pour le trancher net, je ne l'ai pas *vu*, et désormais je ne veux croire que ce que *j'aurai vu*" (p. 1031). As usual these attitudes signify a violent rejection of the phantasy content by the ego.

The most striking aspects of this farce are its suddenness and the ease with which Lucien believes in a manifest absurdity. It seems as though Lucien were only waiting for an excuse to run away. Of course, if Mme de Chasteller had really given birth to a baby, Lucien's flight might be seen as an attempt to avoid doing something worse, such as murdering her. But he makes no attempt to find out the truth, nor even to speak to Bathilde. The suddenness of this turn of events is in every way analogous to the thunderclap which brings about the denouement of *Le Rouge et le Noir*. As in that case, so here too a sudden eruption into consciousness of long-repressed material takes place—and perhaps it is the very same material. I have shown the profound effects produced on Beyle by his mother's "betrayal" of him, the birth of his sister Pauline. Could not Lucien's credulity be attributed to the profound conviction of the reality of this scene in his creator? The results of several months of tireless labor, imaginative and real, are abandoned at the drop of a hat, made worthless by the deep-seated belief that he will be betrayed sooner or later in the cruelest manner. The parallel with Stendhal's own abandonment of his novel is terribly apparent.

For all its similarity to *Le Rouge et le Noir*—the personalities of many characters and their relations to each other, the social and political milieux described, the attitude of the narrator, the denouements—*Lucien Leuwen* is, in a sense, a direct antithesis to the former novel. The relationship between father and son is completely reversed, abnormal hatred being replaced by overweening love. Whereas pure phantasy elements often predominate in *Le Rouge et le Noir*—ladder scenes, duels, prisons, —*Lucien Leuwen* is much more realistic. Only Lucien's duel and Mme de Chasteller's mock parturition come under this heading. The main element of the "family romance," the promotion of the parents, and thus of the child, is no longer a phantasy as with Julien, but a reality; M. Leuwen is rich, witty, influential. Lucien does not reach even the temporary successes of a Julien; he never has the opportunity to say "n'est-ce que ça." Yet, in the final analysis, the two novels are extraordinarily alike, another proof of the statement that, in the unconscious mind, opposites are often identical.

IV

The Child Is Father
of the Child

La Chartreuse de Parme begins with a description of Napoleon's entry into Milan and the resulting profound changes in Milan society. Many critics, after Balzac,[1] have felt that Stendhal ought to have begun his novel with Fabrice's arrival in Waterloo, or at least in Paris, thus excluding these first scenes. From the point of view of esthetic feeling they may well be right. But here, as elsewhere in Stendhal's fiction, artistic considerations were subordinated to other, more powerful motives. One need not go far afield to uncover one of them. In his discussion of Stendhal's attempt to revise his novel in accordance with Balzac's criticisms, Martineau says:

> Dès le 9 février 1841 il semble avoir définitivement renoncé à son grand effort. L'ordonnance de son oeuvre ne sera pas modifiée. Il ne veut plus y toucher "par respect, écrit-il, pour le tableau tendre de Milan en 1796 et pour le caractère de Mme Pietranera."[2]

Behind the juxtaposition of Milan and Mme Pietranera in 1796, one can discern a similar association from Beyle's own life, that between Milan and Angela Pietragrua in 1800. The general consensus of the critics and biographers is given by Martineau in a note to his edition of *La Chartreuse:*

La comtesse Pietranera qui va jouer un rôle important dans cette histoire doit beaucoup, c'est certain, au souvenir d'Angela Pietragrua qui fut à Milan la maîtresse de Stendhal, de 1811 à 1815. Mais celui-ci a idéalisé autant que possible cette "catin sublime" pour pouvoir donner à son héroïne quelques-uns de ses traits. Mme Pietranera emprunte également quelques autres de ses traits, n'en doutons pas non plus, à Métilde Viscontini (p. 1382). [p. 1382]

Aside from the similarity in name (Pietragrua-Pietranera) and certain character traits of the two ladies, there is another element of this first chapter which relates Stendhal's life to the fictional events. In describing the life of the French soldiers in Milan, the author singles out one young officer, Lieutenant Robert, whose experiences are recounted in some detail.[3] During the occupation he lives with the Del Dongo family and is much taken with the Marquise del Dongo and her young sister-in-law, Gina del Dongo (soon to become Gina Pietranera). Stendhal strongly implies that Robert has fallen in love with the marquise. His first impression of her is one of almost supernatural beauty (p. 28), and he soon becomes her escort in society (p. 30). When the French are finally forced to leave Milan, Lieutenant Robert's sadness at saying adieu to the marquise (pp. 31–32) reflects the general mood of the French soldiers, loathe to put an end to so happy a period (p. 30).

The experiences and feelings of Lieutenant Robert differ only slightly from those of Beyle at the time of his entrance into Milan in 1800. Indeed, the very words used in the description are almost the same:

Depuis la fin de mai jusqu'au mois d'octobre ou de novembre que je fus reçu sous-lieutenant au 6e régiment de dragons à Bagnolo ou Romanengo, entre Brescia et Crémone, je trouvai cinq ou six mois de bonheur céleste et complet.

Le croira-t-on, mais tout semblera absurde dans mon récit de cette année 1800. Cet amour si céleste, si passionné, . . . n'arrivera à ce qu'on appelle le bonheur qu'en septembre 1811.[4]

The idealization of which Martineau speaks, aside from being the effect of genuine love, thus refers to the first period when Beyle knew her, not to the years 1811 to 1815 when he was given ample reason for becoming disillusioned.

The analogy between the fictional and the autobiographical accounts is strong enough to warrant the assumption of an identification between Lieutenant Robert and Second Lieutenant Beyle. Robert's love, however, does not go to the representative of Angela Pietragrua—Gina—but to the Marquise del Dongo, her sister-in-law. This transposition is not without significance for the underlying phantasy of the novel, a meaning which I hope to clarify below. First I will follow the fortunes of Lieutenant Robert.

Many allusions in the novel point to the fact that Robert's role in the story is more important than that of occasional lover of the marquise. When introducing Fabrice to the reader, Stendhal employs rather ambiguous language concerning the hero's paternity:

Il venait justement de se donner la peine de naître lorsque les Français furent chassés, et se trouvait, par le hasard de la naissance, le second fils de ce marquis del Dongo si grand seigneur. [p. 33]

Later in this first chapter, the marquise seems unduly preoccupied with what Robert might think of Fabrice's education (p. 37). That her preoccupation is justified Stendhal indicates while Fabrice is on the field of battle at Waterloo, where he joins the escort of a general. "Ce général n'était autre que le comte d'A***, le lieutenant Robert du 15 mai 1796. Quel bonheur il eût trouvé à voir Fabrice del Dongo!" (p. 68) Any doubt as to the point of these allusions is dispelled by a correction which Stendhal made in the Chaper edition to a passage in which the Canon Borda is thinking about Fabrice (Chap. 5, p. 107). Martineau gives the corrected version in a note in the Pléïde edition:

. . . il passait même dans le temps pour fils de ce beau lieutenant Robert, maintenant le général comte d'A***. Il logeait au palais del Dongo, et était le cavalier servant de la marquise. [p. 1398]

The passages quoted above have long been cited by critics to show that Robert is Fabrice's real father. But Fabrice del Dongo, as everyone agrees, is also a representation of Stendhal—an idealized portrait of himself as a youth. The logical conclusion is that, in some sense, Stendhal has constructed a phantasy *in which he becomes his own father.* This is accomplished by representing himself as Lieutenant Robert, the lover of the Marquise del Dongo, and as Fabrice, the offspring of their illegitimate union.

Before attempting to evaluate the significance of this peculiar phantasy, I should like to return to the question of the identity of Gina Pietranera. It was mentioned above that Beyle fell in love with Angela Pietragrua when he came to Milan in 1800, but Lieutenant Robert falls in love with the marquise, not Gina. The question arises then as to the relationship of Gina to the marquise. On the surface Gina is simply the sister of the marquise's husband, the Marquis del Dongo, and thus the aunt of Fabrice. However, the subsequent developments in the novel show another sort of relationship which leads to the heart of the phantasies embodied in it.

When Fabrice is still a child, Gina shows a warm affection for him: "Mais elle était folle de Fabrice" (p. 36). As an adolescent, Fabrice decides to go to France to join Napoleon's army in 1815. Gina's reaction recalls those of Mme de Malivert and Mme de Rênal:

Elle se leva et alla prendre dans l'armoire au linge, où elle était soigneusement cachée, une petite bourse ornée de perles; c'était tout ce qu'elle possédait au monde.
"Prends," dit-elle à Fabrice; "mais au nom de Dieu, ne te fais pas tuer." [p. 48]

.   .   .   .   .   .

C'était avec l'accent de l'émotion la plus vive que la comtesse parlait à Fabrice des futures destinées de Napoléon.
"En te permettant d'aller le rejoindre, je lui sacrifie ce que j'ai de plus cher au monde," disait-elle. [p. 49]

At this point, then, her sentiment toward Fabrice is stronger than mere affection. It is only after Fabrice's return to Italy that the reader is given reason to believe that Gina is in love with him. At first this is stated as a supposition by a third party, Canon Borda, whom Gina has asked to intervene for Fabrice with the government of Milan (p. 107). But Stendhal soon informs us directly of Gina's feelings:

A son retour de France, Fabrice parut aux yeux de la comtesse Pietranera comme un bel étranger qu'elle eût beaucoup connu jadis. S'il eût parlé d'amour, elle l'eût aimé; n'avait-elle pas déjà pour sa conduite et sa personne une admiration passionnée et pour ainsi dire sans bornes? Mais Fabrice l'embrassait avec une telle effusion d'innocente reconnaissance et de bonne amitié, *qu'elle se fût fait horreur à elle-même si elle eût cherché un autre sentiment dans cette amitié presque filiale.* [p. 109, italics mine]

The obstacle to Gina's love is thus her horror at what would amount to an incestuous relationship. The word "filial" is clear.

Gina is not the only one to consider her relationship to Fabrice as that of mother to son. In the next chapter, when Count Mosca has become jealous of Fabrice, he thinks: *"Elle l'aime comme un fils depuis quinze ans. Là gît tout mon espoir: comme un fils"* (p. 154, first italics mine). Fabrice also is aware of this interpretation. At a tête-à-tête with Gina soon after Mosca's jealousy scene, he says:

"La position où le hasard me place n'est pas tenable," se disait-il. "Je suis bien sûr qu'elle ne parlera jamais, elle aurait horreur d'un mot trop significatif *comme d'un inceste.*" [p. 158, italics mine]

In spite of her remorse, Gina is unable to overcome her feelings, and she continues to see Fabrice in both maternal and sexual terms:

Elle trouvait quelque chose d'horrible dans l'idée de faire l'amour avec *ce Fabrice qu'elle avait vu naître;* et pourtant que voulait dire sa conduite? [p. 163, italics mine]

As late as Chapter 25, Gina still insists on this maternal relationship to Fabrice:

"Sauvez Fabrice, et je crois tout! Sans doute je suis entraînée par les craintes folles *d'une âme de mère.*" [p. 442, italics mine]

From all this it can be seen that Gina is a second mother to Fabrice. In theoretical terms, the mother image has been split into two parts, the Marquise del Dongo and Gina Pietranera. A curious confirmation of this deduction is to be found in the corrections to the Chaper edition. During Fabrice's stay in Bel-

gium after the Battle of Waterloo, he tells the peasants who
have given him food and shelter:

"Vous m'avez déjà sauvé la vie une fois en me recevant au moment
où j'allais tomber mourant dans la rue; sauvez-la-moi encore en me
donnant les moyens de rejoindre ma mère." [p. 91]

In the Pléïade edition, Martineau cites Stendhal's correction:
"de rejoindre ma tante Gina Pietranera" (p. 1394). For Fabrice
as well as the author, the two are equivalent.

The purpose of this splitting, or decomposition, is to loosen
the family ties of the two main characters. If the novel were
kept in its present form, only with the Marquise del Dongo
substituted everywhere for Gina, it would arouse repulsion in
the reader rather than the pleasure it now provides. Nevertheless, the difference in age between Gina and Fabrice (the taboo
of generations), and the remaining blood relationship (she is
his paternal aunt) are sufficient to cause the incest barrier to be
invoked. The word is only used in oblique references or in
similes, but nothing ever really happens between the two. In
contrast, since Mme de Rênal is not related to Julien Sorel, but
only his employer's wife, they can become actual lovers.

In Chapter 2, when Fabrice is still a youth, he lives in his
father's castle of Grianta, on the shores of Lake Como. Fabrice,
his mother, his aunt, and his sisters enjoy many outings together, from which his father and his older brother Ascagne are
excluded. One day while they are boating on the lake, a storm
comes up:

La comtesse voulut débarquer au milieu de l'ouragan et des coups
de tonnerre; elle prétendit que, placée sur un rocher isolé au milieu
du lac, et grand comme une petite chambre, elle aurait un spectacle
singulier; elle se verrait assiégée de toutes parts par des vagues fur-
ieuses; mais, en sautant de la barque, elle tomba dans l'eau. Fabrice

se jeta après elle pour la sauver, et tous deux furent entraînés assez loin. [p. 47, italics mine]

The heart of this phantasy is Fabrice's action of saving his aunt Gina, the mother substitute, from the water. In an article entitled "A Special Type of Choice of Object Made by Men," Freud discusses this phantasy:

By a slight change of meaning, which is easily effected in the unconscious—comparable to the way in which shades of meaning merge into one another in conscious conceptions—rescuing the mother acquires the significance of giving her a child or making one for her—one like himself of course. The departure from the original meaning of the idea of 'saving life' is not too great, the change in sense is no arbitrary one. The mother gave him his own life and he gives her back another life, that of a child as like himself as possible. The son shows his gratitude by wishing to have a son by his mother that shall be like himself; in the rescue phantasy, that is, he identifies himself completely with the father. All the instincts, the loving, the grateful, the sensual, the defiant, the self-assertive and independent—all are gratified in the wish to be *the father of himself.*[5]

That Fabrice succeeds temporarily in taking his father's place can be seen from the following incident:

Ces parties étaient charmantes; on invitait à dîner de vieux amis, et l'on se consolait de tout, comme de vrais enfants. Cette gaieté italienne, pleine de *brio* et d'imprévu, faisait oublier la tristesse sombre que les regards du marquis et de son fils aîné répandaient autour d'eux à Grianta. *Fabrice, à peine âgé de seize ans, représentait fort bien le chef de la maison.* [pp. 47–48, italics mine]

Since Gina represents a second mother to Fabrice, these phantasies represent the resurgent sexual and other oedipal wishes of the adolescent before he has gone outside the family to find a new love object. What is presented in symbolic form here has already been realized more directly in the first chapter. There Stendhal represented the wish to be his own father by depicting himself both as the older Lieutenant Robert and the child Fabrice del Dongo. This is in perfect accord with Freud's statement that the child wishes to give the mother a baby as like himself as possible. For the reasons mentioned above, Stendhal could not have Gina actually become pregnant by Fabrice. Hence the author's reluctance to delete these first chapters. Since Gina and the marquise form a doublet, Stendhal's "respect for the character of Mme Pietranera" applies equally to the marquise; both women are derived from Angela Pietragrua and, ultimately, from Mme Beyle.

Italy and Italian women always had a special fascination for Beyle. He spent about half his adult life in that country, and three of his great loves—Angela Pietragrua, Mathilda Viscontini and Giulia Rinieri—were Italian. His preference for Italian music and painting is well known; throughout his life various aspects of Italian life and art formed the subject matter of many of his books. There is a passage in *Henry Brulard* which seems to give the deepest source of this preoccupation:

Un M. Guadagni ou Guadaniamo, ayant commis quelque petit assassinat en Italie, était venu à Avignon, vers 1650, à la suite de quelque légat. Ce qui me frappa beaucoup alors, c'est que nous étions venus (car je me regardais comme Gagnon et je ne pensais jamais aux Beyle qu'avec une répugnance qui dure encore en 1835), que nous étions venus d'un pays où les orangers croissent en pleine terre.[6] Quel pays de délices, pensais-je!

Ce qui me confirmerait dans cette idée d'origine italienne, c'est que la langue de ce pays était en grand honneur dans la famille, chose bien singulière dans une famille bourgeoise de 1780. Mon grand-père savait et honorait l'Italien, ma pauvre mère lisait le Dante. [pp. 101–102]

Like any child, Henri was fascinated by the question of his parents' origin, and the results of his inquiries on this subject obviously made a lasting impression upon him. The displacement from the primary problem, the child's own origin (the secret of birth) is indicated in the lines "we had come from a land," and "I regarded myself as a Gagnon." The main point is that Beyle associated himself and his mother's family with Italy. In a sense, then, his mother was Italian; of course, his father was French. Thus he is reproducing this situation in making Fabrice the son of a Frenchman, Robert, and an Italian woman, the Marquise—Gina. Since the average reader, even so gifted a one as Balzac, is ignorant of these private associations of Beyle, and since they are not developed in the novel, the first chapter can easily seem to be expendable.

Like Julien Sorel and Beyle himself, Fabrice leaves his family during his adolescence. I refer to his famous expedition to Waterloo. It is scarcely a matter of chance that Fabrice is precisely the same age at this point in the novel as was Beyle on his first trip to Italy as a soldier in 1800—seventeen years old. The author points out that Fabrice was two years old when Napoleon entered Milan the second time on June 2, 1800 (p. 33), and the Battle of Waterloo of course took place in 1815. In following Napoleon, Fabrice is imitating not only the author but also his real father, Robert, and his beloved aunt Gina's spouse, Count Pietranera. However, his initiation into adult life away from the protection of the family is something less than heroic.

Indeed, the most significant events of Fabrice's brief career as a soldier are the two scenes in which his horses are stolen out from under him. Since it is really a question of the same phantasy being repeated, only the second one need be considered, the less disguised of the two:

Ce général n'était autre que le comte d'A***, le lieutennant Robert du 15 mai 1796. Quel bonheur il eût trouvé à voir Fabrice del Dongo! . . .
Le maréchal des logis s'approcha de Fabrice. A ce moment notre héros entendit dire derrière lui et tout près de son oreille: C'est le seul qui puisse encore galoper. Il se sentit saisir les pieds; on les élevait en même temps qu'on lui soutenait le corps par-dessous les bras; on le fit passer par-dessus la croupe de son cheval, puis on le laissa glisser jusqu'à terre, où il tomba assis.
. . . Fabrice se releva furieux, et se mit à courir après eux en criant: *Ladri! ladri!* [pp. 68–69]

In the chapter on *Armance* I tried to show that for Beyle, as for many people, there existed the symbolic equation, horse = woman.[7] Since the horse is stolen for Fabrice's father, the Count d'A***, I can surmise that the woman in question is Fabrice's mother or mother substitute. In addition this section of the novel immediately follows the chapters in which Fabrice had symbolically taken over his father's role and had "rescued" Gina. Just as Julien's stay in the seminary at Besançon can be interpreted as punishment and expiation for his earlier relationship to the Rênals, so here Fabrice does penance for his oedipal strivings.

In addition to the loss of his horse Fabrice suffers another punishment before he can escape from Waterloo. He has been ordered to guard a bridge in order to prevent the deserting soldiers from fleeing. Several cavalrymen approach the bridge, and when Fabrice orders them to halt, they decide to cross it by force:

Tous tirent leurs sabres à la fois et tombent sur Fabrice; il se crut mort. . . . Par malheur un de ces coups de pointe blessa un hussard à la main: fort en colère d'être touché par un tel soldat, il riposta par un coup de pointe à fond qui atteignit Fabrice au haut de la cuisse. [pp. 86–87]

This wound seems to represent the other part of the oedipal punishment; he has lost the woman, now he is maimed in the upper thigh region.

Chastized by his martial experiences, Fabrice is more than ready to return home to Italy (Chap. 5). Because of a report made by his brother Ascagne to the Austrian authorities, Fabrice is now *persona non grata* in Milan and goes into a sort of exile in Piedmont. A year or so later he goes to Naples to study theology for four years (p. 144). Meanwhile the author's attention has shifted to the love affair of Gina and Count Mosca, and to the court of Parma where the latter is minister. Mosca, like the Marquis de La Mole, is an idealized portrait of the adult Beyle. He is witty and urbane, adept at political machinations, a somewhat cynical hedonist. Aside from such character traits as those just mentioned, several facts of Mosca's biography correspond to those of his creator. Thus, when he is describing himself to Gina during one of their first meetings, he tells her:

A la chute de Napoléon, il s'est trouvé que, tandis que je mangeais mon bien à son service, mon père, homme d'imagination et qui me voyait déjà général, me bâtissait un palais dans Rome. En 1813, je me suis trouvé pour tout bien un grand palais à finir et une pension. [p. 111]

Anyone familiar with Beyle's life knows how furious he was at his father for undertaking to build a large new house in Grenoble and dissipating his fortune in other unprofitable ventures. Equally known are Beyle's endless pleas and demands to the French government about his *demi-solde* pension.[8]

After speculating on possible models for Count Mosca, Martineau concludes:

> Peut-être est-il encore bon d'indiquer que Mosca représente aux yeux de Stendhal l'homme politique que lui-même, consul, eût voulu être: homme sagace qui conduit et dénoue des intrigues et, en même temps, homme du monde à la fois roué et sentimental qui fait la conquête d'une femme dans sa loge à la Scala. [p. 401]

I might add that Beyle began Chapter 2 of *Henry Brulard* with the categorical statement: "Je tombai avec Nap[oléon] en avril 1814. Je vins en Italie vivre comme dans la rue d'Angivilliers" (p. 45). Unlike Mosca, however, Beyle's political ambitions (he had been an auditor of the Conseil d'Etat and had had hopes for further advancement) never recovered from the blow of Napoleon's fall. Whereas Mosca returns to Italy to become prime minister of Parma, Beyle went to Milan and frittered away seven years.

Just as Lieutenant Robert had come to Milan and made the conquest of the Marquise del Dongo, so Mosca comes to Milan and becomes Mme Pietranera's lover (Chap. 6). Although these latter events are recounted after Fabrice's escapades at Waterloo (Chaps. 2–4), in terms of the chronology of the novel they take place at the same time as the Waterloo episodes. In fact, Stendhal relates that Gina is receptive to the Count's advances partly because of the emotional vacuum created by Fabrice's departure (p. 110).

Thus, when Fabrice joins the two of them in Parma (Chap. 7), his presence threatens the stability of their union. A typical eternal triangle is created, whose only peculiarity is that both the older man and the younger are representatives of the author.

It is in this section of the novel (Chaps. 7–10) that both Gina and Fabrice feel threatened by their incestuous attraction for each other. Mosca too is threatened by the situation, but in a different way. Having received an anonymous letter from the Prince of Parma stating that Gina is having an affair with her nephew, Mosca falls prey to a violent fit of jealousy. His hatred of Fabrice knows no bounds (p. 153). Tormented by curiosity, he goes to observe their behavior together. Their actions, although harmless enough in themselves, arouse his suspicions still further. In an absolute paroxysm of jealousy, "Une idée atroce saisit le comte comme une crampe: le [Fabrice] poignarder là devant elle, et me tuer après?" (p. 156). With a supreme effort Mosca quells the murderous feelings in his heart, or rather he takes flight before the possibility of acting them out (p. 157).

Once again the oedipal situation has been recreated, bringing with it the familiar dangers to each party concerned. It is evident that Gina and Fabrice feel towards each other as mother and son, and that Mosca is aware of this aspect of their relationship. That Mosca himself is looked on as a father can be seen not only from the logic of the situation; it is stated explicitly much later in the novel. In Chapter 22, just after Fabrice has escaped from prison, Ludovic, the Duchess' servant, explains Gina's bizarre conduct in the following manner:

Ludovic vint encore en aide; il dit que madame la duchesse était folle de douleur, à cause de la fièvre continue *du jeune comte Mosca, fils du premier ministre de Parme,* qu'elle emmenait avec elle consulter les médecins de Pavie. [p. 385, italics mine]

Of course the young man in question is none other than Fabrice del Dongo.

As Mosca had hoped, Fabrice is sent away. The latter had

become interested in a young actress, Marietta Valserra, (Chap. 8) and, motivated by feelings of jealousy toward Marietta and by fear of the girl's lover, Giletti, the duchess urges her nephew to visit his family at Grianta. After seeing his family and his old tutor, Abbé Blanès (about whom I will have more to say presently), Fabrice returns to Parma. Shortly thereafter he and Giletti do come to blows, and in the resulting battle Fabrice's adversary is killed. During the remainder of Part 1 (Chaps., 11–13), Fabrice is afraid to return to Parma because he is liable to be punished there for murdering Giletti.

The Marietta-Giletti affair is not simply a random occurrence. It has been prepared for much earlier in the novel and unites several motifs that have recurred throughout. It will be recalled that while at Waterloo Fabrice was punished by having his horse stolen and by being wounded in the thigh. During this same episode he is much concerned with omens and presages. In particular, when given the uniform of a hussard to wear in battle, Fabrice feels that the former owner's deeds will influence his own fate:

Me voici, se dit-il, avec l'habit et la feuille de route d'un hussard mort en prison, où l'avait conduit, dit-on, *le vol d'une vache* et de quelques couverts d'argent! *j'ai pour ainsi dire succédé à son être* . . . et cela sans le vouloir ni le prévoir en aucune manière! Gare la prison! . . . Le présage est clair, j'aurai beaucoup à souffrir de la prison! [p. 55, italics mine]

Later in the episode he returns to these speculations:

Fabrice eût donné tout au monde pour savoir si le hussard Boulot était réellement coupable; en rappelant ses souvenirs, il lui semblait que la geôlière de B*** lui avait dit que le hussard avait été ramassé non seulement pour des couverts d'argent, mais encore *pour avoir volé la vache d'un paysan, et battu le paysan à toute outrance.* Fabrice ne doutait pas qu'il ne fût mis un jour en prison *pour une faute qui aurait quelque rapport avec celle du hussard Boulot.* [pp. 82–83, italics mine]

In the first version of this phantasy Fabrice expresses the thought that he is now the same as the dead Hussard (*succédé à son être*). The crimes he is to commit are expressed more fully in the second version, stealing a peasant's cow and beating the peasant. If taken literally this assertion is absurd; Fabrice almost never comes into contact with peasants and he has no particular interest in, or need for, cows. But the symbolic meaning of this passage eliminates the manifest absurdity. If, namely, the cow represents a woman (just as the horse does),[9] and the peasant simply any man, why then Fabrice might very well be involved in such a situation. In other words the content of this presage is the same as his experiences at Waterloo—losing his horse (cow) and being wounded (beaten)—except that Fabrice now is to have the active role instead of the passive.

During Fabrice's stay with Abbé Blanès, the old priest attempts to predict the young man's future. After noting that Fabrice had been imprisoned at Waterloo, Blanès continues:

"Eh bien, ce fut un rare bonheur, car, averti par ma voix, ton âme peut se préparer à une autre prison bien autrement dure, bien plus terrible! Probablement tu n'en sortiras que par un crime, mais, grâce au ciel, ce crime ne sera pas commis par toi. . . . Je crois voir qu'il sera question de *tuer un innocent, qui,* sans le savoir, *usurpe tes droits.*" [p. 71, italics mine]

Readers have long been puzzled by this episode, not because the abbé makes such predictions, but because, even though Stendhal ridicules Fabrice's superstitious beliefs (p. 168), the author makes them come true, as the later events of the novel show—Fabrice's imprisonment in the Farnese tower, the near death of General Conti, and the assassination of Prince Ranuce-

Ernest IV. In his recent book, *The Tower as Emblem* (Frankfurt am Main, 1967), Stephen Gilman has discussed this episode at length (pp. 33–46). He shows quite convincingly that in it Fabrice's past, present, and future are all united. While Fabrice is in the bell tower where Blanès' observatory is located, the young man is overwhelmed with memories of his childhood at Grianta, of his father's castle and the Lake Como district (pp. 174–75). At the same time, as Gilman is at pains to demonstrate, the abbé's observatory with its tower, *cabane de planches*, orange trees, sparrows, its view of the Alps and of the lake, is a detailed replica, or rather prefiguration of the Farnese tower in which Fabrice will soon be held prisoner (see p. 152). Gilman interprets this convergence of the three tenses as emblematic of the Stendhalian condition for happiness, a liberation from time. Yet the meaning of these presages along with their fulfillment would seem to be the opposite. Of course, for Fabrice as for Beyle, both memory and revery were sources of pleasure; isolation from other people, whether in nature or in the towers, is a prerequisite for a momentary state of happiness. But these states are always transitory because accompanied by danger, anxiety, and the possibility of crime.

In this same episode Fabrice says: "A quoi bon aller si loin chercher le bonheur, il est là sous mes yeux!" (p. 176) In other words, the pleasure that Fabrice feels is caused by his return to childhood (Grianta with its memories), and he wonders why he must ever leave it. But this childhood happiness was the result of fulfilled oedipal desires, and Fabrice's imprisonment in the Farnese tower has the same meaning. All the omens and predictions, including Blanès', concern these same desires. Far from representing a liberation from time, this happiness is predicated on *an escape from time*, that is, from the present and future.

Fabrice is doomed to repeat the same actions, to entertain the same desires, to undergo the same punishments over and over again precisely because he is tied to his past. What he really desires is to be able to love, as he himself constantly says; yet his path to emotional maturity is blocked by his oedipal fixation —at least until he meets Clélia Conti in the latter part of the novel. Thus, when Stendhal discounts Fabrice's musings about these omens, "il était bien loin d'employer son temps à regarder les particularités réelles des choses pour ensuite deviner leurs causes," the author is at once denying Fabrice's insight into his own repetition compulsion and expressing the principal characteristic of maturity, the ability to understand and react to new situations on the basis of the present reality, not in accordance with a fixed pattern determined by childhood perceptions.

On his return from the castle of Grianta, anxious to avoid the Austrian gendarmes, Fabrice meets a valet whose horse he steals (p. 182). Here Fabrice has turned the tables by taking another's horse. The other part of the phantasy is also present, although only in the form of a thought not acted upon:

Ah! si je raisonnais comme Mosca, se dit Fabrice, lorsqu'il me répète que les dangers que court un homme sont toujours la mesure de ses droits sur le voisin, je casserais la tête d'un coup de pistolet à ce valet de chambre. [p. 81]

Now the aggression against the man takes the form of an unconscious wish to kill, rather than to wound or beat him.

In Chapter 11 this phantasy is repeated with no symbolic disguises. Giletti thinks that Fabrice wants to steal his woman, Marietta (p. 194). A fight ensues and this time Fabrice actually murders his opponent (p. 196). Now the omen has almost been fulfilled. In Part 11 of the novel, Fabrice is put into prison because of this crime, as he had foreseen. This confirms the interpretation of the cow as a woman, since he had said that he would be imprisoned "pour une faute qui aurait quelque rapport avec celle du hussard Boulot." What other relationship could there be between their crimes?

Killing Giletti and stealing his woman (in Chapter 12 Fabrice becomes Marietta's lover again while in exile) seems to be a displacement from the corresponding oedipal crimes. The triangle situation with Gina gave rise to an unbearable amount of hostility between Fabrice and Mosca, and the commission of this crime effectively removes Fabrice from the scene. Furthermore, Fabrice's horse was originally stolen by his real father, Count d'A***; the active reversal of this event would thus have the father as intended victim. There is support for this interpretation in the novel. While Fabrice is in exile from Parma in order to avoid being arrested for his crime, Stendhal comments:

Fabrice ne se doutait en aucune façon de ce qui se passait à Parme. Dans le fait, il s'agissait de savoir si la mort de ce comédien, qui de son vivant gagnait trente-cinq francs par mois, amènerait la chute du ministère ultra et son chef le comte Mosca. [p. 216]

Thus the blow given to Giletti threatens to fall on its true object, Mosca, Fabrice's competitor for Gina's love. (In fact, Mosca's eventual fall from the ministry in Chapter 26 is an indirect consequence of this episode.)

Part 1 of *La Chartreuse de Parme* falls into two large sections, each of which has a similar underlying structure. The first section consists of: (1) Lieutenant Robert's experiences in Milan and his siring of Fabrice (Chap. 1); (2) Fabrice's youth, culminating in the rescue phantasy (Chaps. 1 and 2); (3) Fabrice's initiation and expiation at Waterloo (Chaps. 2–5). The second section consists of: (1) Mosca's arrival in Milan and affair with Gina (Chap. 6); (2) the new triangle of Mosca-

Gina-Fabrice (Chaps. 7–10); (3) Fabrice's exile from Parma as punishment for his crime (Chaps. 11–13).

While Fabrice is away from Parma, he has not been forgotten by those who remain there. Indeed, his fate is being sealed by forces over which he has no control, or so it seems. Prince Ranuce-Ernest IV, the ruler of Parma, has personal reasons for desiring Fabrice's downfall. As early as Chapter 7, Stendhal mentions that the prince desires Gina, and that it is out of sexual competition and jealousy of Fabrice that the prince sends the anonymous letter to Mosca which eventually leads to Fabrice's departure from Parma (p. 151).

With such a strong motive as its basis, the prince's hatred of Fabrice does not abate when the latter commits a murder. On the contrary, Ranuce-Ernest seizes this excuse for revenge on both Gina and Fabrice:

En apprenant la mort de Giletti, le prince, piqué des airs d'indépendance que se donnait la duchesse, avait ordonné au fiscal général Rassi de traiter tout ce procès comme s'il se fût agi d'un libéral. [p. 216]

In Parma a liberal is an enemy of the state, so Rassi has, in effect, been ordered to prosecute the criminal as harshly as possible. The Prince's idea of how to punish those who interfere with his desires has already been shown earlier in the novel:

"Mais si j'acceptais les hommages de Votre Altesse," lui disait la duchesse en riant, "de quel front oser reparaître devant le comte?"

"Je serais presque aussi décontenancé que vous. Le cher comte! mon ami! Mais c'est un embarras bien facile à tourner et auquel j'ai songé: le comte serait mis à la citadelle pour le reste de ses jours." [pp. 145–46]

Fabrice's punishment, like his crime, will be almost the same:

"Et la peine?"

"Vingt ans de forteresse, comme Votre Altesse Sérénissime me l'avait dit."

"La peine de mort eût révolté," dit le prince comme se parlant à soi-même, "c'est dommage!" [p. 260]

Worried by the prince's persecution of Fabrice, Gina intervenes on the latter's behalf. She threatens to leave Parma unless the prince promises not to sign Fabrice's sentence and to swear not to renew this *"procédure injuste"* in the future (p. 254). Unfortunately, Count Mosca, who writes out the statement, leaves out this key phrase, and the prince thanks him with a wink (p. 255).

The look of complicity exchanged between Mosca and the prince indicates the similarity of their motives. It will be recalled that Mosca, during his fit of jealousy, had entertained thoughts of killing Fabrice. These phantasies have not left him. Because of this key omission Fabrice is in fact sentenced to prison, where he is exposed to the danger of being poisoned.

Mosca accuses himself of being the cause of Fabrice's death. Even the innocent Clélia Conti has no trouble interpreting Fabrice's arrest:

Ainsi, pensa Clélia, le voilà prisonnier et prisonnier de ses ennemis! car au fond, le comte Mosca, quand on voudrait le croire un ange, va se trouver ravi de cette capture. [pp. 267–68]

Just as sexual competition was the cause of Fabrice's crime, so it is the cause of his punishment, for the prince, with the aid of various courtiers—Mosca, Rassi, Marquise Raversi, General Conti—does manage to capture Fabrice and imprison him in the Farnese Tower. The description of Fabrice's entrance into this prison resembles that of Julien Sorrel's arrival at the seminary in Besançon. Because of its importance, I shall reproduce the passage at some length:

Cette tour Farnèse placée en si belle vue se compose d'un rez-de-chaussée long de quarante pas au moins, large à proportion et tout remplie de colonnes fort trapues, car cette pièce si démesurément vaste n'a pas plus de quinze pieds d'élévation. Elle est occupée par le corps de garde, et, du centre, l'escalier s'élève en tournant autour d'une de ces colonnes: c'est un petit escalier en fer, fort léger, large de deux pieds à peine et construit en filigrane. . . . . A l'une des ex-trémités de cet appartement, on fit voir au nouveau prisonnier une chapelle de la plus grande magnificence; les murs et la voûte sont entièrement revêtus de marbre noir; des colonnes noires aussi et de la plus noble proportion sont placées en lignes le long des murs noirs, sans les toucher, et ces murs sont ornés d'une quantité de têtes de morts en marbre blanc, de proportions colossales, élégam-ment sculptées et placées sur deux os en sautoir. Voilà bien une invention de la haine qui ne peut tuer, se dit Fabrice, et quelle diable d'idée de me montrer cela! . . .

. . . C'est par un corridor obscur placé au centre du bâtiment que l'on arrive à ces chambres. . . . Un conspirateur placé dans l'une de ces chambres ne pourrait pas se plaindre à l'opinion d'être traité d'une façon inhumaine, et pourtant ne saurait avoir de commun-ication avec personne au monde, ni faire un mouvement sans qu'on l'entendît. Le général [Conti] avait fait placer dans chaque chambre de gros madriers de chêne formant comme des bancs de trois pieds de haut, et c'était là son invention capitale, celle qui lui donnait des droits au ministère de la Police. Sur ces bancs il avait établi une cabane en planches, fort sonore, haute de dix pieds, et qui ne touchait au mur que du côté des fenêtres. Des trois autres côtés il régnait un petit corridor de quatre pieds de large, entre le mur primitif de la prison, composée d'énormes pierres de taille, et les parois en planches de la cabane. [pp. 308–310]

Now as one listens to this passage with the "third ear," the strains of a melody quite different from the surface tune can be heard. The various chambers, the spiral staircase leading from one level to another, the mysterious marble columns—all these suggest a rather fantastic picture of the inside of the human body. Above all, the description of Fabrice's prison cell—total isolation from the world, yet one's every movement audible—sounds like a description of the foetus' existence *in utero*. The special arrangement of this chamber, placed inside, yet insulated from the larger room, is analogous to the amniotic sac inside the uterus. In other words, I am suggesting that Fabrice's entrance into prison is built upon a phantasy of return to the mother's body, a rebirth phantasy. The blackness and death heads that he sees would then represent the anxiety felt at entertaining such a forbidden idea.

Many features of the prison episodes contribute to such an interpretation. When Fabrice is first threatened by poisoning, Clélia finds a most ingenious means of getting sustenance to him: she attaches food and a pitcher of water to a rope which he hoists up into his cell (pp. 332–33). Being fed by means of a cord ordinarily occurs only once in one's life—before birth.

The use of figurative expressions, even those of everyday language, is often revelatory of unconscious phantasies. In this same Chapter 12, when Clélia's father threatens to send her away to a convent, Stendhal remarks:

Un seul mot de tout ce discours avait frappé Clélia, c'était la menace d'être mise au couvent, et par conséquent éloignée de la citadelle, et au moment encore où *la vie de Fabrice semblait ne tenir qu'à un fil.* [p. 325, italics mine]

In light of the context of this statement, it is possible to divine the origin of this expression, the *"fil"* in question again being the umbilical cord.

Eventually Fabrice must try to escape from prison. When he

first receives a letter from his aunt Gina, explaining how he is to accomplish this heroic deed, he reacts thusly:

Tout cela est fort beau et fort bien inventé, se dit Fabrice; je dois une reconnaissance éternelle au comte et à la duchesse; ils croiront peut-être que j'ai eu peur, mais je ne me sauverai point. *Est-ce que jamais l'on se sauva d'un lieu où l'on est au comble du bonheur, pour aller se jeter dans un exil affreux où tout manquera, jusqu'à l'air pour respirer?* [pp. 354–55, italics mine]

Alas, the answer to this question is yes. Everyone has been in that place of unsurpassed happiness, everyone has been thrown into this horrible exile called the world, and, what is more, the first impression has always been—asphyxiation!

The amount of time Fabrice spends in prison also provides a clue to the meaning of his stay there. Apparently Stendhal felt that this fact was of great importance, for he repeats it no less than four times. The week before Fabrice escapes, Gina gives him the signal to get ready. Stendhal points out: *"Depuis neuf mois* le malheur extrême avait eu une grande influence sur cette âme ardente" (p. 362, italics mine). In the next chapter, when all Parma expects that Fabrice will soon be put to death, they speculate about the reasons for his disgrace: "Un homme de la naissance de Fabrice n'etait pas mis en liberté *au bout de neuf mois de prison. . . ."* (p. 380, italics mine). As Fabrice is escaping, he thinks: "Combien je suis différent . . . du Fabrice léger et libertin *qui entra ici il y a neuf mois"* (p. 382, italics mine). After Fabrice and Gina are safely out of the state of Parma, Stendhal says: "Fabrice devait à la duchesse l'histoire *des neuf mois passés dans une horrible prison"* (p. 391, italics mine). Nine months, the magic time between conception and birth, how can this meaning be doubted?

If Fabrice's stay in prison represents the foetus' sojourn in the womb, then his escape must be a phantasy of the process of birth. Once again, if close attention is paid to the description of this escape, the underlying phantasy can be discerned:

La duchesse lui avait écrit qu'*il serait surpris par le grand air,* et qu'à peine hors de sa prison, *il se trouverait dans l'impossibilité de marcher;* dans ce cas il valait mieux pourtant s'exposer à être repris que se précipiter du haut d'un mur de quatre-vingt pieds. Si ce malheur m'arrive, disait Fabrice, je me coucherai contre le parapet, *je dormirai une heure, puis je recommencerai.* . . . [pp. 380–81, italics mine]

Fabrice était prêt à agir; il fit un signe de croix, puis attacha à son lit *la petite corde* destinée à lui faire descendre les trente-cinq pieds. [pp. 381, italics mine]

.   .   .   .   .

Il ajoutait que, *poussé comme par une force surnaturelle.* . . . Il défit tranquillement *la grande corde qu'il avait autour du corps.* . . . Il éprouvait de temps en temps *une douleur atroce entre les épaules,* elle allait jusqu'à lui ôter la respiration. Il y avait *un mouvement d'ondulation fort incommode.* [p. 382, italics mine]

.   .   .   .   .

Il y attacha sa troisième corde; elle se trouva un peu trop courte, et il tomba dans un fossé bourbeux où il pouvait y avoir *un pied d'eau.* [p. 383, italics mine]

The whole maneuver is carried out by means of several long cords wrapped around his body—the umbilical cord. The process is intermittent, several times he must stop to rest or even sleep. He feels a terrible pain between his shoulders, is impelled by a supernatural force, is bothered by an unpleasant undulating motion—as though he were a foetus being squeezed forward by the intermittent muscular contractions of the vaginal passage. Finally, he falls into a ditch filled with water, the waters of birth. Like any newborn baby, he makes a great impression on his "mother:" "La duchesse perdit la tête en revoyant Fabrice; elle le serrait convulsivement dans ses bras" (p. 384).

The meaning of this phantasy has been expounded by Freud in the *Problem of Anxiety:*

I add here that the phantasy of returning to the mother's womb is the substitute for coitus of the impotent man (inhibited by the threat of castration). In Ferenczi's sense we can say that the individual who wanted (before) to have his return to the mother's body represented by his genital organ now replaces this organ regressively with his whole person.[10]

In other words, the return to the mother's body in this phantasy is equivalent to the crime of incest.

In my discussion of Part 1, I pointed out that the forbidden attraction between Fabrice and Gina (the mother substitute) is one of the main causative factors of that section of the novel. I have tried to show further that, just as Fabrice is punished by his real father at Waterloo, so the former is imprisoned because of the jealous hostility of the two older men in triangles with Gina and Fabrice, Mosca and the prince. Finally, it was shown that Fabrice's crime is similar to the oedipal transgression, although it is displaced onto harmless persons (Giletti and Marietta) when acted out in reality. In describing the Farnese Tower, Stendhal again indicates the hidden meaning of imprisonment there:

Cette seconde tour, comme le lecteur s'en souvient peut-être, fut élevée sur la plateforme de la grosse tour, en l'honneur d'*un prince héréditaire qui,* fort différent de l'Hippolyte fils de Thésée, *n'avait point repoussé les politesses d'une jeune belle-mère.* [p. 308, italics mine]

The tower was erected in order to house a young man guilty of breaking the incest taboo.

While Fabrice is in prison, meditating on plans for his escape, he thinks in terms which explicitly relate escaping to sexuality, indeed to adultery:

> L'amant songe plus souvent à arriver à sa maîtresse que le mari à garder sa femme; le prisonnier songe plus souvent à se sauver, que le geôlier à fermer sa porte; donc, quels que soient les obstacles, l'amant et le prisonnier doivent réussir. [p. 328]

What has happened here is that, unlike the episodes of Part 1, the punishment and the crime have been condensed into one phantasy. Along with the pleasurable idea of return to the mother's body is the anxiety-laden, punitive side. Thus Fabrice is terrified at the blackness and the death heads he sees when entering the tower. He is frightened at the prospect of leaving his prison: "La duchesse le crut tout à fait fou quand elle lut . . . mots étranges: *je ne veux pas me sauver; je veux mourir ici!*" (p. 345). During the escape Fabrice actually receives two injuries:

> Enfin il arriva au bas de la grosse tour sans autre inconvénient que d'avoir les mains en sang. . . . En tombant de cet arbre, Fabrice se démit presque le bras gauche. [p. 383]

The strange thing about these mishaps is that they were predicted in advance. In her letter to Fabrice the duchess remarks that Count Mosca thinks he (Fabrice) will get away with merely a broken arm, while Ferrante Palla, her other adviser, thinks that he will have just a few abrasions (p. 354). Again Mosca's covert hostility shows through. And of course it was the prince's plan to kill Fabrice that caused Gina to give the latter the signal to escape (pp. 360–62).

Fabrice is not the only one to suffer for his transgressions. His escape has wider consequences than the merely personal effects on himself, Gina and Clélia. Just as his attack on Giletti eventually affected Mosca's fortunes, so his escape ends up by harming the prince. In Chapter 21 Stendhal narrates the story of Ferrante Palla, a rather mad poet who is in love with Gina. When Fabrice was taken prisoner, Ferrante offered his services to the duchess to help her rescue her nephew. She accepted this offer, commissioning him to poison the prince when she gives him the word (p. 370).

Gina's attitude toward the poet is a mixture of wonder, amusement, pity, and maternal affection. In fact there is little difference between her feelings towards Ferrante and those she has for Fabrice. Both men are admirers of Napoleon and both have been condemned by their government. The duchess gives Ferrante her jewels just as she had done with Fabrice before he left for Waterloo (p. 370). Indeed, she is fully aware of the similarity between Ferrante and Fabrice:

"Voilà le seul homme qui m'ait comprise," se dit-elle;" c'est ainsi qu'en eût agi Fabrice s'il eût pu m'entendre." [p. 371]

Who are we to argue with a beautiful and charming woman? Ferrante, by the way, is not insensitive to the duchess' feelings; on the contrary, he exaggerates the importance of her attraction to him:

Suis-je fou, se dit-il, ou bien la duchesse veut-elle un jour, quand je lui aurai donné cette preuve de dévouement, faire de moi l'homme le plus heureux? [p. 370]

Once again the oedipal theme comes to the fore. In return for killing the prince (his "proof of devotion"), Ferrante is to receive the favors of the duchess—he thinks.

Actually, Ferrante's hopes are destined to meet with disappointment, but he and Gina do agree on a signal that is to be followed by the prince's assassination:

"Je puis vouloir sa mort dès demain," continua la duchesse, toujours du même air d'autorité. "Vous connaissez cet immense réservoir d'eau qui est au coin du palais, tout près de la cachette[11] que vous avez occupée quelquefois; il est un moyen secret de faire couler toute cette eau dans la rue: eh bien! ce sera là le signal de ma vengeance." [pp. 370–71]

Once Fabrice is safely out of Parma, Gina tells Ludovic to return and give the signal (p. 388). Ferrante is not dilatory in keeping his promise, as the duchess finds out in the next chapter:

"Le prince de Parme est mort!"
La duchesse pâlit extrêmement; elle eut à peine le courage de dire:
"Donne-t-on des détails?"
"Non," répondit l'archiprêtre;" la nouvelle se borne à dire la mort, qui est certaine."
La duchesse regarda Fabrice. "J'ai fait cela pour lui," se dit-elle. . . . [p. 403]

Again the primal crime is committed, not by Fabrice but by a "mad revolutionary." But it is done at the instigation of the mother figure, Gina, on behalf of the "son," Fabrice.[12] Thus the rebirth phantasy ends with the realization of the second oedipal wish. By condensation and displacement the return to the mother figure's body and the death of the father figure have both been embodied in this phantasy.

For the sake of clarity I have neglected until now any discussion of Fabrice's relationship with the second major female character of the novel, Clélia Conti. In the interest of completeness, not to mention gallantry, I shall now make up for this omission. Clélia's first appearance is made rather early in the novel. After Fabrice's return from France (Chap. 5), he is on his way to Milan with his mother and aunt Gina, when they are accosted by some policemen, who take him for General Conti, Clélia's father. The mix-ups and disguises occasioned by this false arrest allow Stendhal to give much more open expression than usual to the ideas underlying Fabrice's emotional relationships. At first the gendarmes think that Fabrice is General Conti and that Gina is his daughter!

La comtesse sourit à tout hasard, je crois, puis dit au maréchal, des logis:

"Mais, mon cher maréchal, est-ce donc cet enfant de seize ans que vous prenez pour le général Conti?"

"N'êtes-vous pas la fille du général?" dit le maréchal des logis.

"Voyez mon père," dit la comtesse en montrant Fabrice. Les gendarmes furent saisis d'un rire fou. [p. 97]

(This of course is just the reverse of their true relationship, as we have seen earlier in this essay and as is borne out a few pages later, after the real General has been found. "Eh bien! général, vous êtes arrêté, et je vais vous conduire à Milan. Et vous, qui êtes-vous?" dit-il à Fabrice. "Mon fils, reprit la comtesse" [pp. 99–100].)

Because of these equivocations Fabrice is for the moment identified with General Conti; in phantasy he becomes Clélia's father. The mix-up with Gina seems to represent the transference of Fabrice's love from the older woman to the girl, an emotional possibility that will be realized only in Part 2 of the novel. But this tendency is clearly indicated here:

Fabrice, qui rôdait autour de la voiture, s'approcha pour aider la jeune fille à monter. . . .

"Restez sur la route, ne montez pas dans une voiture qui ne vous appartient pas."

Fabrice n'avait pas entendu cet ordre; la jeune fille, au lieu de monter dans la calèche, voulut redescendre, et Fabrice continuant à la soutenir, *elle tomba dans ses bras.* Il sourit, elle rougit profondément; ils restèrent un instant à se regarder après que la jeune fille se fut dégagée de ses bras.

"Ce serait une charmante compagne de prison," se dit Fabrice. . . . [p. 99, italics mine]

As the hero senses, this girl has literally fallen for him!

The identification with General Conti seems to have another meaning, a hostile one. By becoming Clélia's father Fabrice would enter into a more intimate relationship with the girl, but he would also remove the general from the scene; if Fabrice replaces Fabio, then Fabio no longer exists. Both sides of the identification are developed at length in Part 2.

When Fabrice is brought to prison (Chap. 15), Clélia, whose father is jailor of the citadel, observes the new prisoner and recalls their first encounter:

Qui m'eût dit, pensait-elle, que je reverrais [Fabrice] pour la première fois dans cette triste situation, quand je le rencontrai sur la route de Côme? . . . Il me donna la main pour monter dans le carosse de sa mère . . . Il se trouvait déjà avec la duchesse! Leurs amours avaient-elles commencé à cette époque? [p. 267]

There is no need to rehearse the story of Fabrice's and Clélia's love. Every reader of *La Chartreuse* is familiar with these events, and the more hidden emotional developments are almost identical with those of Lucien Leuwen and Mme de Chasteller, which were discussed in the previous chapter. The enormous strength of Fabrice's love is indicated in the following passage:

L'image sublime de Clélia Conti, en s'emparant de toute son âme,

allait jusqu'à lui donner de la terreur. Il sentait trop bien que
l'éternel bonheur de sa vie allait le forcer de compter avec la fille du
gouverneur, et qu'il était en son pouvoir de faire de lui le plus
malheureux des hommes. [p. 323]

The surprising thing—to Fabrice—is that, with the dawning of
this new star on the horizon, the old one which had lit his way
for so many years, is now eclipsed:

Une nuit Fabrice vint à penser un peu sérieusement à sa tante; il
fut étonné, il eut peine à reconnaître son image; le souvenir qu'il
conservait d'elle avait totalement changé; pour lui, à cette heure,
elle avait cinquante ans. [p. 322]

To anyone who has fallen in love and then out again, the
message is clear. When a man is in love, the inner image of the
loved woman is transformed into something unreal, it has a
glow, an aura bestowed upon it by emotion, like the halo with
which medieval artists provided holy people, or like Dante's
vision of Beatrice in the "Tanto gentile" sonnet. When love
has passed, the halo is gone, and although the features of the
image remain the same, it seems dull and washed out in contrast to its former state; hence the impression of old age.

Although Fabrice is convinced that Clélia's image has succeeded to the throne formerly occupied by Gina's, the subsequent events of the novel show that this is only a momentary
victory, the first battle in a long war. I refer to the violent
rivalry that develops between Gina and Clélia from this point
on. Most readers would agree, I think, that the two women are
meant to be, and succeed in being, realistic characters. Their
enmity is thus the natural result of their both being in love with
the same man. However, since the book is told mainly from the
point of view of Fabrice, this rivalry can also be interpreted as
an externalization of the inner processes of the hero. There is

no contradiction between these two approaches; indeed, they dovetail perfectly.

After Fabrice's escape from prison, the duchess is chagrined at her nephew's coldness towards her (pp. 390–91). What galls her especially is the idea that, since Clélia helped Fabrice escape, it was the girl and not she, Gina, who saved him (p. 387).

Moved by her intense jealousy, Gina tries to make certain that Clélia will marry the Marquis Crescenzi. If she cannot have Fabrice, then neither will Clélia (p. 402). At the peak of her mental torture, Gina utters her final word:

J'aimerai Fabrice, je serai dévouée à sa fortune; mais il ne faut pas qu'il rompe le mariage de la Clélia, et qu'il finisse par l'épouser . . . Non cela ne sera pas! [p. 404]

Gina's image is fading, but she will not let it die gracefully. Her successful rival, meanwhile, is in an equally disturbing predicament. Her father is the leader of the "liberal" party of Parma, that is, of the antiregime party; naturally Fabrice, because of his close connection with Mosca, the current prime minister, is on the side of General Conti's political enemies:

Depuis l'arrivée de Fabrice, elle était bourrelée de remords: Voilà, se disait-elle, que mon indigne coeur se met du parti des gens qui veulent trahir mon père! [p. 319]

The matter soon becomes much more serious than simple political treason. In order to get the ropes, which Fabrice needs for his escape, into the prison, the duchess gives General Conti some laudanum; she hopes that everyone will think that he has had a stroke and that in the ensuing confusion it will be easy to smuggle the ropes past the guards. Unfortunately, the dose is too large; even the doctor thinks that Conti's life is in danger (Chap. 21). When Ludovic approaches Clélia to give her the cords, she accuses him of attempted murder: "Je devrais vous faire arrêter; vous ou les vôtres vous avez empoisonné mon père! . . . Avouez à l'instant quelle est la nature du poison" (p. 375). Ludovic tries to convince her that if she reveals his presence and the existence of their plot, she will be killing Fabrice. Horrified, she thinks: "Ainsi, me voilà en dialogue réglé, . . . avec l'empoisonneur de mon père. . . . Et c'est l'amour qui m'a conduite à tous ces crimes!" (p. 375).

In a panic, Clélia prays to the Virgin Mary and makes a vow, whose content she communicates to Fabrice in a letter:

Pénétrée des remords les plus vifs par ce qui a été fait, non pas grâce au ciel, de mon consentement, mais à l'occasion d'une idée que j'avais eue, j'ai fait voeu à la très sainte Vierge que si, par l'effet de sa sainte intercession, mon père est sauvé, jamais je n'opposerai un refus à ses ordres; j'épouserai le marquis aussitôt que j'en serai requise par lui, et jamais je ne vous reverrai. [p. 377]

This vow is the basis for the rest of their love story, one which has often been aptly compared to the tale of Amor and Psyche.[13]

This story can be summarized as follows: The duchess, Fabrice's substitute mother, violently opposes his love for Clélia and does everything in her power to have the girl marry a third party, Crescenzi. Clélia's father is an enemy of Fabrice; the boy's escape almost brings about the older man's death, and the daughter is ridden with guilt at this idea. She feels that it is her fault, even though she knows intellectually that it is not. She swears to the Holy Mother that she will marry Crescenzi and that she will never see Fabrice again, but this vow does not prevent her from making love with Fabrice and even bearing his child (Sandrino). If looked at on the surface, the entire story is so irrational that it almost defies belief. Yet as one reads it, the story is both amusing and believable.

There is, I think, an explanation which makes sense of this fantastic concatenation of events. If, namely, Clélia is interpreted as a sister figure, the whole story falls into place. Mother (Gina) and father (Fabio Conti) forbid the love between brother (Fabrice) and sister (Clélia). They do this partly out of the demands of culture, and partly because of their own hidden attachments (especially Gina vis-à-vis Fabrice). The vow not to *see* Fabrice allows Clélia not to recognize that she is making love with a forbidden person. It is, if you like, a partially successful attempt to repress this idea.

This argument would be more convincing if there were some statements in the novel, analogous to those quoted with reference to Gina and Fabrice, which gave a more direct indication of this hidden relationship. Unfortunately, I have found none. The reason for this seems to be that, whereas nothing ever happens between Gina and Fabrice, he and Clélia do actually make love.

Aside from the reasons adduced above, there is other indirect evidence that Clélia is a sister figure. The analogy between Fabrice's progression from Gina to Clélia and Julien's from Mme de Rênal to Mathilde is generally accepted as valid, and I have tried to show that Mathilde is a sister figure in that novel. In *Henry Brulard* Beyle states that in his childhood canaries were kept in his bedroom and that there were orange trees just outside the room:

Il avait le goût des serins de Canarie, il les faisait nicher et les tenait fort proprement, mais à côté de mon lit. [p. 104]

. . . . .

Ces orangers étaient une véritable manie. . . . Ils avaient les uns trois pouces et les autres un pied de haut, ils étaient placés sur la fenêtre O à laquelle le soleil atteignait un peu pendant deux mois d'été. [p. 105]

These two details correspond to Fabrice's surroundings in prison, where he falls in love with Clélia:

Et d'abord les yeux de Fabrice furent attirés vers une des fenêtres du second étage, où se trouvaient, dans de jolies cages, une grande quantité d'oiseaux de toutes sortes. [p. 310]

.   .   .   .   .

"Ce matin elle vient de faire l'achat de beaux orangers que l'on a placés par son ordre à la porte de la tour sous votre fenêtre. . . ." [p. 315]

Whether or not the inference presented here will be accepted as convincing, I cannot say. In any case, the competition between Gina and Clélia comes to a head in the second prison sequence. With the older prince dead, Gina feels that it is safe for her nephew and herself to return to Parma (Chap. 24). She and Mosca arrange with the new ruler, Ranuce-Ernest V, to have Fabrice's case judged anew. They want him to give himself up at the municipal jail; but Fabrice, anxious to rejoin Clélia, returns to the citadel. General Conti is eager to take his revenge. He was almost poisoned because of Fabrice; now, according to the law of the Talion, he will poison Fabrice. (Here he is repeating the actions of another father figure, Ranuce-Ernest IV, himself killed by poison.)

Clélia soon realizes that Fabrice is going to be poisoned, and she goes to save him:

Fabrice est mort, se dit Clélia on l'a empoisonné à dîner, ou c'est pour demain. . . . S'il vit encore, mon devoir est de le sauver. Elle s'avança d'un air hautain vers la petite porte de la tour. . . .
. . . Elle regarda dans la chambre et vit Fabrice. . . . Elle lui dit: "As-tu mangé?" [pp. 436–37]

Fabrice has not eaten yet, but he does not tell Clélia that:

"O mon unique ami!" lui dit-elle, "je mourrai avec toi." Elle le serrait dans ses bras, comme par un mouvement convulsif.

Elle était si belle, à demi vêtue, et dans cet état d'extrême passion, que Fabrice ne put résister à un mouvement presque involontaire. Aucune résistance ne fut opposée. [p. 437]

In this scene the hidden meaning of "saving," when a man and a woman are involved, comes into the open. Clélia "saves" Fabrice by having relations with him.

At the very same time, in terms of the chronology of the story, Gina is doing a bit of saving of her own. She begs the young prince to send help to Fabrice. He makes a bargain: Fabrice's life for an hour with Gina (p. 443). This promise, which is fulfilled somewhat later (Chap. 27, p. 468), also saves Fabrice. As was pointed out in Chapter 1 of this essay, the phantasy of a boy's being saved by his mother represents the wish to be initiated by her into sexual life. This is precisely what happens here. Gina alludes to this source of the phantasy when beseeching the prince:

"Sauvez Fabrice, et je crois tout! Sans doute je suis entraînée par les craintes folles *d'une âme de mère*." [p. 442, italics mine]

To be sure, although Gina is saving Fabrice, she has relations not with him but with the prince. The latter, however, is another doublet of Fabrice. Freud mentions that fathers are represented in dreams as kings: "Parents appear in dreams as *emperor* and *empress, king* and *queen* or other exalted personnages."[14] In *La Chartreuse*, the exalted personnage is the elder prince, Ranuce-Ernest IV, who, as we have seen, plays the role of a father. His son, the younger prince, is then the child. Stendhal himself used the equation, prince = son, in *Lucien Leuwen*.[15] And when Fabrice was chasing La Fausta (Chap. 13), he was actually mistaken for the young prince:

A ce mot, le comte M*** ... alla se figurer, chose délicieuse pour sa vanité, que ce rival n'était autre que le prince héréditaire de Parme. [p. 230]

It is because of these scenes in which Gina and Clélia rescue Fabrice simultaneously that I mentioned earlier that Clélia's image had not yet completely supplanted Gina's in Fabrice's mind. Here the two are shown to have almost equal strength, but for Gina it is a last, valiant effort. After she keeps her promise with the prince, she leaves Parma and marries Count Mosca, an action which seems to symbolize the withdrawal of her feelings from Fabrice at last (Chap. 27). True to her vow, Clélia marries Crescenzi (Chap. 26) and refuses to look at Fabrice again. Nevertheless she becomes his mistress.

The birth of Sandrino seems to be a repetition of the phantasy of Chapter 1. Like Lieutenant Robert, Fabrice has become the father of a son like himself, but being the offspring of a forbidden union, the boy must die. Fabrice's retirement to the charterhouse and subsequent death complete the penance. The duchess' death, like that of Mme de Rênal in *Le Rouge et le Noir* and Mme de Malivert's retirement to a convent in *Armance* fulfill the wish to be reunited with the mother—at least in death. Clélia's death serves a similar purpose, as is indicated at the very end of the novel: "[Fabrice] espérait retrouver Clélia dans un meilleur monde" (p. 493). This hopeful note reaches the pitch of an ultimate cry of defiance in the last line of the novel, which depicts the future life of Fabrice's two counterparts, the prince and Count Mosca:

Les prisons de Parme étaient vides, le comte immensément riche, Ernest V adoré de ses sujets qui comparaient son gouvernement à celui des grands-ducs de Toscane. [p. 493]

Of such stuff are dreams—and dreamers—made!

V

Love of Knowledge,
Knowledge of Love

In discussing *Lamiel*, most critics have noted the work's lack of continuity, originality, and substance. They agree that it is vastly inferior to Stendhal's other novels. Thus Maurice Bardèche begins his analysis of the novel:

De toute les entreprises de Stendhal, *Lamiel* est probablement la plus difficile à juger, et, sous sa forme actuelle, la plus décevante. Ce qui en a été écrit n'est qu'un démarrage, d'ailleurs lent, pénible, corrigé, alourdi de variantes et de repentirs et finalement touchant à peine au sujet lui-même tel qu'il est indiqué dans les plans annexés au manuscrit.[1]

Prévost expresses a similar, but more laudatory, judgment:

Ainsi ce livre si neuf, parfois si fort, d'une invention hardie et amère, n'est pas seulement inachevé dans son récit; il est incomplet dans sa substance.[2]

He suggests that only a careful revision of the entire novel could have saved it from these defects:

Seule une reprise, une refonte à Paris, durant le dernier congé de Beyle, auraient pu rendre de la substance, du sérieux, un monde jusqu'au bout cohérent à ce livre qui au bout de cent pages part à l'aventure.[3]

The overall impression created by the novel is indeed one of chaos. It begins with a first person narrator who recounts his visits to the Norman village of Carville, describes his own history and that of the principal characters. Then, at the end of Chapter 2, after narrating the events that lead to Lamiel's adoption by the Hautemares, he suddenly leaves the stage, never to return: "Ainsi, ô lecteur benevole, adieu, vous n'entendrez plus parler de moi!"[4] There are at least three different chronologies outlined in the early chapters. The characters' ages and names change from one page to the next. For example, Fédor de Miossens is sometimes called Hector; Count d'Aubigné suddenly becomes Count de Nerwinde.

Above all, Stendhal never succeeded in choosing a central character or plot. *Lamiel* was to be a kind of picaresque novel, something like Lesage's *Gil Blas* or Marivaux's *Vie de Marianne*. As such, it would naturally focus on the successive adventures of the young heroine, Lamiel. As Martineau puts it: "Il s'agit cette fois de retracer l'existence d'une sorte de Julien femelle."[5] Yet from the start another character appeared whose importance grew with each successive version of the work, the hunch-backed Dr. Sansfin. He is first introduced in Chapter 1, a good deal of which is devoted to a description of his character. Much of Chapter 3 is filled with the Doctor's misadventures, and he continues to play an active role in that part of the novel which takes place in Carville.

There is nothing surprising about a novel which has two main characters of different ages, one a youth, the other an adult. Indeed, Stendhal's novels show a regular progression in this respect. In *Armance,* M. de Malivert plays no significant role; in *Le Rouge et le Noir,* M. de Rênal and the Marquis de La Mole are considerably more important, but Julien is almost always at the center of the author's attention; again, in *Lucien Leuwen,* M. Leuwen *père* is a central character but never eclipses his son; finally, in *La Chartreuse de Parme* there are long passages devoted entirely to Count Mosca's life at Milan and Parma, during which Fabrice is literally absent, studying in Naples or exiled from the Parmesan state.

As Stendhal grows older, the role of the older character increases in importance. However, with the exception of *Lamiel* in no case does the author seem unable to choose between the two characters. The *Chartreuse* is in fact a beautiful example of the harmonious integration of the fates of its two male leads. With *Lamiel* the situation is quite different. Proof that Stendhal was never able to find a satisfying resolution to the problem of uniting the two main strands of this work is offered in Martineau's Appendix to his edition of *Lamiel* (pp. 1031–49). There he presents several long passages outlining alternate possibilities of interaction between Lamiel and Sansfin. (The specific content and significance of these variants will be discussed later in this chapter.)

Critics such as Prévost have speculated that, if death had not put an end to his efforts, Stendhal could have ironed out these inconsistencies in a final revision of the novel. To my mind, there seems little basis for such a supposition. It is known that Stendhal generally spent very little time revising his earlier works. When he did make changes, they usually concerned either the style or the order of presentation. He did not alter the plots. I would suggest, therefore, that the disorganized state of *Lamiel* resulted from the author's mental deterioration at the time of writing. This view is admittedly as speculative as that of Prévost, but an acquaintance with Beyle's biography will lend it some support.

It was in the spring of 1839, while he was still correcting the proofs of *La Chartreuse de Parme,* that Stendhal got the idea for his new novel, to be entitled *Amiel.* Not until 1840 and 1841, however, did he write the majority of the chapters that have since been published under the title *Lamiel.* At this time of his life, Beyle's health was rapidly deteriorating. All the neurotic ailments that had plagued him throughout his life were becoming more and more acute. One day as he was working on *Lamiel,* he actually fell into the fireplace.[6]

Suffering from migraine headaches, fainting fits and choking spells, Stendhal was convinced that death was approaching. On September 28, 1840, he drew up his will[7] and in the spring of 1841 he noted: " 'J'ai fait cent fois le sacrifice de la vie, me couchant, croyant fermement ne pas me réveiller' " (p. 386). With such serious symptoms, Beyle consulted a doctor:

On lui avait parlé de M. Séverin, homéopathe de Berlin, comme ayant fait de belles cures à Rome. Il était donc allé, dès le 28 février 1841, le voir. . . . M. Séverin . . . lui débita des phrases à la suite desquelles Beyle entrevit "qu'il s'agissait d'apoplexie *nerveuse,* non sanguine." [p. 387]

Even the doctors of his time recognized that his was a nervous disorder, not an organic one. In the light of modern psychological knowledge, one can surmise that the increase in the severity of the symptoms was due to a reduced capacity of the ego to defend itself against the instinctive wishes. Two of these symptoms, falling and fainting, are often considered as indications of bisexual phantasies (see "Dostoyevsky and Parricide").

During this same period, Beyle fell in love with a woman he

called Earline. In his biography of Beyle, Martineau lays special emphasis on one aspect of this abortive affair:

Jamais on ne vit celui qui le vécut mettre à la poursuite de l'Eros plus d'âpreté désespérée, *plus de complaisance à noter tous les déchirements que lui causaient ses échecs.* Jamais! Même au temps de sa passion transie pour Métilde. Sans vouloir se l'avouer, il devait savoir la 'guerre *Earline*' perdue avant d'avoir commencé. Il avait conscience aussi que c'était sa dernière campagne. Il n'en a pas moins souffert. *Je crois même qu'il a rarement cultivé la douleur avec plus de frénésie.* C'est avec volupté qu'il s'étend sur son lit d'épines et jouit de les briser "à force d'y piquer ses membres palpitants." [pp. 373–74, italics mine]

Thus Martineau himself is aware of the pleasure Beyle derived from entertaining painful phantasies, and the biographer is careful to note that this psychic masochism was greater now than it had been previously. To be sure, Martineau goes on to reject the term 'masochism,' but this rejection is apparently based on a misunderstanding. Martineau seems to think that the word necessarily refers to the actual perversion, whereas it is often used to indicate a purely psychological condition. It is this second usage that I have employed throughout this essay.

As has been mentioned before, the masochistic tendency is closely allied to the feminine identification in a man. It is therefore reasonable to suppose that the increase in masochism during this period of Stendhal's life was due to the increased power of his feminine identification. This circumstance, combined with his reduced ego strength, would help to explain Stendhal's choice of a young girl as the main character of his new novel. In the same way, the other hidden phantasies, such as those centering around Dr. Sansfin, would be able to surface in virtually naked form. And, finally, the weakened ego would be less able to perform its synthesizing function; it would have difficulty integrating the various phantasies clamoring for expression into a meaningful and consistent whole. It seems highly probable that the incoherent form and the often perverse content of *Lamiel* are the result of these unfavorable conditions which attended its creation.

The similarity between Lamiel's story and that of Julien Sorel is quite striking. Each of them begins life in a small provincial town in a half-peasant, half-bourgeois family—the Hautemares in Carville, the Sorels in Verrières. During adolescence each is employed by the leaders of the local nobility, Lamiel as the Duchess of Miossens' reader, Julien as tutor for the Rênals. Both move from their home town to the provincial capital—Rouen and Besançon—and from there to Paris. Furthermore, like *Le Rouge et le Noir, Lamiel* was to end with a great crime, the burning of the Palais de Justice.[8]

Since Julien is in part a representation of Stendhal, the resemblance between Julien's story and that of Lamiel constitutes *prima facie* evidence that Lamiel is also a representation of the author himself. A detailed comparison of the important experiences and attitudes of Lamiel with those of Stendhal as reported in *Henry Brulard* will show that this supposition is well founded.

In describing Lamiel's upbringing, Stendhal states repeatedly that because of their religious and aristocratic pretentions, the Hautemares impose great restrictions on their foster daughter. She is constantly kept under Mme Hautemare's surveillance, must wear good clothes, and must avoid distractions, particularly the peasant children who would be her natural playmates (pp. 896, 902, 904).

Beyle's description of the "Raillane tyranny" of his own youth corresponds in every detail to this picture. A propos of his studies under Raillane, he has this to say:

J'étais sombre, sournois, mécontent, je traduisais Virgile, l'abbé m'exagérait les beautés de ce poète . . . je haïssais l'abbé, je haïssais mon père, source des pouvoirs de l'abbé, je haïssais encore plus la religion au nom de laquelle ils me tyrannisaient.[9]

His great ambition was to be allowed to play with the lower-class children in his neighborhood:

Mon grand malheur était de ne pouvoir jouer avec d'autres enfants; mon père, probablement très fier d'avoir un précepteur pour son fils, ne craignait rien à l'égal de me voir *aller avec des enfants du commun*, telle était la locution des aristocrates de ce temps-là. [p. 106]

Other amusements were equally forbidden to Henri:

J'étais victime de l'éducation aristocratique et religieuse la plus suivie. Mes tyrans ne s'étaient pas démentis un moment. On refusait toute invitation. [p. 113]

It is quite probable that Beyle's memory of Raillane, Chérubin Beyle and his aunt Séraphie—the three tyrants of his youth—was distorted by his emotions toward them. But the important fact here is that he endows Lamiel and her parents with the same characteristics that he felt he and his relatives possessed. This picture corresponds to Beyle's psychological situation, even if it is not a completely faithful reproduction of the historical situation.

The next important point of identification between Beyle and Lamiel is shown in their first sexual experiences. Lamiel's seduction of the tutor, Jean Berville, is described in Chapter 9 of the novel. Toward the end of Chapter 8, Lamiel remarks that she is sixteen years old: "je suis donc à seize ans comme le docteur Sansfin dit que sont les femmes de cinquante" (p. 967). The first sentence of the ninth chapter indicates that a certain amount of time has elapsed: "Pendant les mois suivants, elle s'ennuyait toutes les fois qu'elle était dans la maison de son oncle" (p. 970). Therefore Lamiel must be about sixteen or seventeen years old at the time when she makes love with Berville.

Since she does not know him very well, she is obliged to offer him some money in order to make sure that he will come to their rendezvous in the woods:

"Très bien; je te donnerai dix francs, viens dans les bois mercredi sans manquer, à six heures du soir."

"Oh! pour les dix francs, si mademoiselle le veut, j'irai bien demain mardi, à six heures précises." [p. 972]

When they meet, she has him kiss her and then announces quite bluntly:

"Sans doute, je veux être ta maîtresse."

"Ah! c'est différent," dit Jean d'un air affairé; et alors sans transport, sans amour, le jeune Normand fit de Lamiel sa maîtresse. [p. 972]

Afterwards, Lamiel expresses her dissatisfaction: "Comment, ce fameux amour, ce n'est que ça!" (p. 973)

In *Henry Brulard,* when speaking of his first trip to Italy in 1800, Beyle reports the loss of his innocence:

J'ai oublié de dire que je rapportais mon innocence de Paris, ce n'était qu'à Milan que je devais me délivrer de ce trésor. Ce qu'il y a de drôle, c'est que je ne me souviens pas distinctement avec qui. La violence de la timidité et de la sensation a tué absolument le *souvenir.* [p. 414]

At this time Beyle was about seventeen years old, like Lamiel, and it is more than probable that he "lost his innocence" with a prostitute, that is, by paying his partner just as Lamiel does. A last point of similarity is the sudden passion for mathematics experienced by Beyle and Lamiel. Throughout Chapters 34 and 35 of *Henry Brulard*, Beyle comments on this interest of his youth:

Je veux dire de ma cascade dans les mathématiques. [p. 326]

.   .   .   .   .

J'aimais d'autant plus les mathématiques que je méprisais davantage mes maîtres. [p. 327]

.   .   .   .   .

Mon enthousiasme pour les mathématiques. . . . [p. 329]

While she is living in Rouen with Fédor de Miossens, Lamiel has him teach her various subjects. One day she expresses an interest in mathematics:

Dans ses bizarreries, Lamiel avait recours à toutes sortes d'inventions pour ne pas s'ennuyer; un jour, elle se fit enseigner la géometrie par le duc. Ce trait redoubla l'amour de celui-ci. . . . Sans distinguer tout ce qu'il devait à la géometrie, Fédor l'aimait de passion; il fut ravi de la facilité avec laquelle Lamiel en comprenait les éléments. [p. 991]

However capricious Lamiel may be, it is certainly more than a coincidence that her most unusual whims should correspond in content and in chronology with the events of her creator's life. In fact, it is clear from the evidence presented above that the identification between Stendhal and Lamiel is every bit as complete as that between Stendhal and Julien or Fabrice. That Beyle should, at this point in his life, choose a girl as main character, instead of an effeminate youth as before, is in accordance with the principle of "the return of the repressed"; as time goes on, the repressed material, in this case the feminine identification, comes to the surface in more and more direct form, until at last there is virtually no disguise, except of course that it is projected onto a fictional character.

Lamiel, however, is not the only representation of the author to appear in this novel. Both Fédor de Miossens and Dr. Sansfin share this function, albeit in different ways. Fédor, like Octave de Malivert and Lucien Leuwen, is a student at the Ecole Polytechnique of Paris. Like the other two heroes, Fédor has done what Beyle had failed to do on his arrival in Paris in 1799. Although comparatively little is seen of Fédor in this novel, since the author's attention is concentrated mostly on Lamiel, there are two additional traits which betray his identity with Beyle. The first is his own passion for mathematics and logical reasoning.

The second is his delight in teaching his mistress about literature, the theater, and mathematics. As Martineau points out, Beyle always recommended his newest intellectual discoveries to those he loved:

Henri Beyle a toujours pensé que l'étude des mathématiques apprenait à bien penser en développant la faculté de raisonnement et en apprenant à ne tenir pour vrai que ce qui peut se démontrer. Aussi dès 1800 conseillait-il à sa soeur Pauline de s'adonner aux sciences mathématiques.[10]

From his correspondence with Pauline it can be seen that Beyle did not restrict his suggestions to mathematics alone. Many of his letters are filled with instructions to his sister about life as well as all sorts of intellectual matters. The most characteristic and revealing passage occurs in his letter of May 11, 1804:

Je pense surtout à toi: *dès que je vois quelque chose d'utile, je voudrais te l'expliquer*. Voici l'habitude que je prends: j'écrirai tout ce que je te destine, et, lorsque la feuille sera pleine, je te l'enverrai. *Cela vient de ce que je suis très persuadé qu'on ne peut s'aimer qu'autant qu'on se ressemble.*[11]

Like Fédor, Beyle wishes to explain anything useful to his sister, and with characteristic perceptiveness, he gives as his reason the desire to create a resemblance to himself in the one he loves. Aside from establishing the similarity between author and character, this passage shows the strong narcissistic component in this love, i.e., the desire to find oneself in the love object. An additional confirmation of the fact that both Lamiel and Fédor represent Beyle is to be found in the identity of their ages. Before her departure for Rouen, Lamiel is about seventeen years old; in Chapter 5, Sansfin points out that Fédor, Mme de Miossens' only son, is also seventeen (p. 922). In the novel then, Fédor serves as the masculine component of the bisexual phantasy found so often in Stendhal's works.

Dr. Sansfin is a descendant of the same family as the Marquis de la Mole, M. Leuwen and Count Mosca; the older, cynical man of pleasure who initiates the younger character into the ways of the world. Like his predecessors, Sansfin is thus another version of the adult Beyle, an identity recognized by several critics including Prévost:

En même temps que son imagination créatrice donne toutes ses complaisances à Lamiel, il crée, sans le vouloir, un autre personnage à sa ressemblance—un reflet difforme et douloureux. Dédoublé déjà en Lucien et Leuwen père, déloublé à certains instants en Fabrice et Mosca, il se dédouble enfin en Lamiel, incarnation féminine de Julien Sorel, et amazone de ses rêves de jeunesse, et en Sansfin.[12]

The most direct evidence of this identification is the similarity of their ages: In Chapter 5, Sansfin mentions that he is fifty-eight years old: "Un homme de cinquante-huit ans avec quinze ou vingt mille livres de rente'" (p. 921). According to Martineau:

Le 8 mars 1841, se remettant au travail, [Stendhal] refaisait entièrement les premiers chapitres. Quelques jours plus tard, du 17 au 19 mars, il choisissait un nouveau début et esquissait des pages entières, toutes consacrées au docteur Sansfin et à son père.[13]

Thus it was in 1841 that Stendhal worked on creating the character of the doctor. Since Beyle was born in 1783, he, too, was fifty-eight years old at the time of writing.

In Chapter 6 Sansfin's views on life are expounded, and their resemblance to his creator's philosophy of Beylism can scarcely be denied:

Par exemple, suivant [le docteur Sansfin], le monde n'était qu'une mauvaise comédie, jouée sans grâce, par des coquins sans grâce, d'infâmes menteurs. . . . [p. 934]

. . . Il y a donc doublement à gagner à écouter la voix de la nature et à suivre tous ses caprices: d'abord l'on se donne du plaisir, ce qui est le seul objet pour lequel la race humaine est placée ici-bas; en second lieu, l'âme fortifiée par le plaisir, qui est son élément véritable, a le courage de n'omettre aucune des petites comédies nécessaires à une jeune fille pour gagner la bonne opinion des vieilles femmes en crédit dans le village ou dans le quartier qu'elles habitent. [p. 935]

As is to be expected from the return of the repressed, the libidinal component of this teaching, which is scarcely discernible in Mosca's or the marquis' advice to their young charges, comes to the fore in *Lamiel* since the doctor's main goal here is to seduce Lamiel. At the same time, Sansfin has none of the more appealing qualities of his predecessors, whose realism and frank hedonism allowed them to enjoy life. Sansfin's idea of pleasure has something sinister about it; one has the impression of lechery and perversion in him, a condition symbolized by his physical deformity.

The core phantasy of *Lamiel*, like that of *Le Rouge et le Noir*, is the family romance. In this novel, however, the orphaned state of the main character is no longer presented as a phantasy as in *Le Rouge et le Noir*, nor as a subtle allusion as in the *Chartreuse*, but as an accomplished fact. In this, as in other respects, *Lamiel* gives evidence of the more advanced state of neurotic process, in which the ego is no longer able to defend itself against the irruption of unconscious tendencies.

For Lamiel is in fact an orphan. Her foster parents, the Hautemares, adopt her from a foundlings' home in Rouen (Chap. 2). The immediate cause of this decision is a very peculiar circumstance: the local priest, M. du Saillard, has arranged a little spectacle for the edification of his parishioners in order to convert them to the true faith. At the high point of a sermon delivered by a colleague, M. Le Cloud, on the evils of sin and the hell-fire awaiting heretics, several petards are set off in the church as a kind of graphic illustration of the contents of the speech. Although he is himself the instigator of the show, Du Saillard interprets the explosions as a miracle, a direct intervention of God into the affairs of Carville. Naturally M. Hautemare, in his capacity as beadle, is present along with his wife. After the sermon she tells her husband that they should adopt a little girl, in order to "give a soul to God" (p. 890), since they are childless.

Taken as a whole, the scene is a grotesque farce which Stendhal uses to ridicule his usual *bête noire*, organized religion and superstition. He is careful to expose the very earthly preparations at the bottom of the false miracle, so that Du Saillard and the church in general appear as cynical charlatans intent upon capitalizing on the credulity of a naive populace, in order to frighten them out of any thoughts of revolution against organized authority. But the most peculiar circumstance is that this episode should lead to the adoption of Lamiel and thus her entry into the novel. From this fact alone I would suspect that this spectacle was in some way meant to account for the birth of the heroine, her "entry" into the world. From the emphasis laid on the violent noise produced by the petards, the particular infantile experience involved would seem to be the so-called primal scene. The absurdity and irony of the description would then have the usual significance of rejection by the ego. This interpretation is rendered all the more probable by the presence of little Fédor, and his skeptical reception of the "miracle" he has witnessed.

It will be recalled that one of the typical phantasies associated with the family romance attributes to the mother various illicit sexual activities:

Knowledge of sexual matters gives rise to the tendency to picture erotic situations and relations, impelled by the pleasurable emotion of placing the mother, the subject of the greatest sexual curiosity, in the situation of secret unfaithfulness and clandestine love affairs.[14]

In Chapter 3 the peasant women of Carville impute similar activities to Mme Hautemare, Lamiel's foster mother:

"Ho! là! là! la *madame,* prenez garde de perdre cette *fille de votre frère,* cette prétendue nièce." [p. 897]

    .   .   .   .   .

Qu'appelles-tu fille du diable? dis donc une bâtarde qu'elle a eu en arrière de son mari et qu'elle a forcé ce gros bonhomme butor à adopter, et cela pour lui faire deshériter son pauvre neveu, Guillaume Hautemare. [p. 900]

As an adolescent, Lamiel is taken into Mme de Miossens' house as a kind of lady-in-waiting whose duty it is to read to the duchess. Their relationship does not long remain as one of servant to master, for soon Mme de Miossens acquires a warm affection for Lamiel and wishes to make of her a protégée:

Quand la duchesse fut bien sûre de n'avoir pas fait acquisition d'une petite fille se donnant des airs de demoiselle, *elle se livra avec folie au vif penchant qu'elle sentait pour Lamiel.* . . . La grande dame expliquait à la jeune paysanne normande, fort intelligente, mais ignorante à plaisir, toutes les choses de la vie. [p. 914, italics mine]

The analogy of the situation, and of the very words employed to describe it, with Julien's relationship to Mme de Rênal is patent. However, there is no direct mention here of the mother-daughter constellation. This omission is remedied in the latter part of the novel, when Lamiel, newly arrived in Paris, is taken under the wing of the wife of the proprietor of the hotel in which she lives. "Dès le second jour, Mme le Grand avait dit à sa protégée qu'elle l'aimait *comme sa fille*" (p. 998, italics mine).

As is customary in all of Stendhal's works the main character moves from one foster family to another, the Hautemares, the Miossens and the Le Grands. The primary motives for this phantasy—the feeling of rejection from or disappointment with the parents, the devaluation of their authority, and the longing for continued dependence—are all alluded to by the author. The study of Lamiel's character has already shown that she is constantly seeking advice and instruction about life from parental substitutes—the motif of dependence. The opposite motivation can be seen in Lamiel's numerous expressions of resentment against the restrictions placed upon her conduct by the Hautemares and the duchess. As early as Chapter 4, Lamiel attempts to eradicate any respect she might still have for her foster parents' teachings by accusing them of being stupid (p. 907).

The mixed feelings of rejection, resentment and disappointment are best expressed in Chapter 8. It is immediately after the revolt of July 1830, and Mme de Miossens has gone to Le Havre with her son. As a result Lamiel now lives with the Hautemares once again. At first she is relatively contented, but when Mme Hautemare asks her for some of the secondhand dresses the duchess has given her, Lamiel, oversensitive as usual, is horrified by this "vile request" and concludes: "Je n'ai donc personne à aimer!" (p. 964). In the ensuing conversation, Mme Hautemare ends by telling Lamiel that she is an orphan, a revelation which causes a great shock to the young girl:

> Tout en convenant avec elle-même du peu d'esprit de l'oncle et de la tante, elle avait rêvé une famille à aimer. Dans son besoin de sentiment tendre, elle avait fait un mérite à sa tante du manque d'esprit; elle se sentit toute bouleversée, puis, tout à coup, elle fondit en larmes. [p. 964]

Significantly, it is in the very next chapter that she ventures to make a rendezvous with Jean Berville.

All of Lamiel's relations are marked by one motif—curiosity, the desire to find out about the ways of the world. The Hautemares, the duchess, Dr. Sansfin, Abbé Clément, Fédor and Mme Le Grand all take turns instructing her about life. It is to assuage this curiosity that she spies on the peasant children of the village and that she turns to reading fiction. One of her greatest reproaches against the Hautemares is that they do not tell her the truth about many things: "On ne me dit pas encore ces choses-là, pensa-t-elle, parce que je suis trop petite" (p. 907). This curiosity is more than the normal desire of a young person to learn as much as possible about a world that is still new to her. It has the exclusiveness, the excessiveness and the insatiability of an uncontrollable passion, one that is partly due to an unconscious motivation. Even towards the end of the novel, when Lamiel, now in Paris, has already experienced much, Stendhal repeats at least twice that she is still consumed by the desire to know (pp. 997, 1019).

From the very beginning, Stendhal makes it clear that this passion concerns not merely the general desire to know but is rather a search for an answer to the question: "what is love?" Here again, a motif that was visible in all the novels, particularly the *Chartreuse*, has become a dominant theme in this last work. The passage quoted from Chapter 4 reads in its entirety: "On ne me dit pas ces choses-là, pensa-t-elle, parce que je suis trop petite, c'est comme l'amour dont on me défend de parler sans vouloir jamais me dire ce que c'est" (p. 907). As mentioned above, Lamiel continues to be preoccupied by this question and repeatedly asks her acquaintances about it. One day she tells Abbé Clément:

"Il est un ennemi contre lequel tous les beaux livres que madame me fait lire pour mon éducation tendent à me prévenir; mais on ne me dit jamais clairement ce que c'est; eh bien! monsieur l'abbé, vous, en qui j'ai tant de confiance, qu'est-ce que c'est que l'amour?" [p. 938]

The answers he gives do not satisfy her curiosity, but by his reaction, she senses the emotional importance of the subject: "Je suis parvenue à le piquer d'amour, se dit-elle, il faut qu'il y ait dans cette parole, *l'Amour,* quelque chose de bien extraordinaire" (p. 939). After their conversation Lamiel is thoughtful and still wonders what love is: "Mais, en supposant que l'abbé Clément ait de l'amour pour moi, encore une fois, qu'est-ce que c'est que l'amour?" (p. 943)

One would expect that after her experiences with Berville, Fédor and others, Lamiel would cease to be plagued by this question. In fact its content is merely altered. One day in Rouen she converses about love with a chambermaid from her hotel:

"Mais est-ce que vous n'avez pas eu d'amoureux?"
"Si fait," répondit Marthe à voix basse.
"Et qu'en dites-vous?"
"Que c'est une chose délicieuse."
"Eh bien! rien n'est plus ennuyeux pour moi. Tout le monde me vante cet amour comme le plus grand des bonheurs; dans toutes les comédies, on ne voit que des gens qui parlent de leur amour; dans les tragédies ils se tuent pour l'amour; moi je voudrais que mon amoureux fût mon esclave, je le renverrais au bout d'un quart d'heure."
Marthe restait pétrifiée d'étonnement. [p. 992–93]

Instead of wondering what love is, Lamiel now questions whether other people, such as Marthe, really experience it; in any case, Lamiel decides that it is not for her.

In the early chapters of *Lamiel* the germ of another plot is presented, involving Dr. Sansfin, Lamiel, and the duchess. Stendhal was never able to incorporate this plot element into his novel, but it is of great importance as an indicator of one of the basic phantasies of the work. Many of the supplementary chapters mentioned in the first part of this analysis reveal the author's continuing preoccupation with this story line. In Chapter 5, Dr. Sansfin has been taking care of Lamiel, who has fallen ill from unknown causes:

[Sansfin] s'estima beaucoup lui-même, et du milieu de ses soins une idée folle lui vint à la tête.
"Il faut que j'entreprenne deux choses:
"Me faire aimer de Lamiel, qui a dix-sept ans bientôt et sera charmante quand je l'aurai déniaisée.

"Me rendre si nécessaire à cette grande dame qui a de beaux traits et est encore fort bien, malgré ses cinquante-deux ans, qu'elle se résolve, après un combat de quelques mois ou d'un an, à épouser de la main gauche le médecin de campagne disgracié par la nature." [p. 921]

I have tried to show earlier that Lamiel's relationship to Mme de Miossens was part of the family romance phantasy—that of adopted daughter to foster mother. Sansfin's phantasy then amounts to the project of seducing a woman and her daughter. But since both Lamiel and Dr. Sansfin are representations of the author himself, this phantasy is, at bottom, the narcissistic idea of making love to oneself! Stendhal's imagination did not stop here. The Appendix to *Lamiel* shows that this affair was to be more complicated, and more incestuous, than those Renaissance chronicles that Beyle enjoyed so much. For Lamiel was to marry Fédor de Miossens; then Dr. Sansfin would seduce her:

Pour exemple Sansfin venu faire l'amour à Lamiel devenue duchesse de Miossens. Elle, pour se moquer de lui, lui prépare des dangers en avertissant son mari fort jaloux. . . . [p. 1034]

The idea of a triangle between Sansfin, Lamiel and another man must have haunted Stendhal, for he invented another episode on the same subject. Instead of having Lamiel pay the peasant Berville in order to find out about "love," the author created another character whom he called *"le piéton"*:

Une fois cependant, le piéton put être soupçonné d'avoir manqué à sa discrétion, vertu qui lui était si nécessaire; il se trouva que le docteur Sansfin et lui faisaient la cour à la fille du boulanger. . . . Bientôt il fut connu que la belle boulangère, malgré les quatre mille livres de rente que l'opinion accordait à son père, s'était décidée en faveur du médecin bossu. . . .

C'était ce piéton, fort bien vêtu et renommé à la fois pour son extrême discrétion et pour sa passion encore plus grande pour l'argent, qu'avait choisi Lamiel lorsque sa curiosité avait voulu se former une idée de ce que la jeune fille du pays appelait l'amour. [p. 1046]

In this phantasy then, as well as in the one cited above, the elder version of Beyle enters into a situation of sexual competition and jealousy because of the younger, feminine version. Thus the hypothesis suggested in my discussion of *Lucien Leuwen,* that there was a homosexual component to the hero's jealousy, is given added support by these alternate versions of the core phantasy of *Lamiel.*

In summary, *Lamiel* contains constellations of characters and dominant phantasies which were found in Stendhal's previous novels. The major difference is that trends subjected to a greater degree of distortion in the earlier novels—family romance, bisexual phantasy, sexual curiosity, and narcissism—are all presented much more directly here. A further difference, and one which, I think, has had important consequences for the reception of the novel, is that the political and social aspects of the other novels are drastically reduced in this last, unfinished work. The underlying phantasies have neither been woven together into a coherent unity nor sufficiently transformed into socially meaningful terms; the result, for this reader at least, is that *Lamiel,* like *Armance,* seems more like a study of the abnormal than of a generally meaningful human experience.

Conclusion

In all five novels I have discovered that the psychic content is similar from one work to another. All arise from the same emotional soil; they all express the author's lifelong conflicts stemming from his childhood attachment to his mother, sister, and father. All five manifest the same characteristic defenses employed by Stendhal to cope with these conflicts. Each bears the unchanging stamp of Stendhal's personality, but, like the several offspring of one parent, none resembles the others exactly. These works are by no means identical copies of a single prototype.

When I cast about for the cause of these differences, the first important factor I come up with is the varying strength of the repression operative in the novels. In *Armance* it is excessively strong; in each of the successive novels, with the exception of *Lucien Leuwen,* it grows increasingly weaker until, in *Lamiel,* the hidden wishes receive gratification in virtually undisguised form.

In Stendhal's first novel, the mother-son relationship is veiled in an almost impenetrable cloud of censorship. Octave, of course, does not have relations with Mme de Malivert, nor with Mme de Bonnivet or Mme d'Aumale, the substitute mother figures. This tendency is allowed expression only in symbolic form (his mother's jewels), as an unsuccessful sublimation (Mme de Bonnivet does not convert him), or when desexualized (his platonic relationship with Mme d'Aumale). But Julien, who is merely the tutor of Mme de Rênal's children, does seduce her. And Fabrice is allowed to act out an extensive rebirth phantasy, a crucial part of the novel, in contrast to the fleeting nature of Octave's symbolic gratification; furthermore, Fabrice's surrogate, the young Prince of Parma, does make love to Gina. As I have shown, *Lucien Leuwen* is primarily about the process of love and the relationship to the father, so that it is only natural that the desires for the mother be largely absent. They appear only in Lucien's brief flirtation with Mme de Vaize and in his abortive affair with Mme Grandet. Since the main character of *Lamiel* is a girl, there again the attachment to the mother is of relatively small importance. As part of the family romance, Lamiel is adopted, legally or emotionally, by Mme Hautemare, Mme de Miossens and Mme Le Grand. These relationships are desexualized; otherwise the author would have been obliged to portray a Lesbian affair (such as we find in Balzac's *Fille aux yeux d'or* or Baudelaire's "Lesbos" and "Femmes damnées").

The same general trend can be discerned in all the other important phantasies. Thus, although *Armance* deals almost entirely with a love affair traceable to the brother-sister relationship, Octave spends virtually all his time overcoming his love, avoiding Armance, i.e., defending himself against his desire. Aside from a few moments of relative happiness after his duel with Crêveroche, and platonic happiness at that, there is only one moment of triumph, the marriage and honeymoon, which is described rather vaguely in less than one page. Immediately thereafter he commits suicide. In this respect *Lucien Leuwen* resembles *Armance.* In contrast, Julien and Mathilde actually do make love, as do Fabrice and Clélia. And since Lamiel becomes the daughter, in imagination, of the Duchess of Miossens, the former's affair with Fédor is equally a fulfillment of the brother's desire for his sister.

Likewise the family romance, which finds varied and extended expression in *Le Rouge et le Noir,* the *Chartreuse,* and *Lamiel,* is barely indicated in *Armance* by the simple fact that Octave is the son of a nobleman. M. Leuwen has a high social position and becomes prime minister of France. Furthermore, in two of the later novels the hero becomes a father, the culmination of the family romance. In *Le Rouge et le Noir,* Mathilde's pregnancy is one of the precipitating causes of the denouement, while *La Chartreuse de Parme* contains a still lengthier development of this situation (Sandrino's birth, feigned illness, and eventual death).

The homosexual component also receives clearer and more extended treatment in each successive novel. The partial identification of hero and heroine is constant in the five novels, but otherwise the differences are considerable. In *Armance* these desires are fulfilled only in the persecutions of Octave by the Chevalier de Bonnivet and Commander Soubirane, and the duel with Crêveroche. The other novels contain these elements, too: Julien's duel with Beauvoisis, his persecution by father and brothers; Fabrice's persecution by the marquis and Ascagne del Dongo, his duel with Giletti, the attempted poisoning by General Conti, etc. But in addition, *Le Rouge et le Noir* portrays in detail Julien's relationship with Pirard at the seminary and his condemnation to death by Valenod; the *Chartreuse* has the famous Waterloo episode and the prison scenes; in

Lucien Leuwen the hero's relationship to his fellow officers and superiors, to Coffe and M. de Vaize, are all described at some length; and in *Lamiel* the main representative of the author is actually a girl.

The most striking difference, however, concerns the truly narcissistic tendency represented by the confrontation of two editions of the author in an older and a younger character, the Marquis de la Mole—Julien, M. Leuwen—Lucien, Count Mosca—Fabrice, Dr. Sansfin—Lamiel.

A second, equally important differentiating factor is that of decomposition, a phenomenon treated by Rank in its relation to literary productions.[1] As I use the term it refers to two distinct, but closely related processes, projection and splitting. By the mechanism of projection the author gives external form (a character in the work) to what is really an internal tendency; by the mechanism of splitting, he creates several characters in order to represent several diverse and often conflicting feelings toward the same person. For instance, the priests of *Le Rouge et le Noir* generally appear in pairs, e.g., Pirard and Castanède, a good one and a bad one. They derive their character traits from the author's ambivalent attitude toward authority; the one is a projection of his love attitude, the other of his hostile feelings. But all the priests in the novel are ultimately derived from Stendhal's feelings toward his father, who is represented by several other characters as well.

Now if the novels are compared in terms of this second criterion, a striking progression is noticed. To take the representations of the father, in *Armance* there are M. de Malivert, the Commander, and in a derivative sense, Baron Risset, Crêveroche, and the Chevalier de Bonnivet. Of these five, only Commander Soubirane and Bonnivet play important roles in the plot; their actions almost lead to the permanent separation of the two lovers but end up by precipitating their marriage. In *Le Rouge et le Noir,* the list of such figures becomes much longer: Napoleon, Sorel, M. de Rênal, Valenod, the Marquis de La Mole (in part), the old surgeon, the priests Chélan, Maslon, Pirard, Castanède, Frilair, the Bishop of Besançon, and in the derived sense (imaginary brothers), Sorel's two elder sons, Norbert de La Mole, Croisenois, Luz, and Caylus. Moreover, many of these characters have decisive influences on Julien's life, and one or the other is almost always present and active. A list of the same length could be drawn up for the *Chartreuse* or *Lucien Leuwen.*

The same process is visible with reference to the mother, but it is not nearly so extensive in this case. In *Armance* one finds Mme de Malivert, Mme de Bonnivet and Mme d'Aumale; in *Le Rouge et le Noir,* Mme de Rênal, the maid Elisa, Mme Valenod, Mme de La Mole, Mme de Fervaques and the maid of the La Mole household; in *Lucien Leuwen,* Mme Leuwen, Mme d'Hocquincourt, Mme de Vaize, Mme Grandet; in the *Chartreuse,* the Marquise del Dongo, La Sanseverina, Raversi, Marietta, La Fausta, and the Princess of Parma; and in *Lamiel,* Mme Hautemare, Mme de Miossens and Mme Le Grand. Although the difference in the number of representations is not so great as for the father, their effect on the heroes' lives and the amount of space devoted to them are incomparably greater in the later novels. Hence I am led to a conclusion formulated long ago by Jung and Rank, namely that the emotional importance of a person can be measured by the number of representations he finds in an individual's phantasy productions, as well as by the amount of space devoted to him.[2]

The most interesting variation in the extent of decomposition concerns the hero himself. Thus, although in a sense Armance and Bonnivet represent the author himself, this role is carried mainly by Octave alone. In striking contrast is the situation in the *Chartreuse*. There not only Fabrice, but also Lieutenant Robert, Mosca (in part), the younger Prince of Parma, Ludovic, Ferrante Palla, and Rassi are all representatives of the author. In terms of the conclusion stated in the previous paragraph, this increase of self-representation can be taken as a sign of the author's greater narcissistic regression. Seen from another point of view this observation allows me to make a distinction useful in understanding the psychic determinants of character portrayal in his novels. Until now I have spoken of representatives of the father, for instance, in the crude, and indeed infantile terms of "good" and "bad," explaining them as projections of the child's own feelings of love or hate toward his father. This explanation is perfectly valid as long as I restrict myself to a discussion of the instinctual (id) tendencies underlying the surface story. But it is clearly an insufficient basis for understanding all the particular personality traits of the characters in the novels. Thus Mme de Rênal is an idealized image of the mother, but, although she shares many traits with other characters created by other novelists to fulfill the same function, e.g., Mme de Mortsauf in Balzac's *Lys dans la Vallée*, she is in other respects quite different from them. The point is that she is not only the projection of an inner image but also the resultant of a whole series of real women who played a maternal role in Stendhal's life: Mme Beugnot, Countess Daru, Mathilda Dembowska, Angela Pietragrua, Mme Rebuffel, and ultimately Henriette Gagnon as she really was. The same is true of the father and sister figures. The distinction I wish to make is therefore as follows: there is one class of characters who are composed from the mechanisms of projection and splitting, on the one hand, and from preconscious elaboration on the other (the "models" of the characters); a second class consists almost purely of projections of the author's inner tendencies. The first group includes the representatives of father, mother and sister; the second, those of the author himself.

Immediately upon formulating this distinction, I perceive that it is inadequate to my purpose for several reasons. In the first place, some of the father figures such as Frilair or General Conti seem to have no character other than that of being evil or stupid. Secondly, some of the representatives of the author are based in part on literary models or real people other than himself, e.g., Berthet, Alexander Farnese, or the poet Ferrante Pallavicino (model for Ferrante Palla). Thirdly, a small group are composed of differing tendencies and models: the Marquis de La Mole and Mosca represent, simultaneously or alternately, father, mother, and son, and are built on real models such as Count Molé and Pierre Daru and on the mature Stendhal. Finally, one set apparently has no models—Norbert de La Mole, Croisenois and Crescenzi, to name a few.

It is possible to put some order in this bewildering set of possibilities, without at all reducing its complexity, by introducing the concept of quantity and thereby establishing a series of gradations. At one extreme are characters like Croisenois, whose sole origin is a psychic tendency, that of rival for and sharer of the sister. They have no models because Stendhal himself had no brothers—hence the designation, "imaginary brother." Hence also their "flatness;" they do not impress us as being "real" people. At the other limit are the fully developed characters like M. de Rênal, Mathilde de La Mole, or Gina Sanseverina. They are based on a series of models behind all of whom we may discern the primitive imagos of father, sister and mother, these in their turn being the result of the child's phantasy distortions and the real personalities of the members of his family. This group does impress us as being "real" or "round," to continue E. M. Forster's metaphor.[3] In between we have those who are, although to some extent based on real models, essentially mere expressions of a tendency—Frilair or Ferrante Palla, those who represent a tendency and a current social type —Valenod, the bourgeois parvenu, or Mme de Fervaques, the social climber with religious pretensions. And lastly, there are those who, while representing some tendency, participate greatly in the unconscious model, e.g., Pirard. Obviously these distinctions could be refined still further, but it would be pointless to do so here.

A third source of diversity in the five novels is the extended elaboration of the content by the so-called primary process, that is, the primitive mechanisms of thought found operative in dreams: especially condensation, displacement and symbolism. Of course splitting and projection are also mechanisms of the primary process, but because of their special place in literature, as opposed to other phantasy productions such as dreams or the plastic arts, I feel justified in considering them separately. Both in dreams and in the creation of fiction this regression is made possible by the temporary relaxation of the ego functions which produce rational thinking. But whereas in dreams this relaxation is the result of the ego's withdrawal from the world into sleep, in fiction it is accomplished purposively (but not consciously) by the author's ego in the service of his artistic intention. In both cases the result is twofold, or more precisely, there are two types of regression involved. Unconscious instinctual wishes are allowed to surface, and these wishes, along with preconscious thoughts related to them, are distorted by the primary process. I have already spoken at length of the nature of these wishes in Stendhal's novels. Here I am concerned with the process of distortion.

What I have in mind especially is the mother-son relationship. In *Le Rouge et le Noir,* it takes up about half of the novel; in the *Chartreuse* much more than that. But in *Armance* it is limited to the first chapter, plus a few other allusions and episodes—Mme de Bonnivet, Mme d'Aumale—which, however, also have counterparts in the other novels, e.g., Mme de Fervaques, Marietta, La Fausta. The reason for this difference (in terms of technique, not psychological motivation) is easy to see. Mme de Rênal is not related to Julien; La Sanseverina is Fabrice's aunt; but Mme de Malivert is Octave's mother. Thus his love for her could only be expressed in terms that could be taken simply as an indication of filial, asexual love, or by means of unconscious symbolism—the jewel episode. In *Le Rouge et le Noir,* where there is no family tie, the two are actual lovers. The *Chartreuse* has an intermediate position in this respect. Fabrice's love for Gina is given much more extensive expression than in *Armance,* although mitigated by projection (she loves him, not vice versa); but since she is his aunt they do not becomes lovers. However, she is Mosca's mistress, and she has relations with Prince Ranuce-Ernest V, two surrogates for the author. Hence, although the same oedipal wish is evident in the three novels, because it was not thoroughly elaborated by the primary process in *Armance,* it could only receive scanty gratification there.

My fourth criterion is the quality of the secondary elaboration. This factor, of relatively minor importance in dreams, is absolutely essential in literature. After the wishes have been distorted by the primary process, there results a group of separate elements which form no recognizable pattern; the secondary elaboration takes them and weaves them into a context, or story, that makes sense by the ego's standards, the standards of reality. This function is so important in literature both because the work is written while awake and because the social nature of art requires that others be able to "understand" it. Actually these are two aspects of the same thing since the writer, in judging and correcting his work, puts himself momentarily in the place of his public.[4]

A simple example of this process concerns the jewel episode, which appears in three novels. When it occurs in *Armance* (Chap. 1), the reader is completely taken aback. Stendhal has been describing Octave's passion for study; then, with no transition, he informs the reader that it is late autumn and that Mme de Malivert urges her son to take advantage of the remaining days of good weather by going horseback riding. She buys him a fine English mount, which, however, he refuses to use on the pretext that it cost too much money. In reply his mother tells him that she has bought it with the proceeds of the sale of some of the diamonds which she was going to leave to him in her will. The whole sequence is bizarre; it seems to have no connection with what went before or what comes afterward; in short, it "makes no sense."

The situation is quite different in *Le Rouge et le Noir*. Julien has just finished assembling the fake anonymous letter that Mme de Rênal had instructed him to make. He gives it to her and is about to leave town so that she can arrange matters with her husband, when she tells him:

> "Si ceci tourne mal, ajouta-t-elle avec le même sang-froid, on m'ôtera tout. Enterrez ce dépôt dans quelque endroit de la montagne; ce sera peut-être un jour ma seule ressource."
>
> Elle lui remit un étui à verre, en maroquin rouge, rempli d'or et de quelques diamants.
>
> "Partez maintenant, lui dit-elle." [p. 123]

Here the episode fits naturally into the context of the events of the story. It is well motivated by Mme de Rênal's fears of being exposed as an adulteress and by her trust in Julien.

In Chapter 21 of the *Chartreuse* the same scene is repeated, this time between La Sanseverina and the mad poet, Ferrante Palla. Fabrice is in prison and the duchess has grave fears for his life. She plans to take revenge on the Prince of Parma by having him poisoned. Ferrante Palla is to be the instrument of her vengeance, and she shows her gratitude by giving him a large jewel box filled with diamonds. Here again the characters of the people involved, their current emotional state, and the events of the plot all concur in giving this episode an understandable motivation.

Thus, in all three novels the same phantasy element is present: the mother, or mother figure, gives her son, or his surrogate, her jewels. Because of the universality of certain unconscious symbols, such as this one, the reader "understands" the hidden meaning. In the one case, however, it arouses bewilderment or repugnance in him; in the other two, he finds it perfectly "natural," i.e., understandable in terms of conscious motivation. In the first case, the phantasy has remained, in a sense, private; in the second two, secondary elaboration has made it palatable to the public, a clear example of the importance of the author's artistic skill or technique.

This example has been chosen precisely because its simplicity illustrates the point in the clearest possible fashion. But, in itself, this episode is not of decisive importance to the novels as a whole. Therefore, instead of examining similar minor episodes (compare, for instance, the servant's observation of Mme de Malivert, with Fabrice's enraptured contemplation of Lake Como in Chapter 9), I shall now consider a factor that is absolutely essential—the hero's relation to society.

A comparison of the main characters, Octave, Julien, Lucien, Fabrice, and Lamiel, shows that they have many traits in common. They are all torn by inner conflicts, all have extraordinarily high ideals, all suffer from the incapacity to love, each one is acutely aware of the hypocrisy of others and of himself, and each feels that he is persecuted. Yet, despite these many similarities, they strike the reader, at least while he is actually reading the novels, as being quite different. How can this impression be explained? I will begin by considering only two of the novels, *Armance* and *Le Rouge et le Noir*. When Octave complains about the evils of society, its persecution of truly exalted spirits—such as himself—I feel distinctly uneasy. Why should a young nobelman with every possible advantage, intelligence, good looks, high birth, and great wealth (after the Law of Indemnity is passed) complain about society's persecutions? When he bemoans the lack of energy of the Restoration nobility, I feel tempted to ask, "What have you done to demonstrate moral vigor?" And when he contrasts his own idealism with the baseness of others, I wonder what accomplishments this idealism has led to. How different when Julien expresses the same reproaches! The reason is summed up beautifully in his moving speech to the court:

"L'horreur du mépris, que je croyais pouvoir braver au moment de la mort, me fait prendre la parole. Messieurs, je n'ai point l'honneur d'appartenir à votre classe, vous voyez en moi un paysan qui s'est révolté contre la bassesse de sa fortune."

After admitting his guilt, he continues:

". . . Mais quand je serais moins coupable, je vois des hommes qui, sans s'arrêter à ce que ma jeunesse peut mériter de pitié, voudront punir en moi et décourager à jamais cette classe de jeunes gens qui, nés dans une classe inférieure et en quelque sorte opprimés par la pauvreté, ont le bonheur de se procurer une bonne éducation, et l'audace de se mêler à ce que l'orgueil des gens riches appelle la société." [p. 482]

What seemed absurd in the mouth of the rich nobleman becomes charged with meaning and emotion in the mouth of the poor plebeian whose destiny is controlled by those more powerful than himself.

I am well aware that the emphasis I am laying on this change in the hero's social status is not new to Stendhal criticism. What is new is the light shed on the reason for the importance of this change, for from my study of the content of the novels I have found that the underlying motivation of these feelings, in the case of both Octave and Julien, lay in the very same unconscious conflicts, those of the author. In both cases they are the result of defense mechanisms, especially projection. But whereas Stendhal has placed Julien in a situation in which these defenses can easily be taken at face value by the reader, he has failed to supply Octave with similar justifying circumstances, and thus my uneasiness when reading *Armance*. Unable to share in Octave's defenses, I lose interest in his story; it does not make sense. More important, the failure to occupy the reader's ego allows too great a buildup of guilt created by the forbidden nature of the wishes expressed. This is the main source of the dissatisfaction expressed by Martineau and Atherton in passages cited in Chapter 1.

Now what about Fabrice? He is a pampered son of fate much like Octave, yet it seems that he too is justified. The reason for this is not his social status, but the political situations: his father's reactionary tyranny during the reign of Napoleon (Fabrice's childhood), the oppressive Austrian regime in power after his return from Waterloo, and the monarchical dictatorship that rules Parma, the scene of the latter half of the novel. If the term "objective correlative" has any meaning at all, I would suggest that social structure in *Le Rouge et le Noir* and political structure in the *Chartreuse* are good examples of it. The author has placed his heroes in a wider human context, constructed expressly to make their defenses come true.

What has been said about the heroes' relations to society is equally true of their attitudes toward love. I can understand why Julien should feel trepidation when seducing his employer's wife or daughter; he is mindful of their characters, their social positions, and the "sin" of adultery. Similar obstacles confront Fabrice with regard to the duchess and Clélia. But where is the obstacle that must separate Octave and Armance? They are of the same social class, their fortunes are comparable (after her inheritance), the families do not object, they are devoted to each other. The answer, of course, is Octave's impotence. But, in the first place, that is never mentioned in the novel, and secondly, it is the result, not the cause, of Octave's emotional problems, the same ones that plague Julien and Fabrice. The reader understands this only too clearly in *Armance* because of the very artificiality of the external obstacles that separate the protagonists, e.g., the forged letter. The later novels, while by no means neglecting the aspect of inner conflict in the heroes, offer the reader convincing, although psychologically incorrect, reasons for the heroes' inhibitions, that is, rationalizations in the strict meaning of the term.

In summary, whereas Stendhal offers the reader of *Armance* a series of episodes that have no logical connection between them, in the successful novels he succeeds in weaving similar episodes into a more or less coherent whole that is meaningful to the reader's ego.

My fifth, and last, criterion is that of narrative attitude. In his famous article " 'Psychical Distance' as a Factor in Arts and an Esthetic Principle," E. Bullough gives the following description of this phenomenon:

Distance does not imply an impersonal, purely intellectually interested relation of such a kind [as that of the experimental scientist]. On the contrary, it describes a *personal* relation, often highly emotionally colored, but of a *peculiar character*. Its peculiarity lies in that the personal character of the relation has been, so to speak, filtered. It has been cleared of the practical, concrete nature of its appeal, without, however, thereby losing its original constitution.[5]

This definition of distance is understandable in analytic terms as a description of the peculiar attitude of the more or less mature ego when it indulges in phantasy. Its relation to reality has become sufficiently relaxed so that it can withdraw interest from the outer world and pay attention to its own inner workings. Yet, at the same time, it must constantly be aware of the limits dividing phantasy from reality and be capable of distinguishing between them. A good example of the breakdown of the first condition is that of the student reading a novel in preparation for an examination. In most cases the desire to isolate and remember certain facts, or to make judgments, effectively blocks any enjoyment of that reading. The practical task of learning takes up too much of the student's mental energy. An example of the breakdown of the second condition is a phenomenon that regularly occurs when children give dramatic presentations. The child comes on stage, and, when asked his name by another actor, responds with his real name instead of that of the character he is portraying. The first example would be a case of over-distancing, the second of under-distancing. The assumption is that a proper aesthetic attitude lies somewhere between these two extremes.[6]

What interests me here is not the reaction of specific individuals nor the historical variations in this attitude among given
cultures or segments of society, but the means that the novelist
has at his disposal for influencing the level of involvement of
his readers. Specifically, I am suggesting that, to a great extent,
this function devolves upon the author's narrative attitude, and
that a large class of the problems dealt with under the heading
"the role of the narrator" can be understood psychologically in
these terms.

In order to make the following discussion comprehensible, I
must first enter into a short digression concerning its theoretical
basis. As early as 1907 Rank suggested that the reader of a
fictional work, besides enjoying vicariously the wish fulfillments
and punishments expressed in it, also engages in a partial and
temporary identification with the author of the work.[7] This
suggestion, in conjunction with a remark by Freud in his book
on wit, has been taken up and developed by Kris in light of more
recent developments in ego psychology.[8] Briefly, he states that
the reader, insofar as he reacts aesthetically, re-creates in his
own mind the same processes that occurred within that of the
author during the creation of the work. This identification is
thus carried out on the level of the ego, not the id or superego.
Since the creation of the work involves a certain relaxation of
the ego functions of the author, the reader must do the same.
In these terms, under-distancing means that the reader has
relaxed his control too much; over-distancing, that he has not
done so enough. But what happens if the author himself has
gone too far or not far enough in this direction? Clearly, since
the reader takes his cue, so to speak, from what he finds in the
work, that is, from the author, he will likewise suffer from too
little or too much distancing.

Much of what has been said in the previous sections of this

chapter could be reformulated in these terms since such factors as elaboration by the primary process and secondary elaboration obviously affect distancing, but little would be gained by so doing. I prefer to employ the concept in the one realm where it is especially helpful, that of narrative attitude.[9] This term has several different meanings in current critical usage. It sometimes refers to the presence of a first person or third person narrator, or to narration by one of the principal or minor characters of the story. These meanings can be neglected here since Stendhal always narrates his novels in the third person. It can also refer to the "reliability" of the narrator, that is, the agreement or disagreement between what he says and what actually happens in the story. This usage can also be eliminated from consideration since, although there is an occasional disagreement, Stendhal makes no conscious or sustained effort to exploit such possibilities. Finally, the term can refer to the omnipotence or restriction of the narrator's knowledge[10] and also to his emotional attitude toward the substance of his story and his characters, particularly the hero. It is these two aspects, which are interrelated, that I should like to explore now.

The situation in the first novel is quite simple. With a few exceptions, whenever Octave is on stage, Stendhal either shows us directly what is going on in his mind or else reports it to us with little commentary except such as will better enable us to understand the hero's feelings. For practical reasons I must let one example stand for many:

Avec tout l'orgueil d'un enfant, en toute ma vie, je ne me suis élevé à aucune action d'homme; et non seulement j'ai fait mon propre malheur, mais j'ai entraîné dans l'abîme l'être du monde qui m'était le plus cher. O ciel! comment s'y prendrait-on pour être plus vil que moi? Ce moment produisit presque le délire. La tête d'Octave était comme désorganisée par une chaleur brûlante. A chaque pas que faisait son esprit, il découvrait une nouvelle nuance de malheur, une nouvelle raison pour se mépriser.

Cet instinct de bien-être qui existe toujours chez l'homme, même dans les instants les plus cruels, même au pied de l'échafaud, fit qu'Octave voulut comme s'empêcher de penser. Il se serrait la tête des deux mains, il faisait comme des efforts physiques pour ne pas penser. [p. 134]

This passage, which is worthy of comparison with some of the finest pages of the other novels, occurs when Octave has been revived by a peasant, the day after Octave has realized that he is in love. At first he heaps reproaches upon himself. Then the author begins to speak in an attempt to depict Octave's state more clearly. But notice that Stendhal, although speaking in the third person, continues to show Octave from the inside (e.g., "A chaque pas . . ."). In the next paragraph he brings in a general consideration, man's instinct of self-preservation, both to connect Octave more closely to the reader's experience, and to show how grave his condition is, a process reinforced by the example of the man at the scaffold. Then, after describing Octave's gesture, the author again goes inside his character to tell us why he did this, to stop himself from thinking. The whole passage has an intensely sincere quality; no reader could doubt that this was Beyle's own experience, as indeed we know it was from other sources. The important point for my purpose, however, is that he makes no effort to disassociate himself from Octave. For instance, he fails to point out that, in fact, Octave has not dragged Armance into an abyss. No one but Octave thinks this.

It is true that earlier in this scene Stendhal remarks: "Octave se disait à haute voix des choses folles et de mauvais goût, dont il observait curieusement le mauvais goût et la folie" (p. 133). But this statement strikes the reader as a simple statement of fact—Octave is in a truly pathological state in this scene—not as a kind of disclaimer on Stendhal's part. I realize that I am dealing with intangibles here, but anyone who reads the whole chapter will, I think, agree that the above statement does nothing to distinguish author from character. It is barely noticed in the context, preceded as it is by paragraphs like this one: "Son imagination parcourait rapidement toute l'échelle des actions possibles, pour retomber ensuite avec plus de douleur sur le désespoir le plus profond, le plus sans ressource, le plus digne de son nom; ah! que la mort eût été agréable dans ces instants!" (p. 133). Though this last exclamation might be *erlebte Rede* or *style indirect libre*, the fact remains that in it author and character are completely identified.

When compared with the above, the famous scene from *Le Rouge et le Noir* portraying M. de Rênal's fit of jealousy vividly illustrates that M. de Rênal's torment is no less real and no less well depicted than Octave's.

"A peine levé,—grand Dieu!" dit-il en se frappant la tête, "c'est d'elle surtout [his wife] qu'il faut que je me méfie; elle est mon ennemie en ce moment. Et, de colère, les larmes lui vinrent aux yeux."

Par une juste compensation de la sécheresse de coeur qui fait toute la sagesse pratique de la province, les deux hommes que, dans ce moment, M. de Rênal redoutait le plus, étaient ses deux amis les plus intimes.

"Après ceux-là, j'ai dix amis peut-être," et il les passa en revue, estimant à mesure le degré de consolation qu'il pourrait tirer de chacun." A tous! a tous! s'écria-t-il avec rage, mon affreuse aventure fera le plus extrême plaisir." Par bonheur, il se croyait fort envié, non sans raison. Outre sa superbe maison de la ville, que le roi de *** venait d'honorer à jamais en y couchant, il avait fort bien arrangé son château de Vergy. . . . [p. 124]

The whole scene, however, has become irresistibly funny because of Stendhal's constant interpolations which deflate M. de Rênal's pride. After describing Rênal's despair and fit of tears (comic in itself here), the author calmly makes the scathing remark about the "just compensation," the "practical wisdom" of provincial life. When Rênal seeks to divert his grief by thinking of his accomplishments, Stendhal, in mock complicity, enumerates all the character's petty vanities, and so on. It might be argued that this difference is due to the difference in status of the two characters: Octave is the representative of Beyle's ego; M. de Rênal, that of his father. Although this is true, it is not the whole story, as can be seen from the treatment of Julien himself.

Leafing through the book at random, I find these remarks:

Heureusement pour lui, ce soir-là, ses discours touchants et emphatiques trouvèrent grâce devant Madame Derville. . . . [p. 54]

. . . . .

D'après les confidences de Fouqué et le peu qu'il avait lu sur l'amour dans la Bible, il se fit un plan de campagne fort détaillé. Comme sans se l'avouer, il était fort troublé, il écrivit ce plan.

Le lendemain matin, au salon, Madame de Rênal fut un instant seule avec lui:

"N'avez-vous point d'autre nom que Julien?" lui dit-elle.

A cette demande si flatteuse, notre héros ne sut que répondre. [p. 81]

. . . . .

Si Julien avait eu un peu de l'adresse qu'il se supposa si gratuitement. . . . [p. 84]

Julien tremblait que sa demande ne fût accordée; son rôle de séducteur lui pesait si horriblement. . . . [p. 84]

Quotations of this sort could be multiplied at will.[11] The same process of comic detachment is still more evident in

Stendhal's treatment of Lucien, of Fabrice (e.g., in the episode of the Battle of Waterloo), and of Lamiel. My point is not that Stendhal always mocks Julien and Fabrice; examples can be found in which this is not the case, e.g., the scene of the épee (Chap. 17). Nor do I assert that he never disassociates himself from Octave, since he obviously does so in the following:

Un mouvement instinctif le précipita vers le château. Il sentait confusément que raisonner avec lui-même était le plus grand des maux; mais il avait vu quel était son devoir, et il comptait se trouver le courage nécessaire pour accomplir les actions qui se présenterâient quelles qu'elles fussent. Il justifia son retour au château, *que lui inspirait l'horreur de se trouver seul,* par l'idée que quelque domestique pouvait arriver de Paris. . . . [p. 137, italics mine]

But there is nothing humorous about the italicized interpolation; it sounds more like a serious attempt at explanation. In any case, this type of statement is the exception in *Armance,* whereas it is the rule in *Le Rouge et le Noir* and the *Chartreuse;* that is the important difference. In the first novel, the reader senses that author and characters are one, that this is Stendhal's story; in the others, one feels that there is a separation between them. That there are exceptions merely shows that what is involved is a question of degree.

The result of this lack of distancing in *Armance* is that the reader senses that Stendhal was not in control of his material, but rather that it was in control of him. I have mentioned that one of the principal differences between art and dream is that in art the relaxation of the ego functions takes place within certain limits and that this regression is controlled by the artist's ego. Related to this conception is the assertion that one of the principal sources of pleasure, in artist and public as well, is the sense of mastery over the powerful and dangerous wishes and prohibitions which dominate the unconscious mind. In essence, the observer says to them, "Do your worst, we are still in control of the situation." When the author has failed in this respect, the reader feels, on the contrary, that these primitive forces are too strong; consequently, he grows anxious or experiences guilt feelings and hence is unable to enjoy the work aesthetically. Or, more probably, in reaction to his growing apprehension, he does not allow himself to remain involved with the work on the deepest level; he becomes over-distanced. In both cases the result is the same: he does not appreciate the novel.

In Stendhal's later novels the separation between author and work characteristically takes the form of irony or humor.[12] In 1928 Freud made humor the subject of an essay in which he reaches the conclusion that its peculiar effect is due to an unusually large amount of energy being temporarily shifted onto the individual's superego. After remarking that humor, as opposed to wit or other forms of the comic, arises specifically in situations of danger or distress, he proposes that the person's superego acts toward him in the same comforting fashion that its precursors, the parents, did when he was a child. This position is summarized in the formula: "Its meaning is: 'Look here! This is all that this seemingly dangerous world amounts to. Child's play—the very thing to jest about!' "[13]

One could not ask for a better description of Stendhal's predominant attitude toward Julien and Fabrice. How many times does he say of them, "If they were older, they would have known. . . . ," or "If they had more experience, instead of relying on books for their knowledge of the world . . ."? And almost without exception, these gently ironic remarks are proffered when "our hero" is in some kind of danger. The passages cited above (pp. 297–98) from *Le Rouge et le Noir* all stem from the time when Julien was wooing Mme de Rênal, that is, when he was overcoming his fear of castration. When he fears that he might be the butt of a conspiracy of Mathilde's friends and herself, Stendhal makes the same type of remark (Chap. 15). The most famous humorous episode of the *Chartreuse* is the Battle of Waterloo, which I have shown to be an externalization of the same fear.

To be sure, in these same episodes Stendhal not only uses humor, in Freud's sense, but also irony, bordering on sarcasm at points, and the comedy of situation. But there is no necessary contradiction between these various comic modes. In his essay "Ego Development and the Comic," Kris develops the theory that the mastery of anxiety by the ego is one of the principal functions of the comic. Referring to studies of the origins of comic production and appreciation in children, he states:

In 1929 Herzfeld and Prager published the result of experiments they had made to test children's understanding for fun and the comic. The results are impressive when they refer to the "comic" productions of children in their early years of latency. When we examine the contents of children's drawings which are intended to express something "funny", we gain the impression that what the child represents are objects of the surrounding world which it has just learned to comprehend and to master. Graber's (1931) psychoanalytic observation in a similar case seems to reveal that the deepest problems in the child's life—in Graber's case the repressed fear of castration—may come to be expressed in what the child calls "funny."[14]

This is precisely the case in those scenes from Stendhal's novels, and it is not surprising to find that he uses every means at his disposal—now comic description, now humorous consolation—to master his deepest fear. There is thus a shifting of energy between ego and superego.

There is another connection between these phenomena

which opens up interesting prospects. In criticizing Freud's interpretation of an example given in his essay on humor, Kris says: "I think we are justified here in recognizing a particular form of rebellion against fate: *Self-irony,* a form of the comic which is related to cynicism and sarcasm and bears the stamp of agression" (p. 216). And he adds in a note: "Continued clinical observations suggest to me now (1951) that Dooley (1934) was correct in pointing to the frequent correlation between humor and self-criticism of a masochistic type" (p. 216, n. 19). Now the basic process in masochism, as I have mentioned repeatedly in the course of this essay, is the shifting of an excess of agressive energy onto the superego, which is then directed against the ego and experienced as pleasure. Genetically, this process is characterized by what Reik calls "the flight forward," that is, the individual, unable to stand the buildup of anxiety, accepts punishment (suffering) beforehand in order to reach his gratification. Furthermore, Reik found that the pleasure gained by thus mastering anxiety was often so intense that the desire to retain it obstructed therapy.[15]

All of these phenomena, comedy of situation, irony, and sarcasm, thus fall into place as masochistic attempts to control anxiety, if I make the one simple assumption that Stendhal as narrator takes the role of superego toward Stendhal as "hero" of the novel, the representative of his ego. I have left out humor. But if humor results, as Freud suggests, from a hypercathexis (overcharging with energy) of the superego, then it too can be included in the same sphere of phenomena. I need only suppose that Stendhal's superego used its excess of energy in performing alternately both of the functions it took over from the parents, that of punisher—resulting in masochism—and that of comforter—resulting in humor.

Finally, this theory makes it possible to understand a perplexing situation which, to my knowledge, has gone unnoticed by critics until now. In each of Stendhal's novels, beginning with *Le Rouge et le Noir,* there exists a character who represents "the mature Stendhal," that is, Stendhal in the mother or father identification: the Marquis de la Mole, in *Le Rouge et le Noir,* M. Leuwen (Lucien's father) in *Lucien Leuwen,* Count Mosca in the *Chartreuse* and Dr. Sansfin in *Lamiel.* Yet there is no such character in *Armance.* Now bearing in mind Bergler's description of them as disillusioned, cynical, somewhat hard-boiled men who take it upon themselves to initiate the young hero into the ways of the adult world, but who are also his more powerful rivals, I can show that Mosca is to Fabrice exactly as narrator Stendhal is to hero Stendhal. Since *Armance* was written before this shift in energy had firmly established itself, there is little separation between Stendhal and Octave and no character comparable to La Mole or Mosca.

On the basis of each of my five criteria, Stendhal's novels fall into a graded series. In the earlier works, fewer and less extensive wish fulfillments are expressed; the relative lack of decomposition does not allow a comprehensive expression of the various facets of the conflicts involved; the elaboration by the primary process is strictly limited; the secondary elaboration is most incomplete; and the author has failed to separate himself sufficiently from his material.

In this essay I have employed the methods and findings of psychoanalysis. In so doing I have found it profitable to use a three-pronged approach based on the three factors involved in any communication: the person who wishes to convey something, the author; the means of communication, the novel; and the person who receives the communication, the reader. While my main object of concern was that of any literary critic, the works themselves, I did not hesitate to use data from the author's life or to form hypotheses about the readers' reactions. Many critics seem to feel that it is detrimental to literary studies to use material from one or the other or both of these areas. On the contrary, it seems to me that in a field as complex as literature, and one in which the three factors are so obviously and so intimately interrelated, the critic should take advantage of every possible source of evidence in the attempt to clarify and solve the difficult problems inherent in it. Not only does he thereby gain insight into questions which might otherwise elude his grasp, such as that of artistic creation or aesthetic response, but he attains a better understanding of the work itself.

It is theoretically possible to understand and appreciate a work of fiction without knowing anything about its author. But is it practically possible? In many cases I think not. Or, to put it more judiciously, although partial understanding is possible, many things would be missed. Paradoxical as it sounds, I believe that only the works of the greatest authors can be more fully comprehended without such knowledge, precisely because they have succeeded where other writers have failed, in making their creations speak for themselves. And if I include facts about origins and sources under the heading of biographical knowledge, my case becomes still stronger. Who would claim that there is nothing to be learned from a comparison of Shakespeare's *Hamlet* with earlier theatrical versions and the legend itself? Who would claim that a knowledge of the myth of Phaedra and Hippolytus and the plays of Euripides and Seneca can teach nothing about Racine's *Phèdre*?

The reasons for considering the reader's response are still more evident. Is not the essential difference between a work of literature and its brothers, the dream and the daydream, the fact that it is written with an audience in mind? What sense does it make to speak of the alienation of the artist from society if the fact is not recognized that the artist needs to have a public? Some forms of lyric poetry might be held to be "pure expression." But there is no drama without a stage, or at least a reader. And Stendhal's novels are filled with remarks of the narrator to his reader. There would be no point in creating an unreliable narrator if there were no audience to be mystified by him.

But perhaps the greatest reason for using whatever information can be found is also the simplest—human limitation. So much is unknown, so little known, that the critic is justified, indeed obliged, to make anything and everything serve his purpose—the quest for enlightenment.

Appendix

At the instigation of friendly and not-so-friendly critics, I append a dialogue concerning my method and its relation to traditional literary criticism.

CRITIC: I was not aware that Stendhal had read Freud.

ME: Billiard balls have not read Newton, electrons have not read Einstein. The lack of intellectual formation in these particles does not prevent them from obeying the laws of classical and quantum mechanics.

CRITIC: True, but these particles are not free. Nor do they create works of art.

ME: But men are not free either, at least not in those aspects of their lives in which they are motivated by unconscious, instinctual tendencies. It is precisely these tendencies, *insofar as they are expressed in Stendhal's novels*, that I have studied in this book.

CRITIC: In other words, your book is just a case history, not a work of literary criticism.

ME: No, it is not a case history. A proper case history would concentrate on explaining the origin, nature, and course of an illness. It would use the novels only as evidence of some aspect of the case. I do just the reverse: I use biography as an aid in interpreting the psychic content of the works. And it is to this content that the reader of the novels responds on the deepest psychic level.

217

CRITIC: Aha! You think that everybody is crazy. That sounds like a projection to me.

ME: Thank you for your diagnosis, doctor. I do think that everyone has the capacity to experience in phantasy the desires, conflicts, gratifications, and inhibitions represented in these and other novels. I do think that this imaginative experience forms the core, although not the totality, of reader response to literature.

CRITIC: So you admit that your book deals only with a small part of the novels. It says nothing about Stendhal's art, his style, his narrative technique, his descriptive capacities, his place in the tradition of the novel.

ME: To most of these charges I plead guilty. I do think that my approach has allowed me to explain certain esthetic problems, such as the qualities and defects of the structure of *Le Rouge et le Noir*. I have some insights to offer about esthetic distance, one aspect of narrative technique. But generally you are right. In this respect I am like most critics. Brombert's *Voie Oblique* is a brilliant study of Stendhal's narrative technique, but it has nothing to say about the representation of historical reality in the novels, a subject treated brilliantly by Auerbach. Martineau writes a biography, Durand studies the mythical tendencies of the novels, and so on. My book is not intended to be the be-all and end-all of Stendhal studies, any more than are those of earlier critics. If you disagree with my approach on principle, then all dialogue is impossible. If you are seriously interested in understanding the relationship between depth-psychology and traditional literary criticism, I can do no better than to refer you to Simon Lesser's *Fiction and the Unconscious* and Norman Holland's *The Dynamics of Literary Response*, two excellent studies of the subject.

Notes

INTRODUCTION

1. Matthew Josephson, *Stendhal; or, The Pursuit of Happiness* (New York, 1946), p. 286.

2. Henri Martineau, ed., Foreword to *Stendhal: Oeuvres Intimes*, by Stendhal (Paris, 1955), p. 7.

3. Wallace Fowlie, *Stendhal* (London, 1969), p. 31.

4. Henri Martineau, *Le Coeur de Stendhal: histoire de sa vie et de ses sentiments*, 2 vols. (Paris, 1952–53).

5. Edmund Bergler, *Talleyrand, Napoleon, Stendhal, Grabbe: Psychoanalytisch-Biographische Essays* (Vienna, 1935).

CHAPTER ONE: *The Secret Sin*

1. Three representative views are given below (pp. 22–27 in this essay).

2. In *The Art of French Fiction* (London, 1959), Martin Turnell says that the treatment of such an abnormality is a danger to the novelist:

Although the principal characters in all Stendhal's novels are extraordinary people who are cut off from the society in which they are living, it was only in his first and last novels that he created characters who are abnormal in the medical sense. There are few more difficult or more delicate tasks for the novelist than the portrayal of abnormality. He runs the constant risk of allowing his work to degenerate into a mere case history. [p. 78]

Turnell goes on to say that Octave's abnormal traits are balanced by his normal ones.

By the following apologia Martineau shows that he too is disturbed by this problem:

Octave est donc un fou, un *enragé* suivant l'expression même de l'auteur. Il y a de telles gens par le monde et il était légitime d'en mettre en scène. Si quelque chose nous choque en lui, ce n'est pas qu'il soit si fantasque, c'est que nous n'apercevions pas nettement la nature de son déséquilibre. [Henri Martineau, *L'Oeuvre de Stendhal* [Paris, 1957], p. 338. Hereafter cited as *Oeuvre*.]

Prévost's statement of the problem (see pp. 22–23 in this essay) reveals the same preoccupation. (Jean Prévost, *La Création chez Stendhal* [Paris, 1959], p. 228. Hereafter cited as *Création*.)

3. See also Sigmund Freud, "Psychopathic Characters on the Stage," *Psychoanalytic Quarterly* (1909).

4. Prévost, *Création*, p. 228.

5. Martineau, *Oeuvre*, p. 333.

6. John Humphrey Atherton, "Stendhal and the Uses of Irony" (Ph.D. diss., Harvard University, 1961), pp. 74–75.

7. Ibid., pp. 110–11.

8. Henri Martineau, ed., *Armance*, by Stendhal (Paris, 1962), p. 269, n. 26. All subsequent references to *Armance* are to this edition unless otherwise indicated.

9. It is true that many novels are not named after the main character, but in these cases the title usually refers to an institution, idea, or image which plays a central role in the novel, e.g., *Bleak House, War and Peace, Germinal, A La Recherche du temps perdu*. By giving his novel the title *Armance*, Stendhal leads the reader to expect a work whose main character is Armance; instead, it is Octave.

10. Cited by Martineau, "Notes et Variantes," *Armance*, p. 261. Hereafter cited as "Notes."

11. Cited by Martineau, Introduction to *Armance*, p. xxvii.

12. Martineau, Introduction to *Armance*, p. xxvii, italics mine.

13. Ibid., pp. xxv–vi.

14. Cited by Martineau, "Notes," p. 264.

15. Sigmund Freud, *On Creativity and the Unconscious*, ed. Benjamin Nelson (New York, 1958), pp. 222–23.

16. Martineau, "Notes," p. 298, n. 318.

17. Cited by Martineau, "Notes," p. 263.

18. Stendhal, *Stendhal: Oeuvres Intimes*, ed. Henri Martineau (Paris, 1955), p. 60. All subsequent references to *La Vie de Henry Brulard* are to this edition.

19. Edmund Bergler, *Talleyrand, Napoleon, Stendhal, Grabbe: Psychoanalytisch-Biographische Essays* (Vienna, 1935), p. 78. Hereafter cited as *Stendhal*. This translation and all subsequent ones are my own.

20. Georges Blin, ed., Introduction to *Armance*, by Stendhal (Paris, 1946), p. xxxi.

21. Cited by Martineau, "Notes," pp. 283–84, n.169.

22. Theodor Reik, *Masochism in Sex and Society* (New York, 1962), pp. 115–24.

23. Blin, p. lxvi.

24. Ibid., p. lxx.

25. Sigmund Freud, *Introduction to Psychoanalysis*, trans. Joan Riviere (New York, 1935), pp. 139–40.

26. Marie Bonaparte, *Edgar Poe, Etude Psychanalytique* (Paris, 1933), pp. 349–50.

27. Stendhal, *Stendhal: Romans et Nouvelles*, ed. Henri Martineau, 2 vols. (Paris, 1963–64), 2:295. All subsequent references to *La Chartreuse de Parme* are to this edition.

28. Martineau, *Chartreuse*, p. 1423, n. 1 to p. 295.

29. Stendhal, *Stendhal: Romans et Nouvelles*, 1:1344. All subsequent references to *Lucien Leuwen* are to this edition.

30. Sigmund Freud, *Three Case Histories*, ed. Philip Rieff (New York, 1963), p. 23.

31. "The fantasy embodies a boy's wish that his mother should herself initiate him into sexual life in order to save him from the dreaded injuries caused by masturbation. (The numerous creative works that deal with the theme of redemption have the same origin.)" (Sigmund Freud, "Dostoevsky and Parricide," in *The Literary Imagination,* ed. Hendrik M. Ruitenbeek [Chicago, 1965], p. 347.)

32. On a deeper level it also indicates a frantic attempt to deny the unconscious wish mentioned as its basis.

33. Martineau, *Armance,* p. 302, n. 366.

34. Freud, *Creativity and the Unconscious,* pp. 168–69.

35. Hanns Sachs, *The Creative Unconscious: Studies in the Psychoanalysis of Art* (Cambridge, Mass., 1942).

36. Please note that in this discussion I am not questioning the presence of genuine filial love in Octave (and Beyle). It is only the excessive nature of his attachment which invites interpretation.

37. Réne A. Spitz, *The First Year of Life: A Psychoanalytic Study of Normal and Deviant Development of Object Relations* (New York, 1956), p. 12. Spitz claims that Freud and Georg Simmel were the first scientists to put forth this idea (p. 12).

38. Prévost, p. 232.

CHAPTER TWO: *Happiness' End*

1. Stendhal, *Stendhal: Oeuvres Intimes,* ed. Henri Martineau (Paris, 1955), pp. 1439–40. Hereafter cited as *Oeuvres Intimes.*

2. Stendhal, *Oeuvres Intimes,* p. 1216.

3. Martineau, *Oeuvres Intimes,* p. 1631, n. 2.

4. Stendhal, *Le Rouge et le Noir,* ed. Henri Martineau (Paris, 1958), p. 34. All subsequent references to *Le Rouge* are to this edition.

5. To the English-speaking reader, this passage might seem ambiguous, for the underlined phrase could refer to Croisenois, not

Mathilde. However, Martineau, whose knowledge of the French language and of this novel are not open to question, clearly does not share this doubt. In note 535, he states: "Le duc de Chaulnes n'est pas le père de Mathilde, mais celui de sa mère" (p. 578). Furthermore, I have shown the passage to several native French speakers, without telling them my purpose, and all of them concluded that it meant that the duke was Mathilde's father. When pressed a little, they conceded that there might be some ambiguity, but they still felt that their original interpretation was the more likely one.

6. Otto Rank, *The Myth of the Birth of the Hero and Other Writings*, ed. Philip Freund (New York, 1959).

7. This sentence is mistranslated in Freund's edition of *The Myth of the Birth of the Hero*, so I have corrected it here. The German text reads: ". . . wozu als Triebkraft die Lust tritt, die Mutter, die Gegenstand der höchsten sexuellen Neugierde ist. . . ." Freund renders the passage as: ". . . impelled by the pleasurable emotion of placing the mother, *or* the subject of the greatest sexual curiosity. . . ." (p. 70, italics mine). The word "or" does not appear in the German and its insertion here falsifies the meaning of the sentence. The motive for this error is clear.

8. Otto Rank, *Psychoanalytische Beiträge zur Mythenforschung* (Leipzig, Vienna, and Zurich, 1922), pp. 172–73.

9. In Stendhal's projected article on *Le Rouge et le Noir*, he claims that Mme Michoud had written a similar letter to Mlle de Cordon, Berthet's second love, with equally disastrous effects (*Le Rouge*, p. 256). In fact, there is no proof in the proceedings of the trial that such a letter existed. (See Stendhal, *Stendhal: Romans et Nouvelles*, ed. Henri Martineau, 2 vols. [Paris, 1963–64], 1:715–30.)

10. Here is one of the keys to understanding the importance of Martin Turnell's "walls" in *Le Rouge et le Noir*. See Martin Turnell, *The Novel in France* (London, 1950), pp. 123–208.

11. Because of a disappointment in love Fouqué does not intend

to marry, and Julien suspects that his friend wants him to live with him permanently.

12. This passage was written before I read Gilbert Durand's *Décor Mythique de la "Chartreuse de Parme"* (Paris, 1961), in which the author suggests the same analogy; his interpretation of its meaning, however, differs from mine.

13. "Dostoyevsky's early sympton of death-like seizures can thus be understood as a father identification on the part of his ego, permitted by his superego as a punishment. 'You wanted to kill your father in order to be your father yourself. Now you are your father, but a dead father'—the regular mechanism of hysterical symptoms." (Sigmund Freud, "Dostoyevsky and Parricide," in *The Literary Imagination,* ed. Hendrick M. Ruitenbeek [Chicago, 1965], p. 335.

14. Faguet's argument and the arguments of Rambaud, Prévost, and Martineau are reported in Henriette Bibas, "Le Double Dénouement et la morale du *Rouge*," *Revue d'Histoire Littéraire de la France* 49 (1949): 21–36.

15. Martineau, Introduction to *Le Rouge*, p. iii.

16. Sigmund Freud, *On Creativity and the Unconscious* (New York, 1958), pp. 111–21.

17. Henri Martineau, *Le Calendrier de Stendhal* (Paris, 1950), p. 26.

18. Bibas, "Le double dénouement," p. 35.

19. Ibid., p. 28.

20. See Freud, "Dostoyevsky and Parricide."

CHAPTER THREE: *Unfinished Symphony*

1. Henri Martineau, ed., Preface to *Stendhal: Romans et Nouvelles,* by Stendhal, 2 vols. (Paris, 1963–64), 1:743. All subsequent references to *Lucien Leuwen* are to this edition.

2. Aldous Huxley, *Music at Night and Other Essays* (London, 1931), pp. 157–73.

3. Apparently the subject of Mme Jules Gaulthier's novel was such an episode. It is generally accepted that it was Stendhal's reading of Mme Gaulthier's manuscript which stimulated him to undertake his new novel. (See Martineau's Preface to *Lucien*, pp. 734–38.)

4. Ibid., p. 738.

5. See Chapter 5 of this essay, pp. 186–87.

6. Henri Martineau, *Le Coeur de Stendhal: histoire de sa vie et de ses sentiments*, 2 vols. (Paris, 1952–53), 1: 183–200. Hereafter cited as *Coeur*.

7. Ibid., 2: 92, 172–75, 188–89, 244 ff.

8. This episode is discussed in more detail later in this chapter, pp. 128–30.

9. Martineau, Preface to *Lucien*, pp. 737–41.

10. This is not to dispute the value of this change. Personally, *Henry Brulard* holds more interest for me than *Lucien Leuwen*. I am considering only the effect on the novel and its readers.

11. Stendhal began writing *Henry Brulard* in November, 1835. He returned to *Lucien Leuwen* only once thereafter for a brief period in September-October 1836.

12. Theodor Reik, *Of Love and Lust* (New York, 1957), e.g., p. 279.

13. See Chapter 2 of this essay, p. 43.

14. Henri Delacroix, *La Psychologie de Stendhal* (Paris, 1918); Victor Brombert, *Stendhal et la voie oblique* (New Haven, Conn. and Paris, 1954); Jean Prévost, *La Création chez Stendhal* (Paris, 1959).

15. For example, Delacroix, *La Psychologie*.

16. Edmund Bergler, *Talleyrand, Napoleon, Stendhal, Grabbe: Psychoanalytisch-Biographische Essays* (Vienna, 1935), pp. 99–100.

17. Stendhal, *De L'Amour*, ed. Henri Martineau (Paris, 1957), p. 8.

18. Reik, *Of Love and Lust*, p. 11.

19. Sigmund Freud, *Collected Papers,* trans. Joan Riviere, vol. 2, Clinical Papers, Papers on Technique (London, 1924), pp. 232–34.

20. Martineau, *Lucien,* p. 1509, n. 2 to p. 875.

CHAPTER FOUR: *The Child Is Father of the Child*

1. Honoré de Balzac, *Oeuvres diverses,* ed. Marcel Bouteron and Henri Longnon (Paris, 1940), vol. 3.

2. Henri Martineau, ed., Introduction to *La Chartreuse de Parme,* by Stendhal (Paris, 1961), p. xix. All subsequent references to *La Chartreuse* are to vol. 2 of the Pléïade edition, *Stendhal: Romans et Nouvelles,* ed. Henri Martineau, 2 vols. (Paris, 1963–64).

3. *Chartreuse,* pp. 27–32.

4. Stendhal, *Stendhal: Oeuvres Intimes,* ed. Henri Martineau (Paris, 1955), p. 427. All subsequent references to *La Vie de Henry Brulard* are to this edition.

5. Sigmund Freud, *On Creativity and the Unconscious,* ed. Benjamin Nelson (New York, 1958), p. 201.

6. For Stendhal orange trees are always associated with love. In *Armance* the lovers first kiss near an orange tree; they put their letters underneath this same tree. When Fabrice is in prison, he is delighted to see an orange tree in Clélia's garden. In *Henry Brulard* Beyle mentions an orange tree that he could see from his bedroom. For this reason, and the fact that orange trees are always associated with the younger heroine, I suspect that they were linked with his childhood memories of his sister Pauline.

7. See Chapter 1 of this essay, p. 24.

8. Henri Martineau, *Le Coeur de Stendhal: histoire de sa vie et de ses sentiments,* 2 vols. (Paris, 1952–53), 1:365–66, 400 ff.

9. The symbolic equation, cow = woman, has often been verified. Thus, in *The Writer and Psychoanalysis* (New York, 1950),

Edmund Bergler speaks of a patient:

The idea of the man milking a cow rested on an unconscious . . . substructure. The patient's inner conflict was a masochistic attachment to his mother, later shifted onto his penurious wife. . . . To rebuke the inner reproach of masochistic parasitism he built up unconsciously the defense he wanted to express through sublimation in his picture: "What else are stupid women (cows) good for but to be milked?" (p. 89)

10. Sigmund Freud, *Gesammelte Werke*, ed. Anna Freud et al., vol. 14. Werke aus den Jahren 1925–1931 (London, 1940), p. 170, my translation.

11. That Ferrante is a doublet of Fabrice can be deduced not only from the passages reproduced in the text: in this chapter Ferrante enacts a rebirth phantasy just as Fabrice does; the "cachette" of which the duchess speaks is similar to Fabrice's prison cell; and later on Ferrante practices escaping down a wall using ropes.

12. A more realistic appraisal of the novel could easily show that here, just as with the earlier feelings of guilt experienced by Gina, we are dealing with projection: the son wishes that the mother would do and feel as Gina does, so that he would be relieved of the terrible burden of anxiety and guilt. Stendhal himself indicates this at one point. Fabrice thinks: "J'ai le bonheur de devoir à la duchesse l'absence de tous les maux; de plus, c'est elle qui sent pour moi les transports d'amitié que je devais éprouver *pour elle.* (p. 325, italics mine)

13. For example, Gilbert Durand, *Le Décor Mythique de la "Chartreuse de Parme"* (Paris, 1961), pp. 220–28.

14. Sigmund Freud, *Introduction to Psychoanalysis*, trans. Joan Riviere (New York, 1935), p. 136.

15. See Chapter 3 of this essay, p. 106.

CHAPTER FIVE :   *Love of Knowledge, Knowledge of Love*

1. Maurice Bardèche, *Stendhal Romancier* (Paris, 1947), p. 436.

2. Jean Prévost, *La Création chez Stendhal* (Paris, 1959), p. 385. Hereafter cited as *Création*.

3. Ibid.

4. Stendhal, *Stendhal: Romans et Nouvelles*, ed. Henri Martineau, 2 vols. (Paris, 1963–64), 2:893. All subsequent references to *Lamiel* are to this edition.

5. Martineau, Preface to *Lamiel*, p. 861.

6. Henri Martineau, *Le Coeur de Stendhal: histoire de sa vie et de ses sentiments*, 2 vols. (Paris, 1952–53), 2: 383–84.

7. Ibid., p. 384.

8. Cited by Martineau, Appendix to *Lamiel*, p. 1033.

9. Stendhal, *Stendhal: Oeuvres Intimes*, ed. Henri Martineau (Paris, 1955), p. 107. All subsequent references to *La Vie de Henry Brulard* are to this edition.

10. Martineau, *Lamiel*, p. 1446, n. 1 to p. 991.

11. Stendhal, *Stendhal: Oeuvres Complètes*, ed. Henri Martineau, vol. 50, *Correspondance* (Paris, 1927), pp. 177–78, italics mine.

12. Prévost, *Création*, pp. 375–76.

13. Martineau, Preface to *Lamiel*, p. 866.

14. See Chapter 2 of this essay, nn. 4 and 5.

CONCLUSION

1. Otto Rank, *Das Inzest-Motiv in Dichtung und Sage: Grundzüge einer Psychologie des dichterischen Schaffens* (Leipzig and Vienna, 1927), pp. 63–65.

2. Ibid., p. 309.

3. E. M. Forster, *Aspects of the Novel* (New York, 1927), pp. 108–9. It should be noted that I am in complete agreement with Forster when he asserts that the "flatness" or "roundness" of a character is not the equivalent of his "goodness" or "badness" in terms of aesthetic evaluation of the author's skill or genius. Novels have

plenty of room for, and indeed often require, flat characters as well as round ones. In the nineteenth-century novel the former have, I believe, taken over the function of the "intercalated stories" so common in seventeenth century fiction. Poorly drawn characters are, I think, generally those main characters who act purely out of conscious motivations, who feel no conflicts, and who are always victorious over external obstacles with an absurdly small expenditure of energy. In short, they are the products of the most superficial layers of the author's psyche. In such cases, the author has been unable to plumb the depths of his unconscious; his inspiration has failed (or perhaps he has no talent).

4. These remarks by no means exhaust the question of the public's "understanding" or of the author's means of accomplishing this goal.

5. E. Bullough, " 'Psychical Distance' as a Factor in Arts and an Esthetic Principle," in *A Modern Book of Aesthetics*, ed. Melvin Rader (New York, 1961), p. 406.

6. For a discussion of this problem, see Ernst Kris, *Psychoanalytic Explorations in Art* (New York, 1952), pp. 256–57.

7. Otto Rank, *Der Künstler: Ansätze zu einer Sexualpsychologie* (Vienna, 1907), p. 48.

8. Kris, 251–60.

9. Neither Kris nor Lesser (in his *Fiction and the Unconscious* [Boston, 1957], pp. 178–83) attempts to make this connection. However, Lesser makes some of the following points in a slightly different context (pp. 90–93).

10. This question has been treated at length in Georges Blin, *Stendhal et les problèmes du roman* (Paris, 1954). See also Brombert, *Stendhal et la voie oblique* (New Haven and Paris, 1954).

11. Brombert has done so.

12. Obviously, other novelists use different techniques to achieve a similar result.

13. Sigmund Freud, *Character and Culture*, ed. Philip Rieff (New York, 1963), pp. 263–69.

14. Kris, p. 212.

15. Theodor Reik, *Masochism in Sex and Society*, trans. Margaret H. Beigel and Gertrude M. Kurth (New York, 1962), pp. 115–24, 233–74.

Works Consulted

BY STENDHAL

Beyle, Marie-Henri. *De l'Amour.* Edited by Henri Martineau. Paris, 1957.

———. *Armance: ou quelques scènes d'un salon de Paris en 1827.* Edited by Henri Martineau. Paris, 1962.

———. *La Chartreuse de Parme.* Edited by Henri Martineau. Paris, 1961.

———. *Racine et Shakespeare.* Edited by René Ternois. Paris, 1957.

———. *Le Rouge et le Noir: Chronique du XIXe siècle.* Edited by Henri Martineau. Paris, 1960.

———. *Stendhal: Oeuvres Completes.* Edited by Henri Martineau. 79 vols. Paris, 1927–37. Vols. 21–23, *Mémoires d'un Touriste,* 1929; Vols. 35–37, *Théâtre de Stendhal,* 1931; Vols. 50–59, *Correspondance,* 1933–34.

———. *Stendhal: Oeuvres Intimes.* Edited by Henri Martineau. Paris, 1955.

———. *Stendhal: Romans et Nouvelles.* Edited by Henri Martineau. 2 vols. Paris, 1963–64.

BIOGRAPHIES OF STENDHAL

Martineau, Henri. *Le Calendrier de Stendhal.* Paris, 1950.

———. *Le Coeur de Stendhal: histoire de sa vie et de ses sentiments.* 2 vols. Paris, 1952–53.

Mérimee, Prosper. *Deux Portraits de Stendhal.* Edited by Pierre Jourda. Nogent-le-Rotrou, 1928.

CRITICISM

Adams, Robert Martin. *Stendhal: Notes on a Novelist.* London, 1959.

Atherton, John Humphrey. "Stendhal and the Uses of Irony." Ph.D. diss., Harvard University, May 1961.

Auerbach, Erich. *Mimesis: The Representation of Reality in Western Literature.* Translated by Willard Trask. New York, 1953.

Balzac, Honoré de. *Oeuvres diverses.* Edited by Marcel Bouteron and Henri Longnon. Vol. 3. Paris, 1940.

Bardèche, Maurice. *Stendhal Romancier.* Paris, 1947.

Benedetto, Luigi Foscolo. *La Parma di Stendhal.* Florence, 1950.

Bibas, Henriette. "Le double dénouement et la morale du *Rouge.*" *Revue d'Histoire Littéraire de la France* 49 (1949): 21–36.

Blin, Georges. *Stendhal et les problemes du roman.* Paris, 1954.

———, ed. Introduction to *Armance,* by Stendhal. Paris, 1946.

Blum, Léon. *Stendhal et le beylisme.* Paris, 1930.

Borgerhoff, E. B. O. "The Anagram in *Le Rouge et le Noir.*" *Modern Language Notes* 68 (1953): 383–86.

Bourget, Paul. *Essais de psychologie contemporaine.* Paris, 1885.

———. *Quelques témoignages.* Paris, 1928.

Brombert, Victor. *Stendhal et la voie oblique: l'auteur devant son monde romanesque.* New Haven and Paris, 1954.

Caraccio, Armand. *Stendhal, l'homme et l'oeuvre.* Paris, 1951.

Chartier, Emile-Auguste [Alain]. *Stendhal.* Paris, 1948.

Cordié, Carlo. *Sull' arte della "Chartreuse de Parme."* Florence, 1936.

Croce, Benedetto. *Poesia e non poesia: Note sulla letteratura europea del sècolo decimonona.* Bari, 1923.

Delacroix, Henri. *La Psychologie de Stendhal*. Paris, 1918.

Du Bos, Charles. *Approximations, deuxième série*. Paris, 1927.

Dugas, Ludovic. *Les Grands Timides*. Paris, 1922.

Durand, Gilbert. *Le Décor mythique de "la Chartreuse de Parme":* contribution à l'esthétique du romanesque. Paris, 1961.

Faguet, Emile. *Politiques et moralistes du dix-neuvième siècle, 3e série*. Paris, 1903.

Falcionelli, Alberto. *Nuevos puntos de vista sobre la "Cartuja de Parma" y las ideas de Stendhal*. Cuadernos de Estudios Franceses, no. 1. Mendoza, Argentina, 1949.

Fernandez, Ramon. *Itinéraire français*. Paris, 1943.

———. *Messages, 1ère série*. Paris, 1926.

Fowlie, Wallace. *Stendhal*. London, 1969.

Friedrich, Hugo. *Drei Klassiker des französischen Romans*. Frankfurt am Main, 1939.

Gide, André. *Incidences*. Paris, 1924.

Gilbert, Pierre. *La Forêt des Cippes: Essais de critique*. Paris, 1918.

Gilman, Stephen. *The Tower as Emblem*. Frankfurt am Main, 1967.

Girard, René. *Mensonge romantique et vérité romanesque*. Paris, 1961.

Giraud, Raymond. *The Unheroic Hero in the Novels of Stendhal, Balzac, and Flaubert*. New Brunswick, 1957.

Gourmont, Remy de. *Promenades littéraires, 5e série*. Paris, 1913.

Hemmings, F. W. J. *Stendhal, a Study of His Novels*. London, 1964.

Huxley, Aldous. *Music at Night and Other Essays*. London, 1931.

Hytier, Jean. *Les Romans de l'individu*. Paris, 1928.

Imbert, H-F. "Stendhal et Tom Jones." *Revue de Littérature Comparée* 3 (1956): 351–70.

James, David. "The Harmonic Structure of *La Chartreuse de Parme*." *French Review* 24 (1950): 119–24.

Josephson, Matthew. *Stendhal; or, The Pursuit of Happiness.* New York, 1946.

Jourda, Pierre. *Stendhal, l'homme et l'oeuvre.* Paris, 1934.

Körver, Carl. *Stendhal und der Ausdruck der Gemütsbewegungen in seinen Werken.* Halle, 1912.

Le Breton, André. *"Le Rouge et le Noir" de Stendhal: Etude et analyse.* Paris, 1934.

Levin, Harry. *The Gates of Horn.* New York, 1963.

Liprandi, Claude. *Stendhal, le "bord de l'eau" et la "note secrète."* Avignon, 1949.

Martineau, Henri. *L'Oeuvre de Stendhal: histoire de ses livres et de sa pensée.* Paris, 1951.

Martino, Pierre, *Stendhal.* Paris, 1914.

O'Connor, Frank. *The Mirror in the Roadway.* London, 1957.

Poulet, Georges. "Stendhal et le temps." *Revue Internationale de Philosophie* 16 (1962): 395–412.

Prévost, Jean. *Le Création chez Stendhal. Essai sur le métier d'écrire et la psychologie de l'écrivain.* Paris, 1951.

Richard, Jean-Pierre. *Littérature et Sensation.* Paris, 1954.

Sacy, Sylvestre de. "Le Miroir sur la grande route. Les romans de Stendhal et le roman picaresque." *Mercure de France* 306 (1949): 64–80.

Sells, A. Lytton. *"La Chartreuse de Parme:* The Problem of Composition." *Modern Language Quarterly* 12 (1951): 204–15.

———. *"La Chartreuse de Parme:* The Problem of Style." *Modern Language Quarterly* 11 (1950): 486–91.

Stephan, Philip. "Count Mosca's role in *La Chartreuse de Parme." L'Esprit Créateur* 2 (1962): 38–42.

Taine, Hippolyte. *Nouveaux essais de critique et d'histoire.* Paris, 1894.

Temmer, Mark. "Comedy in the *Charterhouse of Parma*." *Yale French Studies*, no. 23 (1959), pp. 92–99.

Thibaudet, Albert. *Stendhal*. Paris, 1931.

Turnell, Martin. *The Art of French Fiction*. London, 1959.

——. *The Novel in France*. London, 1950.

Ullmann, Stephen. *Style in the French Novel*. Cambridge, 1957.

Wandruszka, M. "Zum Stil Stendhals." *Zeitschrift für französische Sprache und Literatur* 62 (1939): 429–36.

Wardman, H. W. "*La Chartreuse de Parme*: Ironical Ambiguity." *Kenyon Review* 17 (1955): 449–71.

Wicke, Berta. *Stilprobleme bei Stendhal*. Lucerne, 1936.

Zola, Emile. *Les Romanciers naturalistes*. Paris, 1881.

LITERARY THEORY

Booth, Wayne C. *The Rhetoric of Fiction*. Chicago and London, 1963.

Brinkmann, Richard. *Wirklichkeit und Illusion: Studien über Gehalt und Grenzen des Begriffs Realismus fur die erzählende Dichtung des neunzehnten Jahrhunderts*. Tübingen, 1957.

Crane, Ronald S. *The Languages of Criticism and the Structure of Poetry*. Toronto, 1953.

Curtis, Jean-Louis. *Haute Ecole*. Paris, 1950.

Forster, E. M. *Aspects of the Novel*. London, 1927.

Friedemann, Käte. *Die Rolle des Erzählers in der Epik*. Leipzig, 1910.

Friedman, Norman. "Point of View in Fiction: The Development of a Critical Concept." *PMLA* 70 (1955): 1160–84.

Hamburger, Käte. *Die Logik der Dichtung*. Stuttgart, 1957.

Kayser, Wolfgang. "Die Anfänge des modernen Romans im 18. Jahrhundert une seine heutige Krise." *Deutsche Vierteljahrschrift* 28 (1954): 417–46.

Pouillon, Jean. *Temps et Roman.* Paris, 1946.

Rader, Melvin, ed. *A Modern Book of Aesthetics.* New York, 1961.

Schorer, Mark. "Technique as Discovery." *Hudson Review* 1 (1948): 67–87.

Warren, Austin, and Wellek, René. *Theory of Literature.* New York, 1949.
Watt, Ian. *The Rise of the Novel.* Berkeley and Los Angeles, 1964.

PSYCHOANALYTICAL STUDIES

Abraham, Karl. *Selected Papers.* Translated by Douglas Bryan and Alix Strachey. New York, 1953.
———. *Traum und Mythus: eine Studie zur Völkerpsychologie.* Leipzig, 1909.

Bergler, Edmund. *Talleyrand, Napoleon, Stendhal, Grabbe: Psychoanalytisch-Biographische Essays.* Vienna, 1935.
———. *The Writer and Psychoanalysis.* New York, 1950.
Bonaparte, Marie. *Edgar Poe, Etude Psychanalytique.* Paris, 1933.
———. "Du symbolisme des trophées de tête." *Revue Française de Psychanalyse,* fasc. 4 (1927), pp. 677–732.

Freud, Anna. *The Ego and the Mechanisms of Defense.* Translated by Cecil Baine. London, 1942.
Freud, Sigmund. *Character and Culture.* Edited by Philip Rieff. New York, 1963.
———. *Collected Papers.* Translated by Joan Riviere. Vol. 2, *Clinical Papers* and *Papers on Technique.* London, 1924.

——. *On Creativity and the Unconscious.* Edited by Benjamin Nelson. New York, Evanston, Ill., and London, 1958.

——. *Introduction to Psychoanalysis.* Translated by Joan Riviere. New York, 1935.

——. "Psychopathic Characters on the Stage." *Psychoanalytic Quarterly* (1909).

——. *Three Case Histories.* Edited by Philip Rieff. New York, 1963.

——. *Gesammelte Werke, chronologisch geordnet.* Edited by Anna Freud et al. 17 vols. London, 1942–52. Vol. 14. *Werke aus den Jahren: 1925–1931, 1940.*

Holland, Norman N. *The Dynamics of Literary Response.* New York, 1968.

Jones, Ernest. *Hamlet and Oedipus.* Garden City, New York, 1949.

Klein, Melanie. *Contributions to Psycho-Analysis.* London, 1948.
Kris, Ernst. *Psychoanalytic Explorations in Art.* New York, 1952.

Lesser, Simon O. *Fiction and the Unconscious.* Boston, 1957.

Muschg, Walter. *Psychoanalyse und Literaturwissenschaft.* Berlin, 1930.

Phillips, William, ed. *Art and Psychoanalysis.* Cleveland and New York, 1957.

Rank, Otto. *Das Inzest-Motiv in Dichtung und Sage: Grundzüge einer Psychologie des dichterischen Schaffens.* Leipzig and Vienna, 1927.

——. *Der Künstler: Ansätze zu einer Sexualpsychologie.* Vienna, 1907.

——. *The Myth of the Birth of the Hero and Other Writings.* Edited by Philip Freund. New York, 1959.

——. *Der Mythus von der Geburt des Helden: Versuch einer psychologischen Mythendeutung.* Leipzig and Vienna, 1909.

——. *Psychoanalytische Beiträge zur Mythenforschung: Aus den Jahren 1912 bis 1914*. Leipzig, Vienna, and Zurich, 1922.

Reik, Theodor. *The Compulsion to Confess*. New York, 1966.

——. *Of Love and Lust*. New York, 1957.

Reik, Theodor. *Masochism in Sex and Society*. Translated by Margaret H. Beigel and Gertrud M. Kurth. New York, 1962.

Ruitenbeek, Hendrik M., ed. *The Literary Imagination*. Chicago, 1965.

——. *Psychoanalysis and Literature*. New York, 1962.

Sachs, Hanns. *The Creative Unconscious: Studies in the Psychoanalysis of Art*. Cambridge, Mass., 1942.

Spitz, Réne. *The First Year of Life: A Psychoanalytic Study of Normal and Deviant Development of Object Relations*. New York, 1965.

Troy, William. "Stendhal: In Quest of Henri Beyle." *Partisan Review* 9 (1942): 3–22.

Index